IMPORTANT!

What Makes Windows 98 Special?

The most exciting feature of Windows 98 is its seamless integration of Internet Explorer 4, Microsoft's Web browser. **This integration makes possible several exciting new features through its Active Desktop.**

As this book was going to press, there was a legal injunction pending to prevent Microsoft from integrating Internet Explorer 4 with Windows 98. If this injunction prevails, the copy of Windows 98 you purchase may not have Internet Explorer 4 built in.

Without Internet Explorer 4, you will miss out on many of the exciting features described in this book, so we recommend that you get and install Internet Explorer 4 right away. It's easy–*and free!* Just visit Microsoft's Web site (http://www.microsoft.com) and download your free copy of Internet Explorer 4. Run the installation program, and you're ready to go.

Even if you choose not to use Internet Explorer 4, Windows 98 still has many great new features to offer, including more powerful utilities and easier-to-use file management, all of which are covered in this book.

Congratulations on choosing Windows 98! It can be a great tool for making your computer work harder and smarter. Now, sit back and relax, and let this book teach you how to harness the power of Windows 98 for your own PC productivity.

How to Order:

For information on quantity discounts, contact the publisher: Prima Publishing, P.O. Box 1260BK, Rocklin, CA 95677-1260; (916) 632-4400. On your letterhead, include information concerning the intended use of the books and the number of books you wish to purchase. For individual orders, turn to the back of this book for more information.

Learn
Windows® 98

MICHAEL MEADHRA

WITH
FAITHE WEMPEN

PRIMA PUBLISHING

Prima Publishing and colophon are registered trademarks of Prima Communications, Inc. In a Weekend is a trademark of Prima Publishing, a division of Prima Communications, Inc., Rocklin, California 95677.

Publisher: Matthew H. Carleson

Managing Editor: Dan J. Foster

Acquisitions Editor: Jenny L. Watson

Project Editor: Kevin W. Ferns

Technical Reviewer: Bo Williams

Copy Editor: Hilary Powers

Interior Layout: Shawn Morningstar

Cover Design: Prima Design Team

Indexer: Emily Glossbrenner

Microsoft, Windows, and Windows NT are trademarks or registered trademarks of Microsoft Corporation.

Important: If you have problems installing or running Microsoft Windows 98, notify Microsoft at (425) 635-7056 or on the Web at www.microsoft.com. Prima Publishing cannot provide software support.

Prima Publishing and the authors have attempted throughout this book to distinguish proprietary trademarks from descriptive terms by following the capitalization style used by the manufacturer.

Information contained in this book has been obtained by Prima Publishing from sources believed to be reliable. However, because of the possibility of human or mechanical error by our sources, Prima Publishing, or others, the Publisher does not guarantee the accuracy, adequacy, or completeness of any information and is not responsible for any errors or omissions or the results obtained from the use of such information. Readers should be particularly aware of the fact that the Internet is an ever-changing entity. Some facts may have changed since this book went to press.

ISBN: 0-7615-1296-9

Library of Congress Catalog Card Number: 97-69602

Printed in the United States of America

98 99 00 01 02 DD 10 9 8 7 6 5 4 3 2 1

CONTENTS AT A GLANCE

Introduction. xv

FRIDAY EVENING
Getting to Know Windows 98 1

SATURDAY MORNING
Installing and Using Applications 53

SATURDAY AFTERNOON
Customizing Windows 98 105

SATURDAY EVENING
Adding and Configuring Hardware 145

SUNDAY MORNING
Getting Connected to the Internet and Browsing the Web . . . 203

SUNDAY AFTERNOON
Reaching Out with E-mail and News 259

SUNDAY EVENING
Bringing the Web to Your Desktop 317

Appendix - Installing Windows 98 345

Glossary 353

Index 361

CONTENTS

Introduction. xv

FRIDAY EVENING
Getting to Know Windows 98 1

    Welcome to Windows 98 5
        What Is an Operating System and Why Do You Need One? 5
        Why Choose Windows 98? 7
    Starting Windows 98 10
    The Two Faces of Windows 98 12
        Keeping the Classic Style 14
        Adopting the Web Style 15
        Interacting with Active Desktop 16
        Which View Is for You? 17
    Exploring the Windows Desktop 19
        Testing the Taskbar 20
        Using the Start Menu 22
        Using Icons on the Desktop 26
        Introducing the Channel Bar 30
    Take a Break 32
    Opening Windows 32
    Using Dialog Boxes 37
    Exploring My Computer 40
        Exploring a Drive, Folder, or File 42
        Working with Different Views 44

Managing Files and Folders with Windows Explorer....................**44**

    Creating New Folders..**46**

    Renaming Files and Folders..**46**

    Moving and Copying Files and Folders **47**

    Creating Shortcuts..**49**

    Deleting Files and Folders **50**

Closing Windows..**51**

What's Next? **52**

SATURDAY MORNING
Installing and Using Applications. **53**

    Installing and Removing Windows Components......................**55**

    Installing Software **57**

    Removing Software **60**

    Launching Applications..**62**

    Finding Your Way in Any Windows Program **62**

        Issuing Commands **64**

        Selecting Text and Graphics..**66**

        Deleting Text and Graphics **70**

        Using Undo and Redo **71**

        Moving and Copying **72**

        Saving Your Work..**76**

        Closing a File **81**

        Opening a Saved File **82**

        Printing in Windows-Based Programs **83**

        Creating New Documents **85**

    Take a Break..**86**

Exploring the Windows Accessories 86
   Text and Word Processing 86
   Graphics and Imaging 86
   Games 87
   Communications Programs 88
   System Utilities 90
   Entertainment Utilities 91
Setting Up DOS Programs in Windows 98 92
   Installing a DOS-Based Program 92
   Troubleshooting MS-DOS Programs 96
   Some Basic Troubleshooting Tips 97
   Setting Up Shortcuts for DOS Programs 100
Customizing the Start Menu 102
What's Next? 103

SATURDAY AFTERNOON
Customizing Windows 98 105
Customizing the Taskbar 107
   Changing the Taskbar Position 108
   AutoHiding the Taskbar 109
   Changing the Taskbar Size 110
   Managing the System Tray 111
   Working with Toolbars 112
Changing the Look of Your Windows Desktop 115
   Changing the Display Resolution 115
   Hanging New Wallpaper 119
   Changing the Screen Saver..122
   Experimenting with Colors and Fonts 124
   Making Mouse Adjustments...126
   Making Noise with Sounds 128
   Exploring the Windows Themes 130
Managing Your Multimedia Devices 131
   Audio..132
   Video 133
   MIDI 133
   CD Music 133
   Devices 134

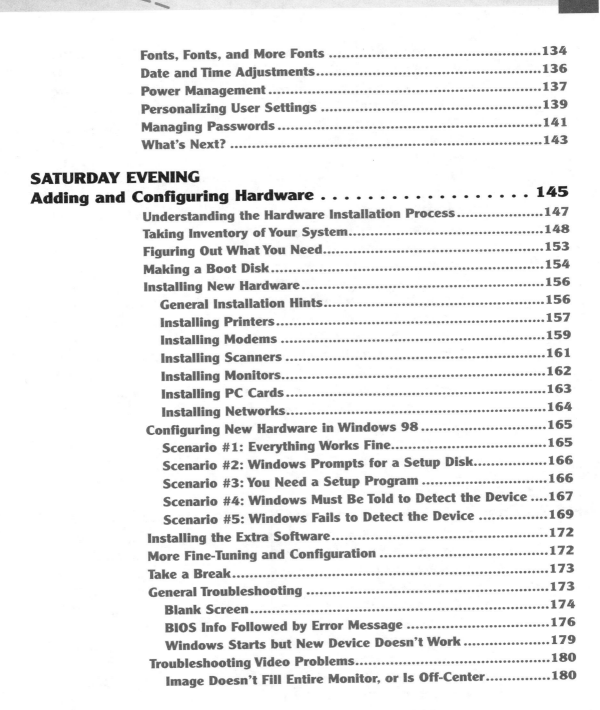

Fonts, Fonts, and More Fonts 134

Date and Time Adjustments..136

Power Management 137

Personalizing User Settings 139

Managing Passwords 141

What's Next? 143

SATURDAY EVENING
Adding and Configuring Hardware 145

Understanding the Hardware Installation Process.....................147

Taking Inventory of Your System...148

Figuring Out What You Need..153

Making a Boot Disk...154

Installing New Hardware...156

    General Installation Hints...156

    Installing Printers...157

    Installing Modems 159

    Installing Scanners 161

    Installing Monitors...162

    Installing PC Cards...163

    Installing Networks..164

Configuring New Hardware in Windows 98 165

    Scenario #1: Everything Works Fine......................................165

    Scenario #2: Windows Prompts for a Setup Disk..................166

    Scenario #3: You Need a Setup Program 166

    Scenario #4: Windows Must Be Told to Detect the Device 167

    Scenario #5: Windows Fails to Detect the Device 169

Installing the Extra Software..172

More Fine-Tuning and Configuration 172

Take a Break...173

General Troubleshooting 173

    Blank Screen..174

    BIOS Info Followed by Error Message 176

    Windows Starts but New Device Doesn't Work 179

Troubleshooting Video Problems..180

    Image Doesn't Fill Entire Monitor, or Is Off-Center...............180

Windows Fails to Detect New Card 181

Display Flickers Noticeably...182

Troubleshooting Modem Problems.......................................184

Windows Doesn't See the Modem.....................................184

The Modem Doesn't Work 185

Windows Sees Modem as Other Device.............................186

No Dial Tone...187

Modem Makes Endless Connection Noises 188

Modem Won't Stay Connected 189

Troubleshooting Sound Problems 190

No Sound, Diagnostic Program Reports Failure..................191

No Sound, Diagnostic Program Thinks It's Fine..................191

Sound Doesn't Work in Specific Program 192

Windows Doesn't See Sound Card....................................193

Windows Sees Card but There's No Sound 194

Windows Sees Card as Other Device................................195

Troubleshooting Printer Problems 196

Windows Doesn't Detect Printer 196

Printer Won't Print 197

Printer Prints with Type Scrunched on Half the Page 198

Printer Prints Garbage Characters 199

Printout Has Black Streaks or Faint Areas.........................199

New Device Works but System Crashes Frequently.................199

What's Next? 201

SUNDAY MORNING
Getting Connected to the Internet and Browsing the Web . . . 203

Getting Windows Ready for an Internet Connection.................206

Choosing an Internet Service Provider 207

Installing the Network Software 213

Establishing a Connection with a Modem 216

Establishing a Connection over a Local Network...................224

Take a Break..225

Browsing the Web with Internet Explorer.............................225

Introducing Internet Explorer...227

Entering Web Addresses..233

Going Back to Where You've Been 235

Keeping a List of Favorite Sites.......................................238

Searching for Information and Web Sites 242
Customizing Internet Explorer 246
What's Next? 257

SUNDAY AFTERNOON
Reaching Out with E-mail and News **259**
Setting Up Outlook Express 261
Installing Outlook Express 263
Starting Outlook Express 263
Setting Up Your E-mail Accounts 265
Setting Up Access to a News Server 277
Configuring Outlook Express Options.........................284
Take a Break...289
Sending and Receiving E-mail with Outlook Express................289
Reading Your E-mail Messages...............................289
Checking Your Mail 293
Composing and Sending E-mail 295
Managing E-mail with Folders...............................303
Using the Address Book.....................................305
Reading the News 308
Connecting to a News Server 309
Finding News Topics 309
Browsing a Newsgroup 311
Reading Messages 312
Following Threads 313
Subscribing to Newsgroups 313
Posting Articles You've Written 315
What's Next? 316

SUNDAY EVENING
Bringing the Web to Your Desktop **317**
What Is Active Desktop?......................................320
Making Windows Act Like a Web Page 322
Choosing the Web Style (or Not)............................322
Customizing Folders 325
Adding Web Content to Your Desktop.......................327
Turning Desktop Web Content On and Off 331

Take a Break..332
Subscribing to Web Content.......................................332
   Subscribing to a Regular Web Site..........................333
   Subscribing to a Channel 338
   Getting Subscription Updates Manually.................341
   Getting Subscription Updates Automatically 342
Offline Viewing...343
What's Next? 344

APPENDIX
Installing Windows 98 345
   Upgrading to Windows 98 from Windows 95 346
   Upgrading to Windows 98 from Windows 3.1 347
   Installing the Windows 98 Upgrade........................349

Glossary. 353

Index 361

ACKNOWLEDGMENTS

We've really enjoyed working on this book, and we appreciate the opportunity to be a part of the *In a Weekend* series. Producing a book such as this is a true team effort, and we'd like to take this opportunity to acknowledge and thank the other members of the team for their contributions. Without their time and talents, this book would not be possible. Jenny Watson, the acquisitions editor, was great to work with, and Kevin Ferns, the project editor, has been a real pleasure. Bo Williams and Hilary Powers made outstanding contributions as technical editor and copy editor, respectively. Shawn Morningstar had the job of transforming the manuscript into the finished pages you see here. Thanks to Matt Carleson, Dan Foster, and the rest of the staff at Prima Publishing for supporting the project. A special thanks goes to Debbie Abshier for acting as liaison with the Microsoft beta team.

ABOUT THE AUTHORS

Michael Meadhra is a freelance writer and consultant. He has written or contributed to more than two dozen computer books on topics ranging from the Windows operating system to graphics programs and personal finance software, including *Organize Your Finances with Quicken Deluxe 98 In a Weekend*, published by Prima. Michael has also served as editor-in-chief of monthly software journals dedicated to helping readers learn to use their software better.

Faithe Wempen, M.A., operates Your Computer Friend, a computer training and troubleshooting business in Indianapolis that specializes in helping beginning users with their PCs. Her eclectic writing credits include over 20 computer books, including Prima's *Learn Word 97 In a Weekend* and *Upgrade Your PC In a Weekend*, plus articles, essays, poems, training manuals, and OEM documentation. Her hobbies include surfing the Internet, doing cross-stitch, and being an active member of Broadway United Methodist Church in Indianapolis.

INTRODUCTION

If you're reading this, it must mean that the title got your attention. *Learn Windows 98 In a Weekend* sounds pretty good, doesn't it? If that interests you, it probably means you have a new or recently upgraded computer with Windows 98 installed and you're looking for some help in learning to use it (or learning to use it better). Now you're wondering if you can actually learn how to use your new computer in just one weekend. Well, the answer is yes, you can! By following the simple, tutorial-style sessions in this book, you can learn how to do the things that most Windows 98 users need to do, from basic operations such as starting programs and working with windows and dialog boxes to installing programs and hardware, customizing your system, and accessing the Internet. And you really can do it all in the space of one weekend—or a similar amount of time spread out any way that works for you.

What This Book Is About

As its title implies, *Learn Windows 98 In a Weekend* is about the Microsoft Windows 98 operating system—the software that provides the working environment for most personal computers sold today. Unlike application programs that are designed to perform a specific task, a computer operating system provides the environment in which you can interact with application programs. This book is about learning how to set up and use the Windows 98 operating system so you can confidently use your computer to perform the tasks you bought it to do. You'll learn how to:

- ✿ Start Windows and launch applications
- ✿ Work with program windows and dialog boxes
- ✿ Manage files and folders
- ✿ Customize Windows 98 settings to make your personal computer more personal
- ✿ Use Windows 98's built-in features and utilities
- ✿ Install and run application programs
- ✿ Set up Windows 98 to work with new hardware and accessories
- ✿ Connect to the Internet and browse the World Wide Web
- ✿ Communicate via e-mail and read newsgroups
- ✿ Automatically get information from the Internet and view it at your leisure

Who Should Read This Book

Learn Windows 98 In a Weekend is for readers who want to learn the basics of using the Windows 98 operating system but don't have the time or inclination to wade through one of those huge reference-style tomes to dig out the information they need. This book is intended for beginning to intermediate users—people who have used a computer before, and may even have used a previous version of Windows, but haven't developed the level of comfort and confidence that comes from mastering the tasks and techniques they need in order to accomplish what they want to do with the computer.

- ✿ Have you been using a Windows-based computer for awhile, but never quite gotten the hang of it?
- ✿ Do you want to develop a level of proficiency with Windows 98 so you can work more confidently and efficiently?

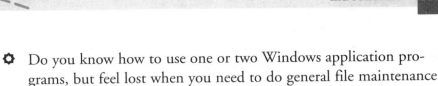

- ✿ Do you know how to use one or two Windows application programs, but feel lost when you need to do general file maintenance or other tasks outside the familiar confines of your applications?

- ✿ Are you fairly comfortable using an older version of Windows, but now you have a new computer with Windows 98 installed and you find yourself disoriented by the differences introduced by the new version of Windows?

- ✿ Do you want to know how to use Windows 98 to get your work done, but without becoming a computer expert or power user?

- ✿ Have you heard about some of the Internet connectivity features of Windows 98 and want to try them out?

If you answered yes to any of these questions, then you should read this book.

What You Need to Begin

All you really need is a personal computer running Windows 98 (or a personal computer running Windows 3.11 or Windows 95, plus a Windows 98 upgrade disk and an extra hour or so to install it). Everything else is optional, but you might want to have the following items on hand:

- ✿ Technical information about your computer system and peripherals and the setup disks provided by equipment manufacturers

- ✿ Installation disks or CDs and documentation for any programs you want to install

If you plan to use the Internet, you'll also need the following:

- ✿ A modem and access to a telephone line or a connection to a local area network that is, in turn, connected to the Internet

- ✿ An account with an Internet Service Provider (or with your corporate network)

- ✿ Your user ID and password and configuration information from your ISP or corporate network

How This Book Is Organized

You can think of *Learn Windows 98 In a Weekend* as a personal tutorial on using Windows 98. It's like having a series of one-on-one training sessions with a knowledgeable friend. The book is organized into seven sessions, each of which can be completed in about two or three hours. (There's even a scheduled break in the middle of each session.) You begin with the basics in the first session, and then add to your knowledge in each subsequent session to build toward the full Windows 98 experience with the Internet integrated into the desktop. The sessions are scheduled from Friday evening through Sunday evening, so you really can cover everything you need in one weekend. However, if you can't devote an entire weekend to learning Windows 98, you can work at your own pace and spread the sessions out—for example, one session each evening for a week will still get it done in a reasonably short time frame. And of course, if you're already familiar with some of the material, you can skim past it.

Here's a summary of what's covered in each session:

- **Friday Evening: Getting to Know Windows 98** starts with an introduction to Windows 98, including a brief history of the different Windows versions. You'll learn about starting Windows and then get an orientation to the Windows 98 desktop, including the taskbar and Start menu and the difference between the Classic and Web styles. This session covers the basics of working with program windows and dialog boxes.

- **Saturday Morning: Installing and Using Applications** covers installing Windows components and using the mini-programs and utilities that come with Windows 98. You'll learn how to install application programs, and how to customize the Start menu and use it to launch programs. You'll discover techniques for using your programs and for opening existing documents, and creating new documents. Finally, you'll learn how to safely remove a program you no longer need.

- ✪ **Saturday Afternoon: Customizing Windows 98** covers the many ways you can customize your Windows 98 environment to suit your own needs and preferences. The session starts with customizing your taskbar and the appearance of your Windows desktop. Then you'll learn how to change Windows system settings for sounds, date and time displays, mouse pointers, and more. You'll learn how to add fonts to your system and discover how to personalize Windows settings for different family members.

- ✪ **Saturday Evening: Adding and Configuring Hardware** shows you how to set up Windows 98 to work with your modem, printer, monitor, and other hardware. You'll learn how to add a scanner or other device to your system, how to use PCMCIA cards in a laptop computer, and how to make sure that your current devices are configured properly.

- ✪ **Sunday Morning: Getting Connected to the Internet and Browsing the Web** outlines the considerations in selecting an Internet Service Provider and then shows you how to establish a connection to the ISP you choose. Then you'll discover how to use the Internet Explorer browser program to surf the Web. You'll learn how to search for Web sites and how to keep a list of favorite sites that you find.

- ✪ **Sunday Afternoon: Reaching Out with E-mail and News** shows that there's more to the Internet than just the World Wide Web. You'll learn how to set up Outlook Express and how to use it to send and receive e-mail and read and respond to newsgroups.

- ✪ **Sunday Evening: Bringing the Web to Your Desktop** gets you started on the road to integrating the Internet into Windows 98. You'll learn to take advantage of Active Desktop to make your Windows 98 desktop look and act like a Web page. You'll also learn how to set up Windows 98 to use Channels and subscriptions to automatically gather information from the Internet and save it for you to read at your convenience.

Special Features of This Book

There are four special elements you'll see throughout the book that offer additional information that you'll find useful.

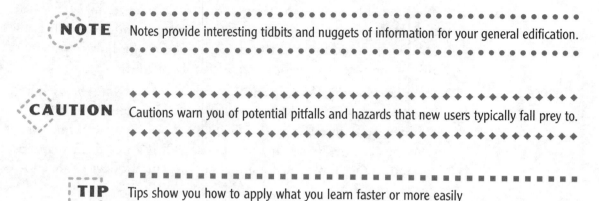

NOTE Notes provide interesting tidbits and nuggets of information for your general edification.

CAUTION Cautions warn you of potential pitfalls and hazards that new users typically fall prey to.

TIP Tips show you how to apply what you learn faster or more easily

---

SIDEBAR

Sidebars present background information or supplemental material that might be interesting or helpful, but not essential.

Instructions for Using Your Mouse

Instructions for mouse operations are written assuming that you are using a two-button mouse configured for default right-handed use. To *click* means to quickly press and release the left mouse button—the one that naturally falls under your index finger—when the tip of the pointer is positioned over the desired on-screen item. To *double-click* means to click the left mouse button twice in quick succession. To *drag* means to position the mouse pointer over an item and then press and hold the left mouse button as you move the mouse to another location, then release

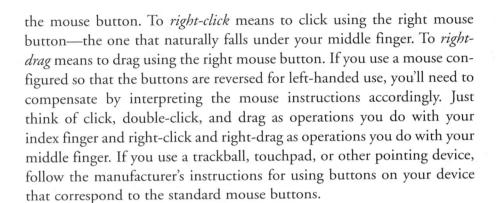

the mouse button. To *right-click* means to click using the right mouse button—the one that naturally falls under your middle finger. To *right-drag* means to drag using the right mouse button. If you use a mouse configured so that the buttons are reversed for left-handed use, you'll need to compensate by interpreting the mouse instructions accordingly. Just think of click, double-click, and drag as operations you do with your index finger and right-click and right-drag as operations you do with your middle finger. If you use a trackball, touchpad, or other pointing device, follow the manufacturer's instructions for using buttons on your device that correspond to the standard mouse buttons.

Web Style versus Classic Style

Windows 98 allows you to choose one of two slightly different styles of accessing objects with a mouse. (This will be explained in more detail in the Friday Evening session.) If you choose the traditional Classic Style, you will click on an on-screen item to select it and double-click on the item to take the default action (usually opening a document or launching a program). However, if you elect to use the Web Style, you will only need to point to an on-screen item (let the mouse pointer rest on the item for a couple of seconds) to select it; clicking on an item will take the default action such as opening or launching it. To avoid confusion about the effect of pointing, clicking, and double-clicking, you'll see instructions to *select* an item. You'll need to execute that instruction by pointing to the item (Web Style) or clicking on the item (Classic Style) depending on which style your system is set up to use. Similarly, instructions to *open* an item will require either clicking on it (Web Style) or double-clicking on it (Classic Style). When you see specific instructions to click, double-click, drag, right-click, or right-drag something without any qualifications about one style or another, those actions will have the same effect regardless of the desktop style.

Getting to Know Windows 98

- ✪ Starting Windows
- ✪ The Two Faces of Windows 98
- ✪ Exploring the Windows Desktop
- ✪ Managing Files and Folders with Windows Explorer
- ✪ Closing Windows

Well, it's Friday evening, the work week is over, and the weekend is beginning. This weekend, you've resolved to do something a little different. Instead of the usual assortment of household chores and errands, you've decided to invest your time in learning how to use the new Windows operating system on the computer that you just bought or upgraded.

Okay, I'll admit that I'm making some assumptions here. It's Friday evening only if you're following the *In a Weekend* format, and I presume that your alternative to spending the weekend learning how to use Windows was going to be chores or something equally boring. (If you had a hot date or a big adventure planned for the weekend, you wouldn't be reading this book, would you?) I'm guessing that you have a new or recently upgraded computer because most people don't study computer operating systems for fun. The odds are that you bought a new computer and it came with Windows 98 installed—or perhaps you are upgrading your existing computer to Windows 98 from a previous version of Windows because you need some of the new features, such as integrated Internet access.

So, now you have a computer system that looks and acts a little (or a lot) different from what you may have used before—and you need to learn how to use it. Furthermore, you're probably anxious to get past the general Windows 98 stuff so you can install and run other programs that will enable you to play games, balance your checkbook, write reports, or whatever it is that you bought a computer to do in the first place.

You might be wondering if you can really master the Windows operating system in one weekend. Yes, you can! Although a weekend isn't enough time to explore every feature, option, and peculiarity of Windows 98 in detail, it's more than enough time to learn about the features you'll need to use on a regular basis. In this evening's session, you'll do the following:

- Get acquainted with the Windows 98 desktop and learn how to work with the windows, dialog boxes, icons, and other objects you find there.

- Get an introduction to the optional Active Desktop and Web Style features and discover some of the ways they can change how you work with Windows.

- Learn to use Windows Explorer and other tools to navigate your system and manage your files.

By the time the weekend is over, you may not be a certified expert on Windows 98 (leave that to the serious computer geeks and their 1200–page reference books that weigh more than some of the computers that run the software). However, you will be acquainted with the Windows 98 operating system and what it can do, and you can develop the confidence that comes from knowing how to use Windows 98 to perform the kind of tasks you need to do regularly.

Before you get started in earnest, there are a couple of preliminary points I need to get out of the way. First of all, you probably read the introduction to this book when you were browsing through it in the bookstore. But if you didn't, please go back and read the introduction now. It contains some important information about how the book is organized and explains some of the special features and terminology you'll see on the following pages.

Also, from here on out, I'll assume that you're using a personal computer with Windows 98 installed. If you still have an older version of Windows installed on your computer and you're planning to upgrade to Windows 98 this weekend, now is the time to do it. Stop right now and turn to the appendix in the back of this book. You'll find some tips and helpful information about upgrading your system to the new version of Windows. After you get Windows 98 installed, come back here and pick up where you left off. (I promise, I won't start without you.)

Welcome to Windows 98

Before you start learning how to use Windows, it's worth taking a moment to consider just what Windows is—the role it plays in making your computer look and behave the way it does. (If you're already familiar with this stuff, feel free to skip or skim over this section.)

Windows 98 continues the legacy of the hugely successful Microsoft Windows operating system. It's an updated version of the software that provides the primary user interface for most of the personal computers used in homes and businesses across the country and around the world today.

What Is an Operating System and Why Do You Need One?

You probably know that computer software involves sets of instructions that tell a computer what to do and how to interact both with humans and with the various hardware components. It's the software that makes the components in your computer work together to behave like a personal computer instead of a timer for a microwave oven, a guidance system for a missile, or a very expensive paperweight.

An *operating system* is the software that creates a platform on which to run other, more specialized software, called *application programs*, that enable you to do things like write a letter, prepare a budget, design a brochure, or sort a customer database. The operating system takes care of housekeeping chores, such as file management, and provides common building blocks for application developers to create their programs. Modern operating systems also furnish much of the human interface for your computer as well by creating the general environment and providing a set of system management tools for the user.

You can think of an operating system as a miniature shopping mall. The computer hardware is the land and the roads, utilities, and other infrastructure. The application programs such as word processors and spreadsheets are individual stores within the mall. And, of course, the computer user is a shopper in the mall.

The mall itself is the superstructure that houses and brings together the stores, shoppers, and infrastructure. The mall supplies the stores with floor space, support services, connections to the infrastructure, and access to shoppers. For the shopper, the mall provides parking and pleasantly decorated common areas, but the main attraction is access to a large assortment of stores in one location.

Similarly, an operating system such as Windows provides a software superstructure that supplies application programs with support services and convenient connections to the hardware and to the computer user. The operating system provides the user with utility programs and some features, but just as the shopper is interested in the stores in the mall, the computer user is interested primarily in the applications that can run on an operating system. Like the mall, an operating system can provide a service to the user by enforcing some standards. You can usually count on all the stores in a mall being open at the same hours; and you can count on all the applications in Windows conforming to certain standards such as a uniform placement and order of menus.

The big difference between computers and shopping is that you don't have to go shopping at a mall, or even a smaller strip shopping center. You can shop at an individual store, make your purchases by mail order, or buy products directly from the manufacturer. In contrast, there's no practical alternative to using a computer operating system if you're going to use a computer at all. (A skilled programmer could write a program that includes its own version of all the services supplied by an operating system, but that's hardly a "practical" alternative.) You don't have to use Windows 98 as your operating system, but you do need to use an operating system of some kind.

Why Choose Windows 98?

All right, so you need to use an operating system. Does that mean you have to use Windows 98? No, it doesn't. There are a number of other operating systems available, such as Unix, MS-DOS, Linux, OS/2 Warp, and Mac OS. They each have their advantages and their loyal following of devoted users. But Windows is the overwhelming favorite operating system and it has become the de facto standard operating system for personal computers.

Not so many years ago, computer operating systems such as CP/M and DOS were text-based. All the communications between user and computer took place by the user typing text commands and the computer responding by displaying plain text messages on the screen. Simple operations such as launching a program or copying a file meant having to memorize arcane commands and file names and type them from the keyboard. One wrong keystroke and the command wouldn't work (or worse, would do something totally unexpected). In contrast, today you can do the same things by using a mouse to move a pointer onscreen and then clicking a button on the mouse when the pointer passes over an on-screen picture that represents the task you want to perform. The whole process takes longer to describe that it does to execute and it's much easier because there are no commands to memorize or mistype. The concept of allowing users to interact with a computer by manipulating symbols on the screen is called a *Graphical User Interface*, or *GUI*. Microsoft Windows wasn't the first computer operating system to employ a GUI, but it is undoubtedly the most popular.

Oddly, early versions of Windows were not very popular at all. Most common business applications such as word processors, spreadsheets, and database programs were designed to run on the text-based MS-DOS operating system. Windows tended to be a niche product used mainly for some graphics applications.

All that changed when Microsoft released Windows 3 in 1990. Windows had matured to the point where it offered a full complement of file management utilities and other system tools, and soon, new versions of many of the popular business applications appeared that were designed to work in the Windows environment. Adding Windows to a DOS-based computer transformed the experience of using a computer by replacing typed commands with mouse clicks in the new GUI. For example, in Windows 3.x, you could launch programs by clicking on icons in the Program Manager window and you could manipulate files by dragging other icons in the File Manager window. Gradually, Windows and Windows-based programs replaced the old standby DOS and DOS-based programs as the standard in homes and businesses everywhere. After a couple of years, Microsoft released Windows 3.1 and Windows for Workgroups 3.11, which added some features and improved performance but kept the basic product the same. All the variations of Windows 3.x create a GUI environment that runs on top of MS-DOS and most of the user interaction goes through Program Manager and File Manager.

Because Windows 3.x works in conjunction with MS-DOS, it must conform to certain conventions and restrictions. Perhaps the most visible of these restrictions is that file names could be no longer than eight characters followed by a period and a three-character extension. Equally important (though less visible) was the requirement that programs designed to run under Windows 3.x used what programmers call 16-bit computer code, despite the fact that modern personal computers (machines with 386, 486, and Pentium processors) run more efficiently when programs use 32-bit computer code.

Windows 95 was the first major overhaul of Windows since Windows 3.x, and it introduced several major changes. First of all, Windows 95 was a complete operating system in itself. Because it was no longer something added onto MS-DOS, Windows 95 wasn't constrained by some of the more troubling restrictions of MS-DOS. As a result, Windows 95—and applications specifically designed to run in Windows 95—could use 32-bit computer code for improved efficiency and better performance. Also, file names in Windows 95 were no longer restricted to eight characters plus an extension, so file names could describe the contents of a file instead of being cryptic abbreviations.

Windows 95 also brought refinements to the graphical user interface—new ways to launch programs and open documents, new buttons to facilitate managing application windows, and new context-sensitive shortcut menus, to name a few. Other new features of Windows 95 included improved networking, new utilities for managing printers and fonts, built-in support for controlling modem connections, and more.

Ever since Microsoft introduced Windows 95, it has enhanced the software with a series of updates. Some of the updates repaired bugs or made minor improvements in existing features and utilities. Other updates, such as Internet Explorer 4, added major new features to the operating system.

Now, Microsoft has released Windows 98—the next step in the evolution of the Windows operating system. Windows 98 builds on the Windows 95 platform and takes it to the next level by incorporating all the upgrades and enhancements that were available for Windows 95 (including all the Internet and Web access features of Internet Explorer 4). Windows 98 also includes many new or improved utilities, lots of behind-the-scenes changes to improve performance, and support for new hardware and technologies such as DVD disks, USB ports, and WebTV for Windows.

Windows is a popular operating system mainly because of the rich assortment of application software designed to run on it. Of course, one of the main reasons there is so much software available for Windows is precisely that it is such a popular operating system. Application software developers know that if they design their programs to run on Windows, they will have the largest possible population of potential customers.

There is another alternative—Windows NT—that contains greatly enhanced network and security features for large corporate environments. Should you use Windows NT instead? Perhaps, but not likely. Windows NT does have some attractive and powerful features (especially for network users), but NT's power comes at a high price in terms of hardware requirements and compatibility problems with a variety of hardware and software. Windows NT is for advanced users and corporate system administrators, not for the average computer user.

NOTE If you're like most computer users, you've never really had to make a choice of computer operating systems. That's because most people buy computers, not operating systems. Of course, the computer hardware isn't of much use without an operating system, but the computer manufacturer normally supplies the appropriate operating system as part of the package when you buy a new computer. Nowadays, that operating system is almost always Windows 98.

Starting Windows

Because the operating system must be running in order to control some of the most basic operations of the computer, the computer system itself starts Windows automatically when you turn it on. This is a marked contrast with Windows 3.x, which relied on MS-DOS being loaded first as the computer's operating system. Then, you would start Windows 3.x by typing the WIN command at the DOS prompt. The process might be automated by the computer's start-up files, but it was two separate steps nonetheless—first load the MS-DOS operating system, then add Windows 3.x. But no more. Windows 98, like Windows 95 before it, is a complete operating system and doesn't require another operating system running on the same computer.

Don't expect the process of starting Windows 98 to be instantaneous, though. It will probably take at least a couple of minutes. When you turn on your computer, the system first runs a series of diagnostics to identify and check out critical hardware components such as the video system, RAM, and hard drives. You'll probably see some text appear on your screen as each major test is completed. Only after the hardware tests are completed does Windows 98 start to load.

You'll know that Windows is starting to load when the Windows 98 logo screen makes its appearance. The logo screen is a sneaky way for Windows to distract you with a fancy graphic while it goes about its chores of checking the video system and other computer components and loading lots of files. Eventually, the logo screen is replaced by the Windows 98 desktop background color and Windows starts loading the various components, utilities, and programs that will make up your Windows environment. When the on-screen mouse pointer finally changes from an hourglass to an arrow, you're ready to begin using Windows.

NOTE If your Windows 98 system is set up to provide access to a network or to track personal preferences for multiple users, you will need to identify yourself to Windows. To facilitate this identification, a Windows Login dialog box will appear during the system start-up. Just type your user name and password in the spaces provided and then click on OK. The first time you log on to Windows, you will need to confirm your password by typing it two more times. (You'll learn how to activate and make good use of the password feature in the Saturday Afternoon session.)

CAUTION This description of the Windows 98 start sequence assumes that Windows is configured to automatically load the GUI. However, it's possible to run Windows 98 in command line mode without the GUI. It's rare, but possible, that a simple menu will appear when you start the computer that allows you to choose between the command line, GUI, and a special troubleshooting configuration called Safe Mode. To use the menu, you simply press the number key corresponding to the operating mode you want Windows to use and then press Enter.

TIP If you want to start Windows in a different mode but the start-up menu doesn't appear automatically, you can bring up the menu by pressing F8 at the moment Windows starts to load. But you'll have to be quick! You must press F8 after the last hardware self-test and before the Windows logo screen appears. The window of opportunity is only about three seconds. To ensure success, I usually start tapping the F8 key rapidly as soon as I see that the hardware tests are nearing their completion.

The Two Faces of Windows 98

After Windows starts and loads all its components and pieces, what will you see then? Well, that depends. You're going to see the Windows *desktop* (that's the background color or graphic and the collection of icons, toolbars, and buttons that appear onscreen and serve as the starting point for everything else you do in Windows). However, the appearance and the features of the Windows 98 desktop can vary dramatically from one system to another. So what you see when you start Windows 98 might not look much like what I see when I start Windows 98. For example, Figures 1.1 and 1.2 show examples of two very different Windows 98 desktops.

The Windows 98 environment is highly customizable. You can change colors, fonts, sounds, and much more. You can turn options on or off and you can adjust settings of various kinds to control how Windows will react in certain circumstances. In fact, there are so many ways to customize Windows that I will devote the entire Saturday Afternoon session to the topic. Still, customizing details like colors and fonts can change the appearance of your Windows desktop, but that doesn't really change the way things work.

However, there are some Windows configuration options that will have a more significant effect on how you do things. Windows allows you to choose between two ways to use your desktop: the Classic Style or the Web Style.

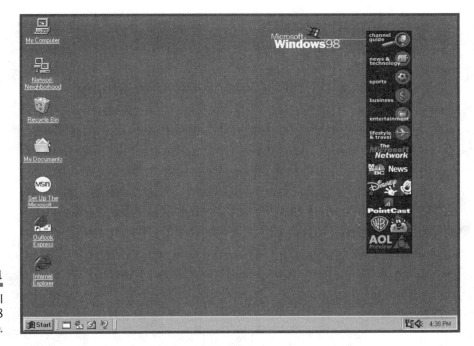

Figure 1.1

This is a typical Windows 98 desktop.

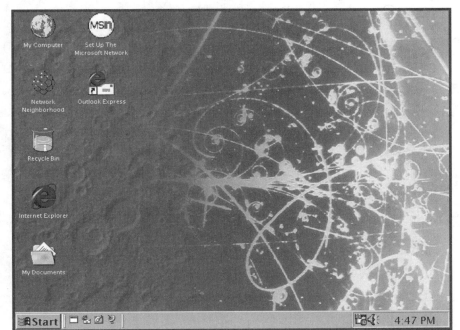

Figure 1.2

This is also a typical Windows 98 desktop.

The two styles give you two different ways to view and interact with the icons that appear on your Windows desktop. Which view you use will make a difference in how you do basic things like point, click, select, and open your programs, files, and documents—fundamental actions that are the very basis of using a graphical user interface.

This business of different views may sound confusing, and it could be, but don't let it throw you. The differences in the views aren't usually a problem unless they catch you by surprise. If you know which view your system is using, you'll know what to expect.

Keeping the Classic Style

The Windows 98 desktop using Classic Style (see Figure 1.3) is nearly identical to the standard Windows 95 desktop. If you've used Windows 95 before, you'll feel right at home with the Classic Style in Windows 98.

Figure 1.3

The Windows 98 desktop in Classic Style

If you previously used Windows 3.x, you may be a little disoriented at first, because the old familiar Program Manager is gone. In its place, you'll find the taskbar at the bottom of the screen and an assortment of icons on the desktop. But once you get past those differences, you'll find that mouse operations are basically the same in Windows 98 Classic Style as what you are used to.

When you're working in Classic Style and you want to select something with the mouse, you move the mouse pointer to the item you want to select and click on it using the left (or main) mouse button. If you want to launch or open an item, you double-click on it. This is standard stuff for anyone who has ever used a Windows- or Macintosh-based computer.

Adopting the Web Style

Windows 98's Web Style (Figure 1.4) departs from the traditional approach of the Classic Style by making the Windows 98 desktop act like a Web page. That is, when you use Web Style, the icons on the Windows 98 desktop react to mouse actions like hyperlinks on a Web page.

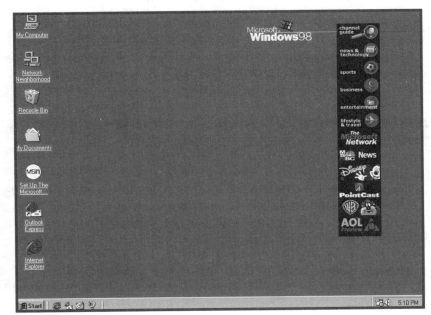

Figure 1.4

Notice the underlined text labeling the shortcut icons. That indicates that this desktop is using Web Style.

To select an icon or other item in Web Style, you simply point to it by letting the mouse pointer rest on the item for a second. You do *not* click on an item to select it in Web Style. Clicking on an icon in Web Style will launch or open the item—the same result that you would get by double-clicking on the item in Classic Style.

In a sense, the Web Style and its point and single-click mouse actions are a radical departure from the norm for a GUI operating system. But there is a certain logic to the Web Style too. The World Wide Web has become so popular that some of the standards developed for use in Web browsers are being adopted for use in other applications as well. So why not use the same techniques in the operating system? Instead of doing things one way when you're surfing the Web and another way in Windows 98, you have the option of applying the conventions of the Web to your Windows 98 desktop.

Another consideration in favor of the Web Style is that it generally requires fewer mouse clicks to get something done. Sometimes that means you can do things faster. But mostly, fewer mouse clicks mean less wear and tear on your mouse—and on the hand that holds it. Also, some people find it awkward to execute a double-click, especially when using some alternate pointing devices such as graphics tablets, trackballs, or the touchpads found on many laptop computers. Web Style comes to the rescue by nearly eliminating the need to double-click.

Interacting with Active Desktop

There's more to the Windows Web Style than just the way icons react to mouse actions. Web Style and its companion feature, Active Desktop, can make your entire Windows desktop act like a Web page. With Active Desktop enabled, your desktop can include text, graphics, backgrounds, hyperlinks, and other interactive elements, just like a fancy Web page—in fact, Microsoft often refers to the Active Desktop feature as viewing your desktop (or folder) as a Web page. You can interact with your Active Desktop by clicking on any of those interactive elements in addition to being able to work with the usual taskbar and shortcut icons. What's more, the same thing can apply to all the folders on your system. You'll learn more about Active Desktop in the Sunday Evening session.

NOTE Although the Web-like interactivity of the Active Desktop and the Web-like mouse actions of Windows 98's Web Style option complement each other and work together to make your desktop act like a Web page, they are two independent features. You can use Web Style without activating the Web page display feature of Active Desktop, and you can enable Active Desktop on a system using Classic Style folder options. The results of the latter combination might be a bit odd, but you can do it.

Which View Is for You?

Classic Style and Web Style both work very well and each one has its advantages. For example, Classic Style is faster and more precise when selecting objects such as files in a folder. On the other hand, Web Style enables you to launch programs and open files with fewer mouse clicks and makes it a little easier to integrate Web content into your desktop and folders. There is even a third option that allows you to create a custom hybrid of the two views by selectively enabling characteristics borrowed from each one. Whatever view you use, it's a trade-off, and in the end you'll have to decide for yourself based on your own personal preferences.

When you first start Windows 98, it might start out in either Classic Style or Web Style. So the first thing you'll need to do is figure out which view is currently enabled. Usually, that's easy to do. Just look for underlined text beneath the shortcut icons on the left side of the screen. That's an indicator that the desktop is in Web Style. Next, point to one of the icons such as My Computer. If the icon and its text label become highlighted without your clicking the mouse button, you're in Web Style. As a final test, click on the My Computer icon. If you're in Classic Style, a single click on the icon will highlight it, but if you're in Web Style, a single click on the icon will open the My Computer window.

Once you know which view is active, you'll know what mouse action to use to select or open an object on the desktop. That tells you all you need to know to be able to start learning how to use Windows 98.

Eventually, you'll want to try both Classic Style and Web Style to see which one you like the best. But you'll need to use each one for several days to give them both a fair trial. There isn't time to do that this weekend along with everything else you need to learn. Besides, I don't suggest trying to switch back and forth between Classic Style and Web Style. If you switch views frequently, it's much too easy to get confused about when to point, when to click, and when to double-click. So I suggest that you pick one view now and stick with it through the weekend, at least until you start exploring the Active Desktop features in the Sunday Evening session.

Switching views is a fairly simple process. If you have any previous experience with Windows 95, you can probably manage the task right now. Otherwise, you may want to read the next section to familiarize yourself with the Windows 98 Start menu and dialog boxes before you change views. When you're ready to change views, here are the steps to do it:

1. Click on the Start button in the taskbar at the bottom of the screen to open the Windows 98 Start menu.

2. Point to Settings in the Start menu and then choose Folder Options from the submenu that appears. This will open the Folder Options dialog box, as shown in Figure 1.5.

3. Click on either the Web Style radio button or the Classic Style radio button, depending on whether you want to select Web Style or Classic Style.

4. Click on OK to close the Folder Options dialog box and apply the selected view to your Windows 98 desktop.

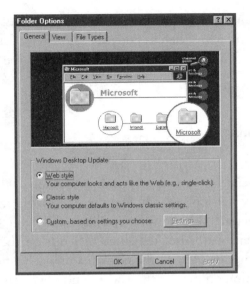

Figure 1.5

Choose between
Web Style and
Classic Style.

NOTE To avoid potential confusion caused by different mouse techniques in Classic Style and Web Style, I'll avoid instructing you to click on something unless clicking will have the same effect in both views. Instead, you'll see instructions to "select" or "open" a desktop icon. If you're using Web Style, you'll point to the icon to select it and you'll click on the icon to open it. If you're using Classic Style, you'll need to click on the icon to select it and double-click on the icon to open it.

Exploring the Windows Desktop

After Windows gets started, you'll see a screen resembling the one in Figure 1.6. This is the Windows 98 desktop, so named because it is the computer counterpart to the top of a typical office desk. It's mostly just open space where you can work on stuff. But the Windows 98 desktop, like your office desk, is also home to an assortment of tools and materials that you can use to help get your work done. On your office desk, you might keep items such as an in basket, a stapler, a telephone, a cup of pencils and pens, a reference book, and a stack of files for a current project. Desk drawers might contain useful items such as notepads, a ruler, a calculator, and other tools and supplies. The Windows 98 desktop contains the following items:

- Desktop background
- Taskbar
- Shortcut Icons
- Channel Bar

Due to the tremendous variety of possible Windows 98 configurations, your desktop may not look exactly like the one shown in the figure. For example, the Channel Bar won't be visible unless you have the Active Desktop feature enabled. Also, the shortcut icons on the left side of the screen might be hidden. Any of the elements might be displayed at a different size or position on the screen. And any number of other items might appear on your desktop that are not shown on the desktop in Figure 1.6. Nevertheless, the Windows 98 desktop shown in Figure 1.6 is fairly typical. It shows all the major components of the desktop in their default positions.

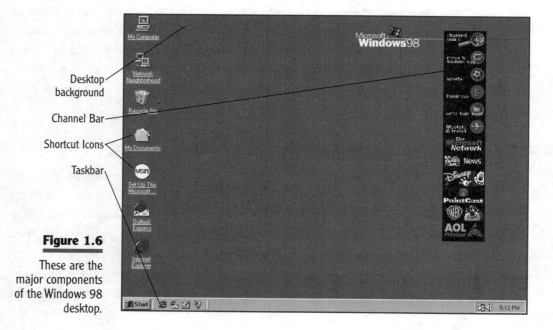

Figure 1.6

These are the major components of the Windows 98 desktop.

Testing the Taskbar

The taskbar is the gray bar at the bottom edge of the desktop. Normally, the taskbar is visible at the edge of the screen, even when you have several application windows open on the desktop. That means that the buttons and icons in the taskbar are almost always available, regardless of what else you're doing in Windows.

The main purpose of the taskbar is to enable you to launch programs quickly and easily and to switch back and forth between any of the programs you might have open and running at any given time. The taskbar (shown in Figure 1.7) is anchored on one end by the Start button and on the other end by the System Tray (the section at the right end of the taskbar where you see the clock display). Between the Start button and the System Tray are one or more toolbars. The most important of these is the program toolbar, which contains a button for each running program.

- **Start Button.** Click on the Start button to open the Windows 98 Start menu, which gives you access to all the programs on your system through a series of nested menus.

- **Toolbars.** Toolbars give you quick access to your programs, documents, Web addresses, and so on by conveniently keeping a set of icons available on the taskbar. For example, the Quick Launch toolbar shown next to the Start button contains icons to launch Internet Explorer or Outlook Express, an icon that will minimize all program Windows to give you access to your desktop, and an icon to use to view Channel content.

Figure 1.7

The Start button at the left and some program buttons in the middle are the common features of the taskbar.

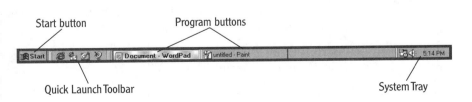

Start button   Program buttons

Quick Launch Toolbar   System Tray

○ **Program Buttons**. The Program buttons provide a quick and easy way for you to get to any program running on your Windows 98 system. Every program window is represented by a button; clicking on a program's button will bring that program window to the foreground where you can work on it. The program window will pop to the front even if you had it buried beneath several other windows. The program buttons on the taskbar eliminate the need for icons on the desktop to represent minimized programs as they did in Windows 3.x. Now, when you minimize a program, it disappears from the desktop except for its button on the taskbar. If you want to restore a minimized program to its regular window size, click on its button in the taskbar.

○ **System Tray**. The System Tray at the right end of the taskbar is normally home to the clock display and the icons that represent utilities and services that are running in the background. For example, some typical inhabitants of the System Tray are Task Scheduler (a program that runs maintenance utilities and other programs at predetermined times) and Volume (an on-screen volume control for your sound card).

Using the Start Menu

The Windows 98 Start menu is actually part of the taskbar, but it's so important it deserves to be considered separately. The Start menu replaces the Windows 3.x Program Manager with a streamlined tool that lets you start programs, find files, get help, and more.

Clicking on the Start button in the taskbar opens the Start menu. A few items in the Start menu, such as Help and Shut Down, will initiate an action immediately when you click on them. However, most of the items in the Start menu, such as Programs, Documents, and Settings, are not typical menu commands at all but are, in fact, the access points for submenus. You can identify the menu headings in the Start menu by the arrowhead that appears to the right of the menu name. Simply pointing to such an item in the Start menu will cause a submenu to open.

The submenu, in turn, may contain a mixture of icons for specific programs, icons for documents, and headings for still more submenus. In some cases, the submenus of the Start menu are nested several layers deep, as shown in Figure 1.8.

The multiple layers of submenus in the Start menu may look a little confusing at first. But they're actually pretty simple to use. For example, suppose you want to write a memo using WordPad, the mini word processor program supplied with Windows 98. First you click on the Start button in the taskbar to open the Start menu. Then you point to Programs in the Start menu to open the Programs submenu, point to Accessories to open another submenu, and finally, start the WordPad program by clicking on the WordPad icon in the final menu. That's all there is to it. Windows 98 launches WordPad and you can start typing your memo as soon as the WordPad window appears.

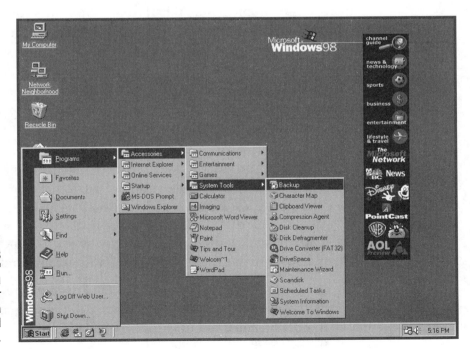

Figure 1.8

The Start menu organizes your programs into a series of nested submenus.

The Start menu can be a little tricky to use with pointing devices such as the touchpads found on many laptop computers. The problem is that when you point to a menu name and then try to move your mouse pointer into the submenu to make a selection there, it's very easy to accidentally touch another menu name with the mouse pointer, which will cause the original submenu to disappear and be replaced by another submenu. Try using the Start menu from the keyboard by pressing the special Windows key. Then you can use the arrow keys to highlight items in the menu. One press of the right-arrow key will move the highlight into a submenu with no chance of accidentally activating a different submenu. Once you highlight the program icon you want, press Enter to launch the program.

Try starting a few more programs with the Start menu. It doesn't matter which ones; just start three or four programs at random to get a feel for working with the Start menu's nested submenus. As you start each program, keep an eye on the taskbar and notice the button that appears there for each program. When you have a few different programs running, click on the program buttons in the taskbar and observe what happens to the corresponding program windows.

If you get too many program Windows open and want to close some of them, try this trick. Right-click on a program button in the taskbar and choose Close from the shortcut menu that appears. Windows will close that program. Pop-up shortcut menus such as this one are a handy feature of Windows. You'll find yourself using the right mouse button quite frequently to access the many Windows shortcut menus.

Of course, there's more to the Start menu than launching programs. Here's a quick rundown on the items you'll probably find in Start menu.

- **Programs.** I've already mentioned the Programs submenu and its nested layers of submenus. In addition to the program icons in those submenus, you might see program icons listed separately at the top of the Start menu. I usually keep icons for the Windows

Explorer and for my word processor on the first level of the Start menu so I can get to them quickly without going through layers of Program submenus.

- ✿ **Favorites.** Windows 98 helps you keep track of a list of favorite sites. Usually the Favorites are Web sites you previously visited with your Web browser, but they could also be documents, folders, or other network resources as well. Having the Favorites menu listed on the Start menu means you'll have quicker access to your favorite sites. Instead of opening your Web browser, displaying a list of favorite sites and then selecting one to visit, you can just make the selection directly from the Start menu. Windows 98 will automatically launch your Web browser if it's needed to view the site. You'll learn more about Favorites in the Sunday Morning session.

- ✿ **Documents.** Windows 98 maintains a list of the documents you've worked on recently. To reopen one of those documents for more work, you can just select it from the Documents submenu. The Documents menu is a highly useful feature that helps Windows 98 work the way you do. After all, the documents that you used recently are the ones that you're most likely to need again soon. It makes sense to have them readily available in a special menu. Of course, if you haven't worked with any documents yet, this submenu will be nearly empty with just a single entry, a link to your My Documents folder (which is also probably empty). So you need to make a mental note to remember to check out the Document submenu again later after it's had the chance to collect a few of your own documents.

- ✿ **Settings.** The Settings submenu gives you access to most of the utility programs and the dialog boxes you'll need to use to configure and customize Windows 98. You'll learn more about these options in the Saturday Afternoon session.

- ✿ **Find.** The Find submenu contains tools to help you find files on your computer, computers on your network, and more.

☼ **Help**. Click on Help in the Start menu to launch the Windows Help system—a window where you can look up all sorts of information about Windows 98. This one is worth exploring when you have the time.

☼ **Run**. Clicking on the Run command in the Start menu will open the Run dialog box shown in Figure 1.9. When the dialog box appears, you can type the name of a program or a DOS command and click on OK. Windows 98 will launch the program or open an MS-DOS Console window and execute the DOS command. You probably won't use this feature very much, but it can come in handy at times. (Just wait till Saturday morning, and you'll see what I mean.)

☼ **Log Off**. The Log Off command allows one Windows 98 user to log off so another user can log on without having to reboot the computer or completely restart Windows.

☼ **Shut Down**. This command enables you to shut Windows down when you're ready to turn off your computer. You'll learn more about this process at the end of this evening's session.

Using Icons on the Desktop

After you get the hang of using the taskbar and Start menu, it's time to turn your attention to the icons on the left side of the desktop. Actually, icons can appear anywhere on the desktop, but by default they start out on the left side, as shown in Figure 1.10. Some icons, such as My Computer, are permanent residents of the desktop—Windows 98 will not allow you to move them anywhere else. Other icons, such as those for files you're working on, might be on your desktop only temporarily until you find a more appropriate place to store them permanently.

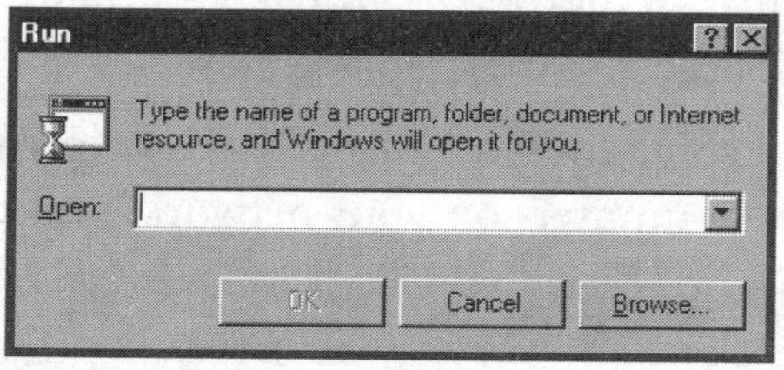

Figure 1.9

GUIs are nice, but sometimes it's faster to type a command in the Run dialog box.

Run dialog box showing: Type the name of a program, folder, document, or Internet resource, and Windows will open it for you. Open: [   ] OK | Cancel | Browse...

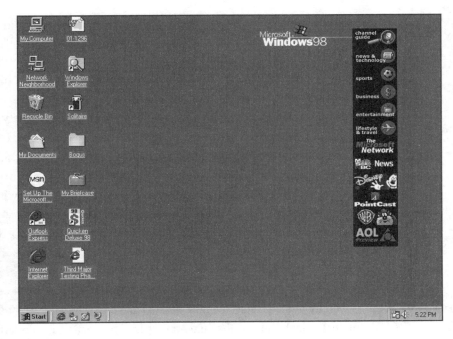

Figure 1.10

By default, desktop icons are arranged in a column on the left side of the screen.

Another kind of icon that might appear on your desktop is called a *shortcut* icon. A shortcut is a small file that contains a link to a parent file, usually a program or a document file, that is located elsewhere. A shortcut icon looks and acts very much like the icon for the parent file. In most cases, the only way you'll know you're using a shortcut is if you notice the small arrow symbol in the lower left corner of the icon. If you click (Web Style) or double-click (Classic Style) on a shortcut icon, Windows will open the parent file that the shortcut is linked to. This lets you do things like keep an important document file stored in an appropriate folder somewhere with a bunch of related documents, but still have a shortcut icon for that file on your desktop where it is instantly available.

Working with icons on the desktop is simple, but this is one of the activities where there is a noticeable difference between Web Style and Classic Style. Probably the most common action you'll take with an icon is to open the file or program the icon represents. To do this in Classic Style, you double-click on the icon, but if you're using Web Style, a single click will do the same thing.

You can do other things with icons besides open a program or file. You can rename, copy, move, or delete icons. (Later on this evening, I'll show you how to create shortcuts and how to manipulate shortcuts and other files. Remember that all the techniques I'll show you for working with files and folders will work on the desktop as well.) And just as you can move stacks of paper around to different locations on your office desk, you can move icons around on your desktop. To move an icon, just drag it from its starting position and drop it in its new location. You can also drag icons and drop them on other icons to perform actions. For example, dropping a document icon on a folder icon will move or copy the document to the target folder. Similarly, dropping a document icon on the icon for a printer tells Windows 98 that you want to print the document on that printer.

◆◆◆◆◆◆◆◆◆◆◆◆◆◆◆◆◆◆◆◆◆◆◆◆◆◆◆◆◆◆◆◆◆◆◆◆◆

 **CAUTION**   If you try to move an icon on the desktop and discover that it won't stay where you put it, that probably means the Auto Arrange feature is enabled. Auto Arrange automatically arranges your desktop icons in a neat column on the left side of the desktop. If you want to position icons elsewhere on the desktop, you'll have to disable the Auto Arrange feature. It's easy to do; you just right-click on the desktop, point to Arrange Icons in the shortcut menu that appears, and then click on Auto Arrange in the submenu. Now you'll be able to put your desktop icons anywhere you please.

◆◆◆◆◆◆◆◆◆◆◆◆◆◆◆◆◆◆◆◆◆◆◆◆◆◆◆◆◆◆◆◆◆◆◆◆◆

The best way to learn how to use icons on the desktop (or anywhere else for that matter) is with hands-on practice. Unfortunately, the default selection of desktop icons doesn't give you a lot to work with. So, for now, you'll have to be content with opening My Computer or My Documents and moving some of the other icons around on your desktop. Later, after you learn to create shortcut and file icons, you can try working with icons for other types of files and experiment with some drag-and-drop techniques.

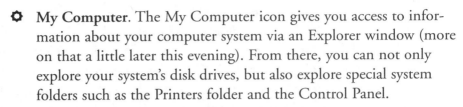

The following list will give you an idea of what some of the standard desktop icons do:

My Computer

- ○ **My Computer**. The My Computer icon gives you access to information about your computer system via an Explorer window (more on that a little later this evening). From there, you can not only explore your system's disk drives, but also explore special system folders such as the Printers folder and the Control Panel.

Network
Neighborhood

- ○ **Network Neighborhood**. If your computer is connected to a Windows-based network, the Network Neighborhood icon will open a window where you can browse through network resources to locate a shared computer, drive, folder, or printer. When you locate a network resource, you can use the Network Neighborhood window to work with that resource almost as if it were located on your own computer. (Unfortunately, you can't easily remove the Network Neighborhood icon from your desktop, even if you have no use for it because you're not connected to a network.)

Recycle Bin

- ○ **Recycle Bin**. When you delete files and folders in Windows, they're not really gone. Instead, they're stored temporarily in a special folder called the Recycle Bin. The Recycle Bin icon gives you access to that folder. You can open it up and examine the files that have been deleted. If you find a file that was deleted by mistake, you can restore it to its original location. I'll show you how a little later this evening.

Internet
Explorer

- ○ **Internet Explorer**. Normally, the Internet Explorer icon on the desktop provides a quick and easy way to launch the Microsoft Internet Explorer Web browser. However, before you can use Internet Explorer, you must configure the program with information about how you access the Internet. Until that is done, opening the Internet Explorer icon will launch the Internet Connection Wizard instead of the Web browser. There's no need to go through the process right now, as it's covered in the Sunday Morning session.

My Documents

⚙ **My Documents**. This icon serves as a window into a folder where you can store your document files. (You don't have to store your documents in the My Documents folder, but several popular applications use the My Documents folder as the default location for saving the files you create.) If you're using Windows on a new machine, the My Documents folder is probably empty. After you create some documents and store them in the My Documents folder, you'll be able to work with them just as you do files in any other Explorer window.

There are probably some other icons on your desktop. For example, you might have an icon for Outlook Express, the Internet e-mail companion program to Microsoft Internet Explorer. You might also have another icon that will launch a program to walk you through the process of signing up for an Internet access account on the Microsoft Network. The purpose of most desktop icons will be obvious from their text labels; you can figure out others by trying to open them.

Introducing the Channel Bar

So far, the components of the Windows 98 desktop have been essentially the same as their counterparts on the Windows 95 desktop. Aside from some relatively minor differences and improvements in Windows 98, the taskbar, Start menu, and desktop icons should all look familiar if you have used Windows 95—especially if you're using Classic Style in Windows 98.

The Channel Bar may not be as familiar. Although it's not entirely new to Windows 98, the Channel Bar only became available to Windows 95 users in the last few months before Windows 98 was released. The Channel Bar was introduced as part of the Internet Explorer 4.0 upgrade, but even among Windows 95 users who installed the upgrade, it was unusual to see a computer with the Channel Bar enabled.

The Channel Bar is a box containing a set of buttons that enables you to link to some specially designed Web sites—sites that are set up to allow your computer to automatically download information from the Internet and save it for you to view later, at your leisure. Some call this *push* technology.

If you have Active Desktop enabled and are viewing your desktop as a Web page, the Channel Bar will probably appear as a column of buttons on the right side of your desktop, as shown in Figure 1.11. Despite appearances, the Channel Bar is really a window (the border and title bar are hidden, but they magically appear if you point to the top button in the Channel Bar). And, like other windows, you can move and resize the Channel Bar if you so desire.

If you're not taking advantage of all the Active Desktop features, you won't be able to see the Channel Bar on your desktop. But don't worry about missing out on channel content. You can still view channel content in the Internet Explorer browser window. You just won't be able to do it directly on your desktop.

Figure 1.11

The Channel Bar is only available when you view your desktop as a Web page—in other words, you have Active Desktop enabled.

You'll learn how to work with channels and channel content in the Sunday Evening session. Until then, just ignore the Channel Bar—you can't do much with it until you establish an Internet connection and configure the channels anyway.

Take a Break

It's time to look at something besides the computer screen and the pages of this book for a few minutes. So take a break already. Get up and let the dog out or go get yourself a snack. When you come back, I'll cover the basics of using windows and dialog boxes, and then I'll show you how to use some of those desktop icons and buttons to do something useful such as explore your system and manage your files.

Opening Windows

Next up on the agenda, a quick look at windows—those ubiquitous on-screen boxes that are the namesake of the Windows operating system.

The basic concept is that each program gets its own movable, resizable on-screen box, called a *window,* in which to display its operations. You can have several program or application windows open and displayed onscreen at the same time (see Figure 1.12), and the windows can overlap without interfering with each other in much the same way that you can have several sheets of paper from different projects in an overlapping stack on your office desk.

You can maximize an individual window so that it fills the entire screen. You can also minimize a program window so that it's hidden from view without closing the program or the document you were working on. Simply clicking on the program's button in the taskbar will restore the minimized program window to its previous size. You can pick up where you left off without taking the time to relaunch the program or reopen the document.

Figure 1.12

You can have several programs running at one time, each in its own window.

You can work with the contents of only one window at a time (the one in the foreground) but you can easily switch to another window by clicking on the window or on the associated taskbar button to bring the desired window to the foreground.

The details of each program window will vary greatly depending on the activities you need to perform in that program and, to a certain extent, on the software developer's style. But nearly all program windows share many of the same components—easily recognized standard features that you will use to manipulate and interact with the window itself rather than the document or data within it. The WordPad window shown in Figure 1.13 is a good example of a typical application window. The following list describes how you can use some of the features of a typical program window.

Title Bar
Menu Bar
Toolbar

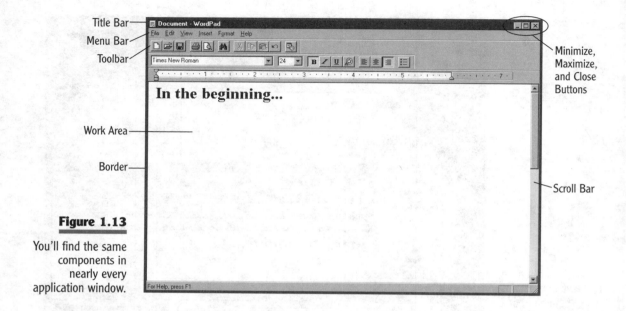

Minimize, Maximize, and Close Buttons

Work Area

Border

Scroll Bar

Figure 1.13

You'll find the same components in nearly every application window.

○ **Border.** The window border is more than just the edge of the program window; it's a tool for resizing the window. To resize a window, position the mouse pointer so that its tip sits atop the window border. When the mouse pointer changes to a double-headed arrow, drag the border to make the window larger or smaller on that side. If you do this at a corner of the window, you can drag diagonally to adjust two adjacent sides of the window at one time.

○ **Title Bar.** The Title Bar is the colored bar across the top of the window that lists the name of the application and the name of the current document. The Title Bar changes color to indicate which program window is currently active. To move a window, position your mouse pointer on the window's Title Bar and then drag the Title Bar to the new window location.

 TIP   Double-clicking on a window's Title Bar will maximize the window instantly, or if it is already maximized, restore it to normal size.

- **Minimize, Maximize, and Close Buttons.** These three buttons are located in the title bar in the upper right corner of each program window. Click on the Minimize button on the left (the one with the dash) to minimize the window. It will disappear from view but remain in memory; you can get it back by clicking on the program's button in the taskbar. Click on the Maximize button in the middle to maximize the window, or if the window is already maximized, to restore the window to normal size. Click on the Close button on the right (the one with the X) to close the window. Closing the window will shut down the program and remove it from memory.

NOTE If you've been using Windows 3.x, you may be accustomed to using commands on the Control menu, accessed by clicking on the Control button in the left end of the title bar, to minimize, maximize, restore, and close windows. In fact, you may be wondering what happened to the Control button. Actually, the Control button is still there, it's just disguised as a document icon. Click on this icon and you will see the familiar Control menu.

- **Menu Bar.** The Menu bar appears just below the title bar in a program window. It presents a list of top-level menu names. When you click on a menu name, a drop-down menu of related commands appears beneath it. Then you can click on one of the menu items to initiate an action, open a dialog box where you can adjust a variety of settings, or display a submenu of additional choices. Windows conventions specify the normal order of the menus starting with File on the left and going to Help on the right. As a result of this standardization, there's a good chance that you'll know where to find certain common commands in a typical Windows program even if you've never used it before.

- **Toolbar.** The Toolbar (which generally appears just below the Menu bar) contains one or more rows of buttons. Each button corresponds to a frequently used option or command in the program and is usually identified with an icon or pictograph instead of a text label (although toolbar buttons sometimes have text labels as well). Clicking on a button has the same effect as choosing the corresponding command or option from the menus, but the button is usually faster and more accessible.

✿ **Work Area.** The work area is usually a large open space occupying most of the window. It is used by the program to display the document or data that you're working on. In the example WordPad window, the work area is where you type and format your word processor document and preview what it will look like. In other programs, the work area might be quite different. The work area is really just the space where the program does whatever it's supposed to do.

✿ **Scroll Bars.** If a document is too large to be fully displayed within the confines of the work area, Windows will add a scroll bar to the side, and sometimes to the bottom, of the work area. The work area becomes an aperture through which you can view a portion of the document, and the scroll bars enable you to control what portion of the document is displayed in the work area. The length of the scroll bar represents the size of the document and the gray slider box represents the proportional size and position of the viewing aperture. To change what portion of the document you're viewing, simply drag the slider along the scroll bar. The small arrowhead buttons at each end of the scroll bar enable you to move the slider box in smaller increments.

Okay, it's your turn. Get in there and try it. Open your own WordPad window and try moving, resizing, minimizing, maximizing, and closing the window. Type something into a WordPad document until it's too big to fit in the work area and then use the scroll bars to move around in the document. Open some other application windows (try Notepad and Paint, both found on the Programs, Accessories menu) and try moving them about on the desktop. Practice switching back and forth from one program to another. Remember, you can switch to another program by clicking on its window or by clicking on its button in the taskbar.

Using Dialog Boxes

Pointing and clicking will take you only so far when it comes to interacting with Windows and with many of your Windows applications. Sometimes you will need to enter information or select options and settings that just aren't practical or convenient to present onscreen as menus or as individual icons or buttons. The solution to this problem is a graphical device called a *dialog box*, a sort of on-screen form where you can fill in the blanks, make selections from lists, and choose various combinations of options and settings. After you make your selections in the dialog box, you click on an OK button (or something equivalent) to close the dialog box and apply the settings.

Dialog boxes are ubiquitous. They show up everywhere, in Windows itself and in nearly every Windows-based program. Dialog boxes are used to present and gather all sorts of information, but despite their tremendous variety, dialog boxes rely on just a few simple formats for presenting your options and gathering information from you. You will be able to respond appropriately to almost any dialog box you see if you are familiar with the following:

- **Text Boxes.** Text boxes, like the ones shown in Figure 1.14, may be the easiest data entry device to understand. The proper use of a text box is almost self-evident. The prompt or label will tell you what kind of information is expected. Click on the text box to move the cursor into that box, and then type the requested information with the keyboard. That's all there is to it. The only problem with text boxes is that typed information is prone to spelling and typographical errors.

- **List Boxes.** List boxes do just what the name implies—they present a list of choices in a box. You select an item from the list by clicking on it.

- **Drop-Down List Boxes.** A drop-down list box, such as the Name box in the middle of the dialog box shown in Figure 1.15, may not look like a list at first glance because it shows only a single value in the box. However, the list will appear when you click on the little arrow button at the right end of the box. You scroll through the list and select an item by clicking on it. After you make a selection, the list disappears and the selected item is displayed in the box.

○ **Buttons.** Most dialog boxes contain buttons. At the very least, there will be an OK button and a Cancel button. Click on OK to close the dialog box and record the settings or click on Cancel to close the dialog box without changing the current settings. Other buttons will be labeled according to their function. Often, clicking on a button in one dialog box will open another dialog box.

○ **Radio Buttons.** Radio buttons, such as the ones shown in Figure 1.16, are used to present a list of mutually exclusive options. Radio buttons get their name because they work like the preset tuning

Figure 1.14

Text boxes are easy to understand, but they require you to type in information.

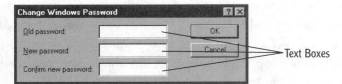

Figure 1.15

What could be simpler than selecting an option from a list?

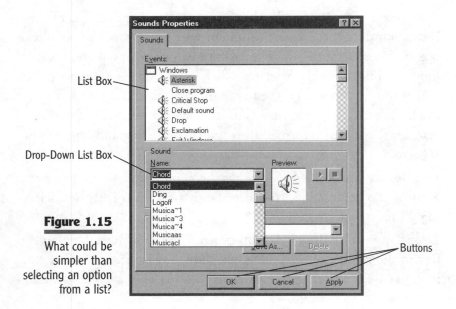

buttons on an old car radio—selecting any button automatically deselects the previous selection. You can easily identify radio buttons because you'll see a list of options, usually surrounded by a box, with a small circle beside each option. Only one circle will have a dot in it.

✿ **Check Boxes**. Check boxes are used to present options requiring individual on/off decisions. A check box appears as a small square ballot box beside an option description. A check mark in the box indicates the option is enabled. If the box is empty, the option is disabled. Clicking on a check box toggles the check mark on or off.

✿ **Tabs**. Tabs, such as those in the dialog box shown in Figure 1.17, provide a way to access multiple pages of options in one dialog box. Clicking on a tab displays a different set of options in the dialog box. You can move from tab to tab reviewing and adjusting settings without having to close and reopen the dialog box for each page.

✿ **Sliders**. Sliders allow you to set a value by visually positioning a marker to indicate where the desired value should fall in a range. Sliders are particularly useful when the underlying numerical value would be difficult for the user to relate to because of unusual measurements and standards. To use a slider, you drag the marker along the range line and drop it at the appropriate place.

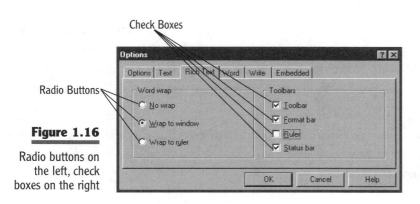

Check Boxes

Radio Buttons

Figure 1.16

Radio buttons on the left, check boxes on the right

Tabs —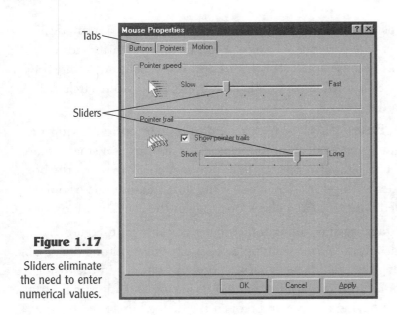

Sliders —

Figure 1.17

Sliders eliminate
the need to enter
numerical values.

Exploring My Computer

My Computer

In the upper left corner of your Windows desktop, you'll probably find an icon labeled My Computer. (It might have been moved or renamed, but it's there unless all the icons on your desktop are hidden.) When you locate the icon, open it. Windows will open a window similar to the one shown in Figure 1.18.

Take a good look at this window. For the moment, ignore the contents of the window and whether it's displayed as a Web page. Just look at the window itself, noticing things like the menus and the toolbar. You need to get to know this window because you're going to be seeing a lot of it.

The window you've been examining is called the Explorer window. Yeah, I know, it says My Computer in the title bar. But that title varies depending on what Windows is showing in the window. The generic name for the window is Explorer.

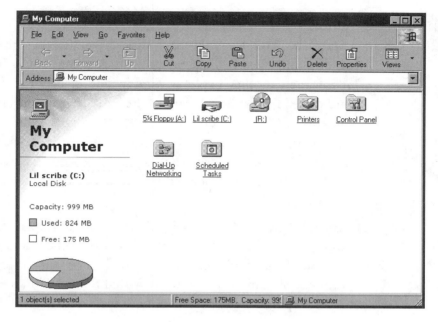

Figure 1.18

When you open My Computer, Windows uses an Explorer window for the display.

Windows uses Explorer windows to display just about everything. For example, in addition to My Computer, the Network Neighborhood, the Recycle Bin, and the My Documents folder all appear in Explorer windows. Go ahead, open them up and see the resemblance. Opening and closing lots of windows is good practice at this point.

Despite some minor variations to accommodate the needs of the window contents, they are all Explorer windows. You'll see more Explorer windows tomorrow as you work with features such as the Control Panel and the Printers and Dial-Up Networking windows.

Now let's return from the general idea of Explorer windows to examine the contents of one particular Explorer window—My Computer. You'll notice that the My Computer window contains icons for each of your disk drives, plus icons for some special system folders. There's no detail, so you can't do much with these few icons, but My Computer serves as a starting point from which to launch an exploration of your system.

Exploring a Drive, Folder, or File

(C:)

Locate the icon for your hard disk drive (C:) in the My Computer window and open it. Depending on the settings you're using, Windows might open another Explorer window and display the contents of your hard drive in it, or the contents of the hard drive might simply replace the contents of My Computer in the open Explorer window. Either way, the result is a window that looks something like Figure 1.19. Instead of a few icons for your system drives and a few more icons for system folders, the window is filled with folder and file icons, reflecting the contents of your hard drive.

Bogus

Now take the next step. Pick a folder icon and open it. As you might expect, Windows will display the contents of the folder in the Explorer window. If that folder contains other folders, you can continue to drill down deeper and deeper into the nested folders. Windows will continue to use Explorer windows to display the contents of folders. However,

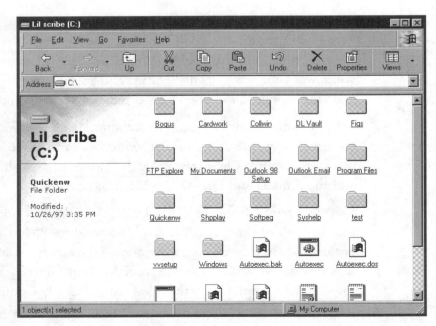

Figure 1.19

The Explorer window gets more crowded when displaying the contents of a drive.

Windows will leave the Explorer windows behind if you try to open an individual file. If the file is a registered document type, Windows will open the application that uses the kind of file and will then automatically load the file into the program for viewing or editing.

After digging down several layers deep in nested folders, you might need to get back up to the top level of the drive where you started. One way to get there would be to click on the Up button in the Explorer window toolbar. Each time you click on the button, Windows will display the contents of the parent folder one level higher than the current level. The Up button is a great way to move up a level or two. However, bigger moves are faster and easier using the Address box. Click on the arrow button in the Address box to display the address list shown in Figure 1.20. You can click on an item in the list to go directly to any parent folder or any top-level drive or system folder.

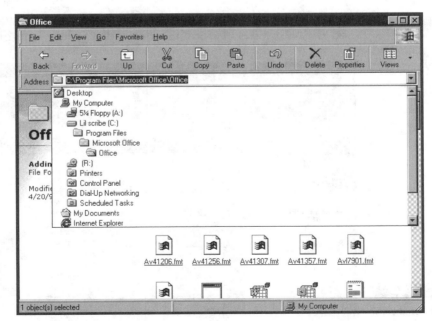

Figure 1.20

The Address list gives you instant access to any top-level drive or folder.

Working with Different Views

Views

You may have noticed that there was plenty of room in the Explorer window for all the icons in My Computer, but when you displayed the contents of the entire drive, things got crowded. The default view—large icon—isn't very practical for handling large numbers of folders and files. Fortunately, the Explorer window offers some optional views. In addition to the large icons, you can choose one of two arrangements using smaller icons or a detail view (see Figure 1.21) that displays additional information about each folder and file. Clicking on the Views button in the toolbar will cycle through the four available views in Explorer.

Managing Files and Folders with Windows Explorer

You could use Explorer windows to manage your files and folders. All the tools are there to let you create, copy, move, rename, and delete folders and files. However, I don't recommend it. There's nothing wrong with

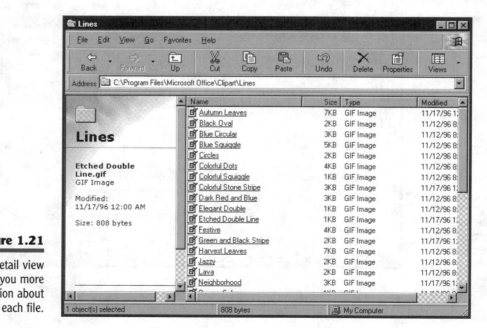

Figure 1.21

The detail view gives you more information about each file.

Explorer; it's just that there is a better tool available for file management—Windows Explorer.

To open Windows Explorer, click on the Start button on the taskbar, point to Programs, and then choose Windows Explorer from the submenu. When Windows Explorer appears onscreen (see Figure 1.22) you'll see that it's really another Explorer window, but this Explorer window has one very significant addition. The All Folders bar that appears on the left side of the work area provides a convenient tree-hierarchy display of your entire system. You can display as much or as little detail as you want in the All Folders bar. Click on the plus symbol beside a drive or folder to expand that branch of the tree and display the next level of detail. Click on a minus symbol beside an expanded drive or folder to collapse that branch. You have individual control over every drive and folder. Click on any drive or folder shown in the All Folders bar to display its contents in the main Explorer window on the right.

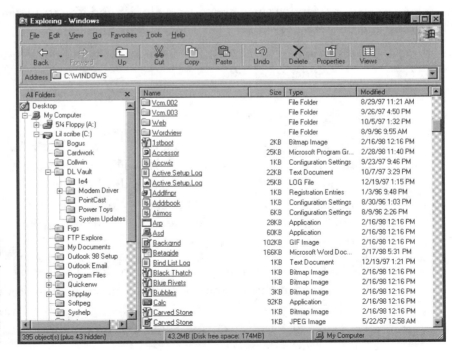

Figure 1.22

The All Folders bar transforms a plain Explorer window into the supercharged Windows Explorer.

Now that you have had an introduction to Windows Explorer, the Windows file management tool, it's time to try out some of the file management techniques you'll probably need in the future.

Creating New Folders

One common task that you will undoubtedly need to perform regularly is create a new folder where you can keep the files for a project. When you need to create a new folder, just follow these steps:

1. Display the contents of the drive or folder where you need to create the new folder. In other words, if you want to create a "Junk" folder that is a subfolder of the "C:\Bogus" folder, you need to start with C:\Bogus displayed in Windows Explorer.

2. Right-click on some unoccupied white space anywhere among the file and folder portion of the display. When the shortcut menu appears, point to New and then choose Folder from the submenu. Windows will create a new folder and give it the temporary name, "New Folder." That name will be highlighted.

3. Type in your name for the new folder and press Enter. Your new folder is ready to use.

Renaming Files and Folders

Renaming files and folders is another common task. You might discover that you made a typo when you originally named a file, or you could decide that the "My Stuff" folder needs a better name—"My Good Stuff" perhaps. (Okay, maybe changing "Contract-version 3" to "Contract-Final" is a better example.) Whatever your reason for the name change, it's easy to do by following these steps:

1. Display the contents of the parent folder of the file or folder you want to change and scroll the Explorer window so that the file or folder you want to change is visible. That is, you want to see the file or folder's icon and name, not the contents of the folder you're trying to change.

2. Right-click on the item you want to change and choose Rename from the shortcut menu that appears. Windows highlights the name of the selected file or folder.

TIP If you're using Classic Style mouse actions, you can skip the shortcut menu when you want to rename a file or folder. Just click on a file or folder once to select it and then click on it again to highlight the name so you can rename it. Of course, you have to be careful to click on the text of the name, not the file's icon, and you need to pause for a second or so between clicks so Windows doesn't think you meant to double-click on the item.

3. Type in the new name and press Enter. Windows Explorer records the new name for your file or folder.

TIP You don't have to retype the entire file or folder name to make a small change. After Windows Explorer highlights the name, you can use the left- and right-arrow keys to move the cursor through the file name so you can edit the existing name by erasing and retyping selected characters.

Moving and Copying Files and Folders

Perhaps the most common file management task is moving or copying files and folders from one folder to another folder or drive. You might make a copy of a file to send to a co-worker or copy a folder and all the files it contains so you have a backup of an important project. You might move document files from one folder to another to improve the organization of your hard disk and make the files easier to find.

There are several techniques for moving and copying files in Windows. For example, you can drag and drop files from one Explorer window to another. However, this seemingly simple operation can get confusing because Windows follows different rules depending on whether you are moving files between folders on the same drive or moving them to a different drive. You can also move or copy files to an invisible temporary storage area called the Windows Clipboard using the Cut or Copy buttons on the Explorer window toolbar and then display another folder in Explorer and use the Paste button to copy the files from the Clipboard into that folder. But this technique can be confusing because it's hard to keep track of what is stored on the invisible Clipboard. I prefer the technique described in the following steps because it works the same way every time regardless of whether you are copying or moving between drives or between folders on the same drive.

1. In the right side of the Windows Explorer window, display the contents of the folder containing the file or folder you want to copy or move.

2. Make sure the target location you want to copy or move to is visible in the All Folders bar in Windows Explorer. You may need to scroll down the All Folders list and expand some drive or folder branches to get the target folder visible. Don't click on the target folder or drive, just make sure it's visible in the All Folders bar.

NOTE Actually, the target location doesn't have to be a drive or folder icon in the All Folders bar of the Windows Explorer. It could be an Explorer window or an open spot on your desktop instead. Just be sure that it's available onscreen and not obscured by another window.

3. In the right side of the Windows Explorer window, select the file or folder you want to move or copy.

4. Right-drag the selected file or folder icon from the right side of the Windows Explorer window and drop it on the icon for the target drive or folder in the All Folders bar. (Remember, right-drag means to click and hold the right mouse button as you drag an object, and then release the button to drop the object at its target destination.)

5. Choose either Move Here or Copy Here from the shortcut menu that appears when you release the mouse button. Windows Explorer will move or copy the file or folder to its new location depending on which option you select.

TIP If you accidentally drop the file or folder you're trying to move or copy onto the wrong folder in the All Folders bar, simply choose Cancel from the shortcut menu to abort the operation. Then try again.

TIP You can select several individual items (files, folders, or both) in one folder and copy or move them to another drive or folder all at once. To select multiple items, press and hold Ctrl as you select one item and then another. Each additional item will be highlighted without deselecting previously selected items. Then, when you drag any selected icon to a new location, all the other selected items will come along with it.

CAUTION You can usually move document files around anywhere you want, but don't move or rename program files or the folders that contain them. If you move or rename a program file or any of its essential support files, Windows may not be able to run the program the next time you need it.

Creating Shortcuts

How would you like to have a shortcut icon on your desktop that links to the document file for that big report you're working on? It's easy to do. The technique is a slight variation on the one you just learned for moving or copying files. Just right-drag a selected folder or file icon from Windows Explorer and drop it on the desktop. Then choose Create Shortcut(s) Here from the shortcut menu. The shortcut icon appears on your desktop. (If the Auto Arrange feature is enabled, the shortcut icon may not stay where you dropped it. Windows will immediately move the new shortcut icon into the columns with your other desktop icons. You may need to minimize or move some open Windows before you can see your new shortcut icon.)

Deleting Files and Folders

Computer desks are like people; they tend to accumulate excess baggage and clutter—in this case, in the form of outdated files. Sooner or later you'll need to get rid of some of those unwanted files or folders. When the time comes, you can select a file or folder in Windows Explorer and then use any one of the following simple techniques to delete it:

- ✪ Right-click on the selected file or folder icon and choose Delete from the shortcut menu.
- ✪ Click on the Delete button in the toolbar.
- ✪ Press Delete on the keyboard.
- ✪ Drag the selected file or folder icon from Windows Explorer and drop it onto the Recycle Bin icon located on your Windows desktop.

No matter which technique you use to delete the file or folder, the results are the same. Windows doesn't completely delete the file or folder immediately. Instead, it moves the deleted item into a temporary storage area known as the Recycle Bin. This gives you some protection in case you mistakenly delete the wrong file or folder.

NOTE   If (perhaps I should say when) you need to recover a deleted file from the Recycle Bin, all you have to do is open the Recycle Bin (it's just another Explorer window) and locate the file or folder you want to recover, then right-click on it and choose Restore from the shortcut menu. Windows will move the file or folder out of the Recycle Bin and restore it to its previous location, where it was before you deleted it.

The Recycle Bin doesn't store deleted files indefinitely. The size of the Recycle Bin is limited, and when it gets full, Windows automatically discards the oldest files to make room for newly deleted files and folders. This system works pretty well because it ensures that the files and folders you're most likely to need to recover—the ones that you recently deleted—are available in the Recycle Bin. If a file has been languishing in the Recycle Bin for a while and you haven't recovered it, you probably won't need to.

TIP You can permanently delete all the files in the Recycle Bin by right-clicking on the Recycle Bin icon and then choosing Empty Recycle Bin from the shortcut menu. You might want to do this to make sure some sensitive files you deleted are really gone or to recover the disk space being occupied by the files in the Recycle Bin.

Closing Windows

There's one last thing to cover before bringing this session to a close—and that's exiting Windows. There's a wrong way to do it, and a right way. The wrong way to leave Windows is to simply turn off your computer. Doing this has the potential to cause all sorts of problems because it doesn't give Windows an opportunity to do some important housekeeping chores such as closing programs, saving documents, and cleaning up temporary files.

The right way to exit Windows and shut down your computer system is to follow these simple steps:

1. Click on the Start button on the taskbar and choose Shut Down from the Start menu. Windows will open the Shut Down Windows dialog box, as shown in Figure 1.23.

Figure 1.23

Pick the way you want to exit Windows.

2. Choose Shut Down (or one of the other options) and then click on OK.

3. Wait for Windows to shut down. Depending on the speed of your system and how many programs and files were open, this could take anywhere from a few seconds to a minute or so. (One of the minor improvements in Windows 98, as compared to Windows 95, is that the shutdown process is faster, so you won't have to wait quite as long as you did with Windows 95.) Windows 98 will be able to automatically shut off the power on most newer computers when the shutdown process is finished. If Windows can't shut down the power automatically, it will display a message onscreen when it is safe for you to manually turn the power off.

What's Next?

I hope the next thing you plan to do is get a good night's sleep. If you're following the plan, it's Friday evening and it's probably getting kind of late. So take a little while to relax and unwind, and then hit the sack. Tomorrow morning you'll learn how to install and use application programs in Windows. And that's just the beginning. There's more fun stuff to learn in the Saturday Afternoon and Evening sessions. Then on Sunday, I'll show you how to connect Windows to the Internet.

Installing and Using Applications

- ⚙ Installing and Removing Windows Components
- ⚙ Installing Software
- ⚙ Removing Software
- ⚙ Finding Your Way in Any Windows Program
- ⚙ Exploring the Windows Accessories

N ow that you know how to use Windows, it's time to *do something* with it. Having Windows without something to do is like having a hammer with nothing to build. To get some benefit out of Windows, you need to install and run some applications. (*Application* is a fancy word for a computer program that helps you do something useful or fun, like write a letter or play a game.) In this session you'll learn how to install and run all kinds of applications.

Installing and Removing Windows Components

Before you go out and buy a bunch of applications to run with Windows, check out the great free programs (a.k.a. Windows components) that come with it. Some are utilities, some help you with the Internet, and others are simple versions of practical applications that let you format text and draw pictures. There's a real mixed bag of them! I'll introduce you to them a bit later in this chapter.

The catch (and it's only a small catch) is that the default installation routine doesn't set up the whole set of freebies for you. If you got Windows 98 with a new computer or you upgraded from Windows 95, your system is probably missing a few of the helpful components that you might want. Here's how to check, how to grab any goodies that aren't installed, and how to get rid of any that are installed already that you know you're never going to use:

1. Click on the Start button in the taskbar and then choose Settings, Control Panel.

Add/Remove
Programs

2. Open the Add/Remove Programs icon. The Add/Remove Programs Properties dialog box will appear.

3. Open the Windows Setup tab. A list of all the Windows components appears, as in Figure 2.1. Here's a key to what you see:

   ✿ Each of the items on the Components list is a category of program (like Accessories or Communications).

   ✿ Categories with a blank check box next to them have none of their programs installed.

   ✿ Categories with a check mark in a white box have all of their programs installed already.

   ✿ Categories with a check mark in a gray box have some of their programs installed.

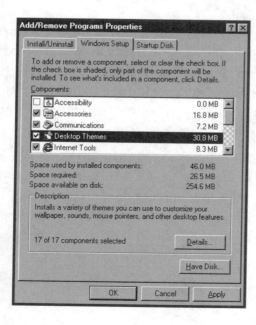

Figure 2.1

You can install (or remove!) Windows 98 components from here.

4. Pick a category that you want to explore and click on it. Then click on the Details button to display a list of the programs that fall under that category.

5. Click on a check box to select or deselect that program as desired. Placing a check mark installs the program; removing a check mark removes a program. Look in the Description area below the list to see what the selected program is for.

 NOTE As an exercise, try installing a Desktop Theme. Click on Desktop Themes on the list, and then click on Details. You see a list of themes. Click on the check box next to one that appeals to you (I like Inside Your Computer). The Desktop Themes Support item is also required, so a box pops up asking you whether you want to install it too. Click on Yes. Now both items are checked. Click on OK to return to the list of categories.

6. When you're done with the category, click on OK to return to Figure 2.1. Then repeat Steps 4 and 5 until you have checked out all the categories and chosen what you want.

7. Click on OK again to accept your changes. If prompted to do so, insert the Windows CD and click on OK to continue. You may be prompted to restart Windows; if so, click on OK to do it. Table 2.1 lists a few of the cooler components that you might want to install, and why.

There are also some components that you might want to consider uninstalling. For example, if you don't have a modem or other connection to the Internet, ditch the entire Online Services and Communications categories.

Installing Software

After you've exhausted the free programs that come with Windows, you may still want more. If so, you'll want to buy more programs at your local software store. You can buy an amazing variety of programs that will do everything from balance your checkbook to design your new deck.

TABLE 2.1 WINDOWS COMPONENTS

Category	Program	Purpose
Accessories	Desktop wallpaper	Provides extra images and patterns for your desktop (covered later in this chapter)
Accessories	Games	Four games you can play, including Freecell, a great Solitaire variation
Accessories	Mouse pointers	Allows you to change the appearance of the mouse pointer to any of several cool shapes
Desktop Themes	(any or all of them)	Schemes of colors, sounds, pictures, mouse pointers, and more, organized around specific themes (like baseball and space)
Internet Tools	FrontPage Express Web Publishing Wizard	Tools for creating Web pages and transferring them to a Web server

NOTE   Make sure that the programs you buy are designed to run under Windows 95/98. Such programs will run best on your system. If you buy a program designed to run under Windows 3.1 or DOS, it may not work as well.

When you buy a new program, it comes either on a CD-ROM (most common) or a floppy disk (less common). If it's a CD-ROM, it might have AutoRun capability; if that's the case, the setup program starts automatically, and you just have to follow the prompts that appear.

If you pop in the CD-ROM (or disk) and nothing happens, you'll have to start the installation program yourself. There are two ways to do it: the easy way and the foolproof way.

The easy way is to open the My Computer icon on the desktop, and then open the drive icon for the drive containing the new program. (Click on it in Web Style, or double-click on it in Classic Style.) If the setup program

starts at that point—great. If it doesn't, then a list of the files on the disk appears. Select the setup program from that list to start the installation process. (Look for a program called Setup.exe, Install.exe, or something similar.)

NOTE   If you see several files named Setup on the list of files, you may not be sure which one to choose. On some systems, the display is set up so that file extensions (the letters after the period in the name) are hidden for some files. This can cause the problem you're experiencing: several files may appear to have the same file name. To fix this, in the My Computer window, open the View menu and choose Folder Options. Click on the View tab, and click to remove the check mark from the Hide File Extensions For Known File Types check box.

The other way is more foolproof because you don't have to identify the setup program from any list. Just do the following:

1. Close all open applications.
2. Make sure the disk containing the new program is inserted in the appropriate drive in your PC.
3. Choose Start, Settings, Control Panel.

Add/Remove Programs

4. Open the Add/Remove Programs icon. The Add/Remove Programs Properties dialog box appears.
5. Click on the Install button on the Install/Uninstall tab (see Figure 2.2).
6. Follow the prompts that appear. Windows searches for the installation program for the new application and runs it.
7. If prompted to do so, restart the computer. (If you don't restart when it's recommended, your computer may lock up if you try to run the new program.)

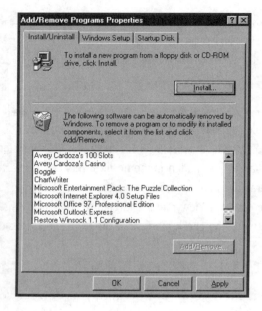

Figure 2.2

When you use the
Install button,
Windows searches
for the installation
program file
for you.

Removing Software

You may have noticed in Figure 2.2 that a list of installed programs
appears in the Add/Remove Programs Properties dialog box. (Take
another look now if you didn't.) The best way to remove a program that
you no longer want is to uninstall it from there. If you simply delete the
program files from your hard disk, traces of the program will be left
behind in the Windows Registry, and in time these traces can bog down
your system.

The *Windows Registry* is a special file that keeps track of what is installed in Windows
and what your preferences are (colors, icon placement, which applications to use for
certain file types, and so on). It is possible to use a Registry editing program to go in
and manually clean out the remains of improperly removed programs, but this is very
dangerous for a beginner. If you make an improper change, Windows 98 may stop
working. Why borrow trouble? Use Add/Remove Programs and stay safe!

To uninstall a program, follow these steps:

1. Close all open programs.

2. Choose Start, Settings, Control Panel.

Add/Remove Programs

3. Open the Add/Remove Programs icon. The Add/Remove Programs Properties dialog box appears (Figure 2.2).

4. Click on the program that you want to remove, and then click on the Add/Remove button.

5. Follow the prompts. Depending on the program, the uninstallation may happen immediately without further prompting, or you may have to make some choices.

6. When the uninstallation finishes, click on OK to close the dialog box informing you of it.

Here is some guidance for dealing with the questions the uninstallation routine may ask you:

❖ If it asks whether you want Automatic or Custom removal, choose Automatic.

❖ If it asks whether you want to restart your computer, choose Yes or OK.

❖ If it asks whether you want to remove a shared file or shared component, choose Keep (or No, whatever the program asks). You want to keep all shared files, for safety's sake, in case some other program needs them. If Remove None is an option, choose that, answering the question once and for all for the entire uninstallation.

● ●

NOTE Keeping all shared files is by far the safest route to take when you remove a program. However, safety has its price in the form of unneeded files left on your system. If you are confident of being able to correctly identify the locations of the files the uninstall program offers to delete, you can probably go ahead and let it delete any files in the program's own folder and sub folders. Make sure you keep any shared files stored in the Windows folder or sub-folders of the Windows folder.

● ●

❖ If it asks whether you want to remove internal data files, choose Yes.

Launching Applications

You can run any installed program from the Start menu. Click on the Start menu and point to Programs, and a list of installed programs opens. Some (like Windows Explorer) are right there on the Programs menu, but most of the others are organized into submenus, usually with easily interpreted names. (*Accessories* has the Windows 98 accessory programs in it, for example.) Figure 2.3 shows the Accessories submenu open. When you see the program you want to run, click on it to run it.

Finding Your Way in Any Windows Program

Once you know how to ride a bicycle, you can ride pretty much any bicycle, right? The brakes may work a little differently, or the basket may be in a different place, but the skills you need are similar.

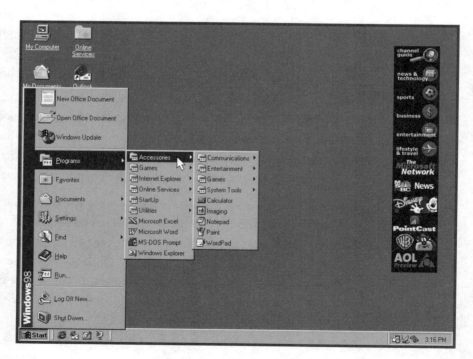

Figure 2.3

Run a program by choosing it from the Start menu.

It's the same with Windows-based programs. Once you catch on to the basic skills, you can apply them to almost any Windows program. (The exception is games—most games have their own unique interfaces that don't correspond to standard Windows 98 controls. With a game, you must rely on the instructions that come with it to figure out how to maneuver.)

For the examples that follow, I'll be using WordPad, a simple word processor that comes with Windows. To start WordPad, choose Start, Programs, Accessories, WordPad. The WordPad program opens, as in Figure 2.4.

Some of these controls are similar to the controls you learned about in the Friday Evening session, but it won't hurt to review them now.

- ✿ **Menu bar.** All Windows-based programs have a menu bar. Each word on the bar is a menu name. Click on the menu name to open the menu, and then click on the command you want to select it.

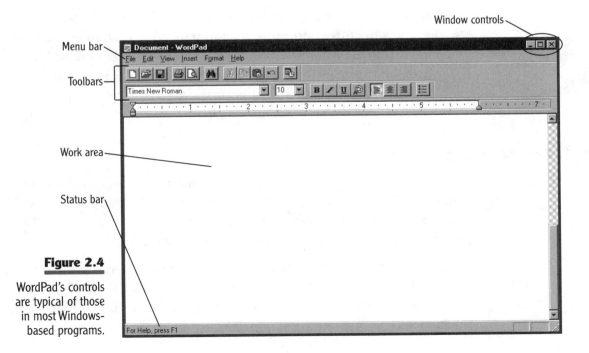

Window controls

Menu bar

Toolbars

Work area

Status bar

Figure 2.4

WordPad's controls are typical of those in most Windows-based programs.

- **Toolbars.** Most Windows programs have one or more toolbars. (WordPad has two.) The buttons on the toolbar represent shortcuts to menu commands. For example, the rightmost button on the top toolbar in Figure 2.4 is the New button, and it is a shortcut for opening the File menu and clicking on the New command.

TIP

To find out what a particular button does, point the mouse pointer at it to see a pop-up name (a ToolTip). Then look in the status bar for a brief description of the button.

- **Status bar.** The status bar reports any special messages or status indicators to the user. For example, in Figure 2.4, the Status Bar reminds you that you can press F1 for help.

- **Work area.** The center of most Windows programs is the work area, where you type or draw or do whatever it is that the program is used for. In WordPad, text you type appears there.

- **Window controls.** As you learned in last night's session, each window has three buttons in the top right corner. From left to right, they are Minimize (shrinks the window to a bar on the Task bar), Maximize or Restore (toggles between making the window full-screen size and making it normal size), and Close (closes the window and the program running it).

Issuing Commands

There are several ways to issue the same command in a Windows-based program. One way is to click on a button on the toolbar. Another is to open a drop-down menu from the menu bar and click on a command on it. Figure 2.5 shows the opened Edit menu in WordPad.

Notice in Figure 2.5 that some of the menu commands are dimmed. This means that you can't use them at the moment. For example, in Figure 2.5, the Links command is dimmed because there are no links in the open document.

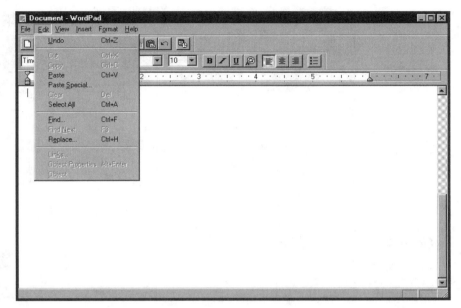

Figure 2.5

Click on a menu
name to open it.

Notice also that some commands have key combinations beside them, such as Ctrl+X for the Cut command. These are *shortcut keys*. They remind you about keyboard alternatives to using the menu commands. For example, if you have selected some text and want to cut it, you could open the Edit menu and click on Cut, or you could hold down the Ctrl key and press the X key. Both work the same. As you get experienced with a program, you will remember the shortcut keys for the operations you perform the most, and you may find them faster and easier to use than the menu commands.

Now take a look at the View menu, as shown in Figure 2.6. This menu contains two other types of commands. First, notice that the first four commands have check marks next to them. These are *toggle* commands, like light switches. Each time you click on one, it changes its state. In Figure 2.6, all four commands are turned on.

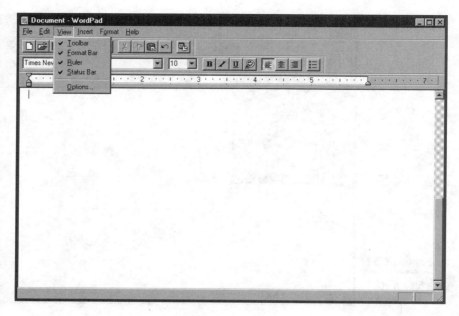

Figure 2.6

The View menu
shows other types
of commands.

At the bottom of the View menu is an Options command. Notice the
ellipsis (...) following the command. An ellipsis means that when you
select that command, a dialog box appears requesting more information
or clarification of what you want.

Selecting Text and Graphics

It's very important to get the hang of selecting, because this is something you'll need to do over and over in Windows-based programs that
manipulate text (like word processing programs) or graphics (like Paint
or PowerPoint). When you select something, you're telling the program:
"The next command that I give you should apply to the selected material." After you select, you can issue almost any command—you can tell
the program to change the object's appearance, copy or cut it, and so on,
and the command will just affect what you selected, not the rest of the
file. The same principle applies whether you're selecting files in an
Explorer window or selecting text in a Word document.

Go ahead and type some sample text right now in WordPad. Don't worry if it's nonsensical. Type a few paragraphs out of this book if you don't know what to type! As you type, you'll notice that you don't have to press Enter at the end of the line. When you fill up a line of text, you can just keep typing—WordPad automatically drops down the next line. You only need to press Enter to mark the end of a paragraph. After you enter some text, you can use it to practice the skills in this and the next few sections.

When you select text, it appears in *reverse video*. That means that if it was formerly black text on a white background, it appears as white text on a black background. Figure 2.7 shows some selected text in WordPad. When a graphic object is selected, it appears with *selection handles* around it, which are little black squares. Figure 2.8 shows a selected graphic image.

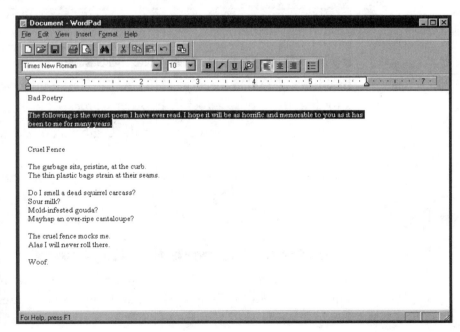

Figure 2.7

Here, an entire paragraph of text is selected.

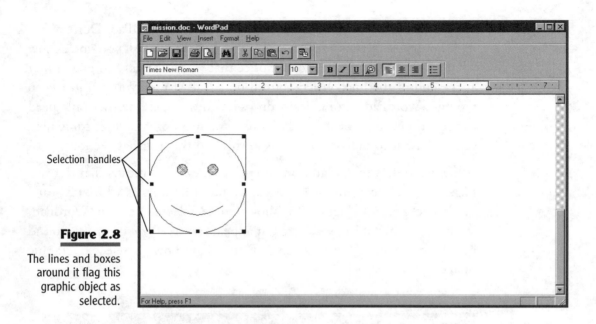

Selection handles

Figure 2.8

The lines and boxes around it flag this graphic object as selected.

Selecting Text with the Mouse

To select a graphic object, just click on it. The simplest way to select text is to drag the mouse across it. In other words:

1. Position the mouse pointer at the beginning of the text that you want to select.

2. Hold down the left mouse button while you move the pointer to the end of the text.

3. Release the mouse button. The text remains selected, as in Figure 2.7.

Selecting Text with the Keyboard

Some beginners find it difficult to select text with the mouse because it requires them to precisely position and move the mouse. An alternative way to select is:

1. Position the insertion point where you want the selection to start (as you learned in the preceding section).

2. Press Shift and use the arrow keys to extend the selection where you want it.

3. When the area you want is selected, release Shift. The text remains selected, just as if you had used the mouse.

There are also some shortcuts for selecting, with both the keyboard and the mouse. Table 2.2 shows the mouse methods that work in many Windows-based programs, and Table 2.3 describes the keyboard ones.

TABLE 2.2 SELECTING WITH THE MOUSE

To select this	Do this
A word	Double-click on the word.
A graphic	Click on the graphic.
A line of text	Move the pointer to the left of the line until it changes to a right-pointing arrow, and then click.
Multiple lines of text	Move the pointer to the left of the lines until it changes to a right arrow, and then drag up or down. (This works in most word processors, but not in all programs.)
A sentence	Hold down Ctrl, and then click anywhere in the sentence. (Does not work in all programs.)
A paragraph	Triple-click anywhere in the paragraph. (Does not work in all programs.)
Multiple paragraphs	Move the pointer to the left of the paragraphs until it changes to a right arrow, and then double-click and drag up or down.
A large block of text	Click at the start of the selection, scroll to the end of the selection, and then press Shift and click.
An entire document	Move the pointer to the left of any document text until it changes to a right arrow, and then triple-click.

TABLE 2.3 SHORTCUT KEYS FOR SELECTING	
To extend a selection	**Press**
To the end of a word	Ctrl+Shift+Right Arrow
To the beginning of a word	Ctrl+Shift+Left Arrow
To the end of a line	Shift+End
To the beginning of a line	Shift+Home
To the end of a paragraph	Ctrl+Shift+Down Arrow
To the beginning of a paragraph	Ctrl+Shift+Up Arrow
One screen down	Shift+Page Down
One screen up	Shift+Page Up
To the end of a window	Alt+Ctrl+Page Down
To the beginning of a document	Ctrl+Shift+Home
To include the entire document	Ctrl+A

Deleting Text and Graphics

To delete a graphic, select it and press Delete on the keyboard. You can delete text in two ways: you can delete one character at a time, or you can select a group of characters and delete them all at once. To delete one character at a time, you can:

✿ Position the insertion point to the right of the character you want to delete, and then press Backspace. This is good for simple typing errors that you catch on the spot; just Backspace over your mistake and retype.

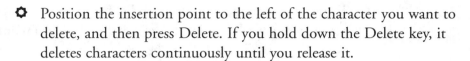

- Position the insertion point to the left of the character you want to delete, and then press Delete. If you hold down the Delete key, it deletes characters continuously until you release it.

There are also several equally good ways to delete blocks of text. The tricky part, actually, is selecting the text to be deleted. If you have caught on to selecting (see the preceding section), deleting should be no problem for you. Select the text to delete, and then do any of these:

- Press the Delete key or the Backspace key.
- Choose Edit, Clear. (This only works if the program offers this command; not all do. It's most common in spreadsheets.)

You can also Cut something to the Clipboard to delete it. This doesn't really delete it, but rather places it in "limbo," as you'll learn later in this session. If you never use the Paste command to move it out of limbo, it's effectively deleted. The following are the various ways to cut:

- Choose Edit, Cut.
- Press Ctrl+X.
- Click on the Cut button on the toolbar.
- Right-click on the selected text and choose Cut from the shortcut menu that appears.

Go ahead and experiment with deleting bits of the sample text you've typed in WordPad. That's what it's there for, after all.

Using Undo and Redo

Now that you've deleted big chunks of the sample text you worked with in WordPad, it's time to learn about a real life-saver of a feature: Undo. Undo allows you to reverse actions you've taken. In WordPad, you can undo only the one most recent action, but in more sophisticated programs like Microsoft Word, you can undo many more actions—and some programs even let you decide how much space to devote to this sort of protection.

To undo an action, just choose Edit, Undo or press Ctrl+Z. Some programs give you an Undo button on the toolbar. (WordPad has one, as pointed out in Figure 2.9.) If the program you are working with has such a button, you can use it instead of the menu command.

Some programs (like Microsoft Word, for example) have a Redo button on the toolbar. Redo is the opposite of Undo. If you have undone something erroneously, you can redo it by clicking on the Redo button. If you haven't undone anything, the Redo button will be dimmed out.

Moving and Copying

Now comes the fun part! You're going to learn how to move and copy selections from your document to other locations. (See, I told you selecting was an important skill.) This works in almost any Windows-based program.

You can move things around within the same document (like rearranging paragraphs or words), or you can move or copy them to other documents

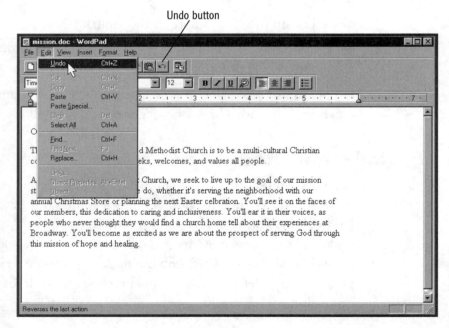

Undo button

Figure 2.9

Undo your last action with the Undo button on the toolbar or the Edit, Undo command.

or even files in other programs. For example, you can move some text from WordPad into one of the other Windows accessory programs, like Paint. The sky's the limit.

The thing that most confuses beginners is that there are so many different methods for moving and copying! It's really mind-boggling. Windows-based programs typically provide a lot of ways because everybody has their own ideas about what's easy, and the program authors apparently want to please everyone's tastes.

Just for simplicity, I'm going to break it down into two big categories: *cut, copy, and paste* (methods that involve the Windows Clipboard), and *drag-and-drop* (methods that involve dragging selections with the mouse).

Cut, Copy, and Paste

Take a moment to ponder this thing called the Windows Clipboard. Think of it as a holding tank, floating somewhere out there in Windows-land. Nearly all Windows-based programs have access to this Clipboard.

When you use the Cut command in any Windows program, the program takes whatever you had selected and moves it to the Clipboard. It disappears from the document you were working on. In contrast, when you use the Copy command, the program makes a copy of the selection and moves the copy to the Clipboard. The original remains in the document.

Now suppose you're ready to use the material on the Clipboard. You position your insertion point where you want the material to go, and then issue the Paste command. Because all Windows programs share the same Clipboard, you can issue that paste command from any Windows program, effectively sharing data from one program with another.

Whatever is on the Clipboard remains there until one of these things happens:

- ✪ You cut or copy something else to the Clipboard (from any program).
- ✪ You shut down Windows 98 (or the power goes off).

Because the material stays there, you can paste it multiple times. For example, if you wanted your name pasted in five different spots in a document, you could copy it once to the Clipboard and then move the insertion point to the right spots and issue the paste command five times.

Got that? Good. Now you're ready to try it out. Follow these steps:

1. Select some text in your sample document. (It doesn't matter how much or how little, for this exercise.)
2. Choose Edit, Cut.
3. Reposition the insertion point somewhere else in the document.
4. Choose Edit, Paste.
5. Choose Edit, Paste a few more times, to see additional copies pasted in.
6. Repeat the steps using Edit, Copy, in Step 2, instead of Cut.

Remember how I said there were so many different ways do to it? Well, here are your choices:

To cut, you can:

- Click on the Cut button on the toolbar, if your program's toolbar has such a button. (It typically looks like a pair of scissors.)
- Choose Edit, Cut.
- Right-click on the selection and choose Cut from the shortcut menu.
- Press Ctrl+X.

To copy, you can:

- Click on the Copy button on the toolbar, if your program's toolbar has it. (It is usually directly to the right of the Cut button.)
- Choose Edit, Copy.
- Right-click on the selection and choose Copy from the shortcut menu.
- Press Ctrl+C.

To paste, you can (after repositioning the insertion point):

- Click on the Paste button on the toolbar (if your program has one).
- Choose Edit, Paste.
- Right-click on the insertion point and choose Paste from the short-cut menu.
- Press Ctrl+V.

Drag-and-Drop Editing

People who are comfortable using a mouse usually love drag-and-drop. People who can't quite get coordinated with the mouse avoid drag-and-drop like the plague, and with good reason: it can be tricky getting the mouse pointer positioned just right.

Not all Windows-based programs support drag-and-drop, but most do, including WordPad, Word, Excel, PowerPoint, and the whole line of products produced by Microsoft. All the major word processing competitors do too, like WordPerfect and Word Pro.

Drag-and-drop involves dragging the selected text to a new location, the same way that you drag icons around in Windows 98 (or drag the cards in Solitaire!). Follow these steps to move selected text:

1. Select some text. (Any text will do.)
2. Position the mouse pointer over the selection so that the pointer turns into an arrow (rather than an I-beam).
3. Hold down the left mouse button and move the mouse to drag the text to the desired location. The mouse pointer turns into an arrow with a rectangle around it to show that it's taking your selection with it.

◆ ◆

CAUTION   Drag-and-drop works best if the desired location is also visible on the screen; if it's not, you have to drag all the way up or down the screen to make it scroll, and it sometimes scrolls faster than you would like. If possible, try to scroll the display or arrange the windows so that both the old and new locations are visible at once before you start the drag-and-drop process.

◆ ◆

4. Point the mouse pointer at the spot where you want to drop the selection (see Figure 2.10), and then release the mouse button.

You can also use drag-and-drop for copying; just press and hold Ctrl before you press the mouse button and don't let it up until you've released the mouse button. When you're copying, your mouse pointer has a little plus sign next to it.

Saving Your Work

Almost all Windows-based programs provide a means for you to save your work. (And the few that don't do so usually save your work automatically,

Mouse pointer

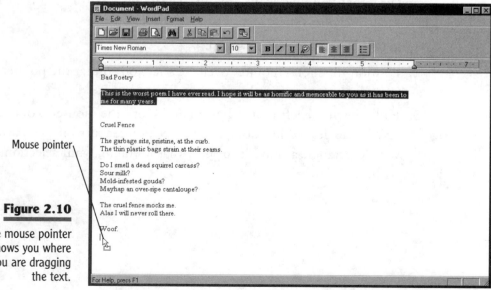

Figure 2.10

The mouse pointer shows you where you are dragging the text.

so you don't have to bother with it.) The command for saving is almost always File, Save (in other words, open the File menu and click on the Save command). There is usually a toolbar button for saving too; in WordPad it's the third button from the left on the top row (the one that looks like a floppy disk).

WHAT HAPPENS WHEN YOU SAVE?

You can think of your computer's memory as the top of your desk and your hard disk as a drawer in the desk. When you work in a program, you're working on the top of the desk, just as you would when you write a letter or add numbers by hand. When you exit the program or turn off your computer, it's like a janitor comes in and scoops everything from your desk surface into the garbage. Everything in memory is wiped out. If you want to preserve something you've been working on, you have to copy it to the hard disk so that it's safely stashed away in a drawer where the janitor can't get it. Copying it to the hard disk is called *saving*.

After a document has been saved, a copy exists on your hard disk that you can open, which you'll learn to do later in the session. The copy stays on your hard disk until you delete it. Each time you make changes to a document, you must save it again for the changes to be reflected in the copy stored on your hard disk.

When you issue the Save command, a Save As dialog box appears, asking you for a file name to assign to the document you're saving, as in Figure 2.11. Type a name in the File name box (replacing any default name that's already there) and click on the Save button.

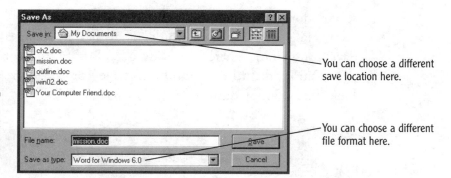

Figure 2.11

When you save a file for the first time, Windows programs prompt you for a name.

Names can be up to 255 characters and can include spaces. For practical purposes, however, you should keep the names reasonably short, such as Smith 8-97 or Henson Report. You can include spaces in your file names, and most symbols (although not < > ? or *). You usually don't have to type the extension on the end of the name (like .doc or .xls), because the program adds that automatically.

◆◆

CAUTION   If you are going to be sharing files with someone who uses DOS or Windows 3.1, you should stick to eight-letter names with no spaces, for compatibility. Otherwise, the truncated versions of your file names will appear strange to DOS/Windows 3.1 users. For example, a file called Robert Smith Letter.doc will become Robert~1.doc.

◆◆

Changing the Folder or Drive

If you have not used many Windows 98 programs, the file navigation system may seem foreign at first. You must use it whenever you need to change the drive or folder in a dialog box that saves or opens files. You'll encounter it in the Save As dialog box (see Figure 2.11) and also in the Open dialog box covered later in the session.

To change to a different drive, you must open the Save In or Look In drop-down list. (The name changes depending on whether you're saving or opening a file.) Figure 2.12 shows this drop-down list in the Save As dialog box. From it, choose the drive on which you want to save the file.

Select the drive
from this list.

Figure 2.12

Use this drop-down
list to choose a
different drive.

Next, you must select the folder where you want to save the file (or open
it from). When you select the drive, a list of the folders on that drive
appears. Double-click on the folder you want to select.

Table 2.4 explains the buttons and other controls you see in the Save As
and Open dialog boxes, as well as in other Windows 98 dialog boxes you
may encounter.

TABLE 2.4 BUTTONS FOR CHANGING DRIVES AND FOLDERS IN WINDOWS 98 DIALOG BOXES		
Button	**Name**	**Purpose**
	Up One Level	Moves to the folder "above" the one shown in the Save In box (that is, the folder in which the current one resides).
	View Desktop	Shows the items on the Desktop (useful if you have a data file there)
	Create New Folder	Creates a new folder within the one currently displayed.
	List	Shows the folders and files in the currently displayed folder in a list.
	Details	Shows details about each file and folder.

Saving a Document Subsequent Times

After a document has been saved, you can resave it in most Windows-based programs using the same file name and location by doing any of the following:

- ✪ Click on the Save button on the toolbar. (The Save button may look different in some other programs, but there's usually one available.)
- ✪ Press Ctrl+S.
- ✪ Choose File, Save.

If you need to reopen the Save As dialog box—to specify a different name or location, for instance—choose File, Save As, and then save the file as you did the first time.

Saving in Other Formats

In the Save As dialog box you may have noticed the Save as Type drop-down list. It enables you to save your file in a variety of other formats designed for use with other programs. The exact formats the drop-down list offers depend on what program you are using. Sophisticated programs like Word give you many more options than you see in WordPad.

NOTE   Sometimes you have to stretch a bit to find a common format between two programs. For example, suppose that you have a co-worker who uses only WordPerfect. All you have is WordPad in Windows 98, and WordPad doesn't export in WordPerfect format. You could export your document in RTF (Rich Text Format), however, which WordPerfect can import. Get a list of acceptable formats from your co-worker, and pick the one that will give you the most detail from the program you're using. Your last resort should be plain text (ASCII), which strips out all formatting.

To save in another format, just save the file using the Save As dialog box, but before you click on Save, open the Save as Type drop-down list and select a different type, as shown in Figure 2.13. Then click on Save.

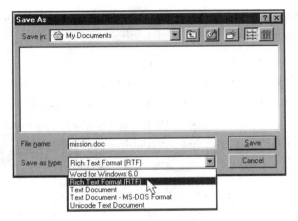

Figure 2.13

In most Windows-based programs, you can save your work in other formats for compatibility with other programs.

Closing a File

When you save a file, it remains onscreen in the program that created it, so that you can continue to work on it. When you're finished working with the file, you can close it in either of two ways:

- You can exit the program. The document closes when the program closes.

- You can close the file and keep working in other files in that program.

To quit a program, just close its window. You can choose File, Exit, or click on the window's Close button.

Programs differ in whether they allow you to have more than one file open at once. WordPad, for example, does not, and neither do most of the Windows accessory programs (like Paint and Hyper Terminal). When you start a new document, the currently open one is closed. To work on a different file in WordPad and programs like it, simply open a different existing file (File, Open) or start a new one (File, New).

Other programs let you have multiple files open at once. (Word and many other Microsoft Office programs are like this, as well as similar programs from other developers.) In these programs, to close a document and leave the program open, do any of the following:

- ✪ Click on the document window's Close button. If the document window is maximized, the Close button is the lower of the two X's in the top-right corner. If the document window is not maximized, the X is at the right end of the document window's title bar.

- ✪ Choose File, Close (not available in all programs).

- ✪ Press Ctrl+W (not available in all programs).

When you close the document, if you have made any changes to it since you last saved it, the program will ask if you want to save your work. Click on Yes or No, depending on what you want. If you click on Yes and the document has not yet been saved, the Save As dialog box opens, which you learned about earlier in this session.

Opening a Saved File

There's no point in saving your documents to your hard disk unless you are, at some point, going to open them again. When you open a file, you redisplay it onscreen, where you can modify it further if you want.

To open a saved file in almost any Windows-based program, follow these steps:

1. Do one of the following to open the Open dialog box, as shown in Figure 2.14:

    - ✪ Click on the Open button on the toolbar.
    - ✪ Choose File, Open.
    - ✪ Press Ctrl+O.

2. If the file you want to open appears, click on it. Otherwise, change the drive and folder displayed as needed to find it. (Refer to "Changing the Folder or Drive" earlier in this session for help.)

3. Click on the Open button or double-click on the document file name. The document opens onscreen.

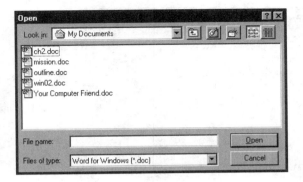

Figure 2.14

Choose the saved
file you want to
open and then click
on the Open
button.

Printing in Windows-Based Programs

 The easiest way to print is to click on the Print button on the toolbar, if the program you are working with has such a button. It doesn't get much simpler than that. When you click on this button, the default printer prints the active document, one copy of the entire thing.

TIP
In some programs, you can point to the Print button on the toolbar and a little box pops up telling you the name of the default printer. This is useful if you have more than one printer and you change back and forth between them. It does not work in WordPad, but it does work in Microsoft Word and many other Microsoft products. Try it.

The default print options work well if you want the default settings, but many times you will want to use a different printer to print more than one copy, print less than the entire document, or select some other special settings when you print. To set your print options, use the Print dialog box. It varies somewhat from program to program, but it will always have the same basics: number of copies, print range, printer to use, and so on.

1. Choose File, Print, or press Ctrl+P. The Print dialog box appears. Figure 2.15 shows the one for WordPad.

What range to print

Figure 2.15

The Print dialog box enables you to choose nonstandard print settings like a different number of copies or pages.

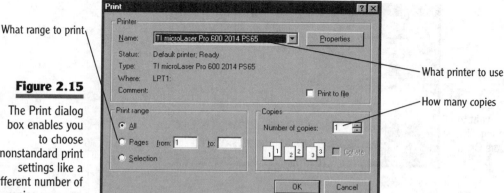

What printer to use

How many copies

2. Set any options in the Print dialog box that you want. (These are fairly self-explanatory.)

3. Click on OK to print.

All Windows programs feed their print jobs through a single print queue for each printer. After you have sent a job to the printer, a little printer icon appears in your system tray. You can double-click on it to open the print queue for that printer, or you can choose Start, Settings, Printers, and then select the printer (see Figure 2.16).

The print queue window lists all print jobs waiting to be printed. From the print queue window, you can do any of the following:

✪ Select a print job and then pause it or delete it by using Document, Pause Printing, or Document, Cancel Printing menu commands. To restart a paused print job, select Document, Pause Printing again.

✪ Select a print job and drag it up or down the list to change its position in the queue so that it prints sooner or later than other print jobs.

✪ Pause the entire printer with Printer, Pause Printing.

✪ Cancel all pending print jobs with Printer, Purge Print Jobs.

✪ Change the printer's setup with Printer, Properties.

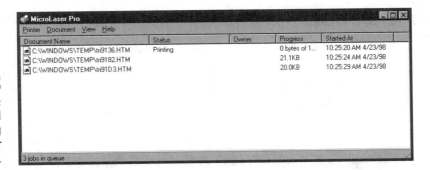

Figure 2.16

The print queue window lists and controls pending print jobs for the printer.

NOTE Occasionally, Windows will pause a printer queue automatically if it detects a possible problem with the printer, such as a paper jam. Normally, Windows will be able to resume printing automatically as soon as you correct the problem with the printer. But some-times Windows may not be able to tell when the printer error has been fixed. (This usually happens when working with an older printer.) In that case, you'll need to open the printer queue window and un-pause the printer manually.

Creating New Documents

In most programs, you can start a new document at any time by choosing File, New. Some programs also have a New button on the toolbar you can click.

As I mentioned earlier, some programs can have only one file open at once, so when you start a new one, the old one closes. Other programs don't have this limitation, so you can start as many new documents as you like. In such programs, you can switch among the open documents by choosing the one you want from the Window menu. (Not all programs have a Window menu; WordPad doesn't, for example, because it does not allow more than one file, or window.)

Take a Break

Congratulations! You've made it halfway through this morning's session. Stand up, have a stretch, and give your eyes a rest. This is a great time to get a snack from the fridge. When you get back, you'll start exploring the goodies on the Windows 98 Start menu.

Exploring the Windows Accessories

Windows 98 comes with some pretty great freebies, as I mentioned earlier. In addition to WordPad, which you've seen, there are over a dozen small applications ("applets") that you can enjoy.

Text and Word Processing

In this category fall programs that let you type, save, and print text. WordPad (Start, Programs, Accessories, WordPad) is the most powerful of the lot; you can use it instead of any of those high-priced word processors on the market if your needs are relatively simple.

Another text processor is Notepad (Start, Programs, Accessories, Notepad). Notepad creates and saves text-only files, with no formatting. It's a useful utility for editing system files and for creating plain-text files that you want to share with people on very different computers (like Macintosh or UNIX systems).

Graphics and Imaging

Windows includes several programs that help you create and manipulate graphics. Paint (Start, Programs, Accessories, Paint) is a favorite with children. It lets you draw lines and shapes and color them with any of hundreds of colors. Figure 2.17 shows a fun project in progress in Paint.

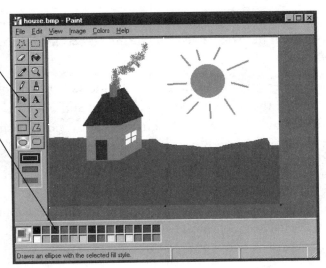

Click on a tool and then draw on the canvas.

Click on a colored square to choose the pen color.

Figure 2.17

Even kids can create pictures with Paint.

TIP After you've created a picture in Paint, you can use the File, Set As Wallpaper command in Paint to make your picture appear on the Windows desktop.

Another graphics program that comes with Windows 98 is called Imaging (Start, Programs, Accessories, Imaging). This is a fancier program, designed primarily for editing images rather than creating them. You can use it to control a scanner and to edit photos and other pictures by rotating, flipping, changing colors, and so on.

Games

Windows 98 comes with four games, all on the Start, Programs, Accessories, Games list.

Freecell is a strategy-rich solitaire game. Adults love it because almost every hand is winnable with the right strategy. (I have a friend who claims to have never lost a game of this. If she loses, she simply restarts, and replays the hand until she wins it.) There is also the traditional Solitaire game, which hasn't changed much since it was introduced in the original Windows 3.0.

Minesweeper was introduced with Windows 3.1. The object of this one is to find all the mines on the playing field and mark them as such, while clearing away all the tiles for squares that do not contain mines. Figure 2.18 shows a game in progress.

Hearts is the old-fashioned card game you probably already know how to play, but updated so you can play it over a network if your computer is connected to one. (You can also play with three computer opponents if you don't have access to other human players.)

Communications Programs

Besides Internet Explorer (the Web browser, which you'll learn about on Sunday), Windows 98 has several other programs that help you get information from one computer to another. They're all located in Start, Programs, Accessories, Communications.

Dial-up networking is the broad banner under which almost all of your connections via phone lines to other computers fall. As you'll learn on Sunday, you set up a dial-up networking connection to connect with an Internet Service Provider (ISP).

Figure 2.18

Minesweeper is one of four games that you get free with Windows 98.

Hyper Terminal is a standard terminal program, like the old Terminal program in Windows 3.1 and like commercial programs you may have used such as Procomm. It connects your computer to another over the phone lines in a direct and straightforward way, without any of the special protocols that enable you to see graphics. You might use it, for example, to connect to a BBS (a proprietary online service) set up by an individual or a company. Figure 2.19 shows a Hyper Terminal session.

The Direct Cable Connection is useful when you have data to transfer between two computers that are both located in the same place. For example, if you got a new computer, you could transfer all your data from the old hard drive to the new one by connecting the two with a cable and then using this utility.

Finally, Phone Dialer maintains an address book of phone numbers, and at your request dials your telephone for you (provided your modem is connected to your telephone). It sounds convenient, but most people rarely use it because it is more trouble to start the Phone Dialer program and choose a number to dial than it is to simply pick up the phone receiver and dial the number yourself.

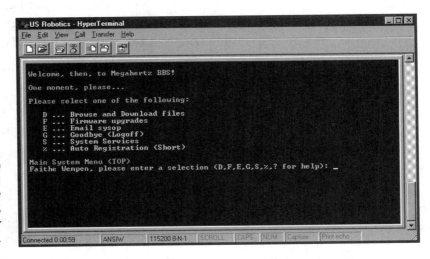

Figure 2.19

HyperTerminal offers text-only connections to BBS systems and other computers.

System Utilities

The Windows 98 system utilities are a tinkerer's dream. So many opportunities to tweak your system to make it run a little better! Each of the system utilities can be accessed from Start, Programs, Accessories, System Tools.

- **Character Map** shows every character from any font you have installed, in a table format. You can pick characters that you normally can't access with the keyboard and cut and paste them into documents.

- **Compression Agent** tweaks the performance of any compressed drives you may have (see DriveSpace).

- **Disk Cleanup** offers suggestions of files you can safely delete to save space on your hard disk.

- **Disk Defragmenter** consolidates the empty space on your hard disk into one big pool, and places all parts of each file together contiguously, so that programs run better.

- **Drive Converter (FAT32)** converts a 16-bit file system to a more efficient 32-bit one. (You use this utility only once.)

- **DriveSpace** runs a compression program on your hard disk that enables it to store about twice as much data as before. (You can't use this on a 32-bit file system like the one that Drive Converter creates.)

- **Maintenance Wizard** helps you schedule routine maintenance tasks such as running Disk Defragmenter and ScanDisk.

- **Resource Meter** displays a graphical indicator of how much the system's resources are being taxed at a given moment.

- **ScanDisk** checks your hard disk for errors and fixes them.

- **Scheduled Tasks** is another, less-automated way of scheduling regular maintenance. Tasks set up with Maintenance Wizard appear here.

- **System Information** provides detailed information about all hardware components installed and all software currently running.

- **Welcome to Windows** is an interactive tour and instruction booklet for beginners.

TIP

Put your computer on a maintenance program! Computers, just like cars, need to be tuned up regularly to stay at their peak performance. Let the Maintenance Wizard set up a regimen that includes regular ScanDisk, Disk Cleanup, and Disk Defragmenter sessions.

Entertainment Utilities

Windows 98 offers many multimedia tools (that is, tools that control sounds, videos, CDs, and so on), all located in Start, Programs, Accessories, Entertainment. As the technology for playing media clips has advanced, so have the tools in Windows.

NOTE

A *media clip* is any file that contains a sound, a video, a picture, a movie, or some other sight-and-sound bit of data.

Some of the utilities can play more than one type of clip. For example, Media Player is an extremely versatile tool that plays not only sounds and videos but also tracks from audio CDs. The CD Player program also plays audio CDs, but it offers additional controls (such as the ability to program a list of tracks to play) specifically for them (see Figure 2.20).

NOTE

When you pop an audio CD into your CD-ROM drive, Windows detects it and automatically starts the CD player, so you should never have to run it from the Start menu.

The ActiveMovie Control is a player designed specifically for Active-Movie-format video clips. This kind of clip is commonly found on the Internet. Sound Recorder works with your microphone or audio CD input to record your own media clips, which are then stored on your hard disk.

Figure 2.20

You can play
audio CDs with
the Windows
CD Player.

You'll also find a Volume Control in this group, but it's the exact same volume control that you can access by double-clicking on the little speaker icon in the bottom right corner of the desktop (next to the clock).

Rounding off the entertainment options are Interactive CD Sampler and Trial Programs. (You need to have the Windows CD-ROM in the drive to run these.) They install and present what are essentially advertisements for other products. If you like shopping, I guess you could call these "entertainment." (I had a good time playing with the Dilbert Desktop Games demo.)

Setting Up DOS Programs in Windows 98

Sad but true, not all programs you buy are designed for Windows. Some programs, especially those found in bargain closeout bins, are designed to run under DOS. Such programs might perform just fine under Windows 98, or they might not run at all. You just never know. (That's why those programs were in the closeout bin.)

Installing a DOS-Based Program

Enough of this gloom and doom; you might as well hope for the best. Your DOS-based program might work just fine under Windows 98. All you can do is install it and see.

1. Insert the CD-ROM or floppy disk for the program into your drive.

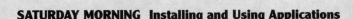

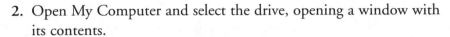

2. Open My Computer and select the drive, opening a window with its contents.

3. Scan the list of files, looking for the setup program. It may be called Setup.exe, but it could be something else instead, like Install. Figure 2.21 shows the installation CD for a DOS-based game, for example. Check the documentation that came with the program if you can't find the name. When you locate it, open it to start the installation.

4. If the installation program appears in a pinched-looking window, rather than full-screen, press Alt+Enter to make it fill the entire screen.

5. Follow the prompts to complete the installation. If you are not sure what to pick for a particular option, stick with the default. If the program asks whether you want it to automatically detect your sound card and/or video display, choose Yes. If the program asks whether you want to set it up to be launched from within Windows, choose Yes (of course).

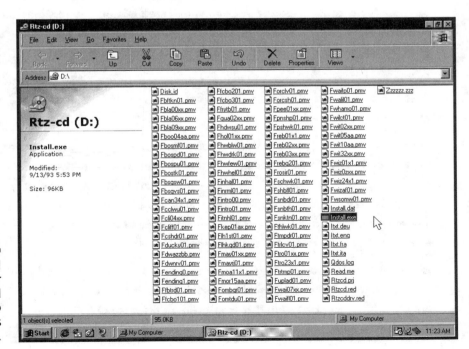

Figure 2.21

Here's a typical installation disc for a DOS-based game. The setup program is highlighted.

WHY ARE DOS GAMES SUCH A PAIN?

DOS-based word processors and the like usually run very well under Windows 98. The main problems usually come from DOS games. The reason is that game designers have, from the very start of computing, pushed the limits of what they have to work with. Give them a video screen that displays a given resolution of picture, and they'll figure out a way to make it display a better resolution. Give them a CD-ROM drive, and they'll figure out a way to stream video images from it into the game. Give them the possibility that the user has a sound card, and they'll build cool sound effects into the game. You get the idea. While people who design business applications generally try to design their program to run on an average system, game designers design their games to run best on top-of-the-line systems.

The games you'll find in the closeout bins now were designed anywhere between three and five years ago, when everyone had DOS systems. DOS was a real pain for game designers, because the user might have any of 20 different sound cards and 20 different video card types. Painstakingly, the designers built in support for multiple types of devices, and set up complicated installation routines that detected the types in use. The result was that you could play awesome games on your DOS system.

In Windows 95 and 98, however, things are very different. Windows handles the differences between video cards and sound cards, so the differences are transparent to the programs that run.

Your DOS program, however, doesn't know that Windows 98 is in control of those factors, so it tries to do its thing to detect and install the right drivers in the old, complicated way. This sometimes works in spite of itself, but many times it falls flat on its face. For one thing, the game may list 20 different sound cards and ask you to choose which you have, but five years ago, when the game was made, your sound card didn't exist, so it's not on the list!

All of this is why, personally, I stay far away from any games that do not say "Designed for Windows 95" or "Designed for Windows 98" on the box. It doesn't matter if it's a great bargain if it won't run on my system.

◆ ◆

CAUTION If the program wants to modify your setup files (Config.sys and Autoexec.bat), choose No. These modifications should not be necessary, and can even be harmful, since Windows 98 does not expect such modifications and may not be compatible with them.

◆ ◆

6. When the program finishes, do any of the following as needed:

   If a DOS prompt appears, type **exit** to return to Windows.

   If you see a message saying that you need to restart the computer, choose Start, Shut Down, Restart the Computer.

7. Back in Windows, reopen My Computer and navigate to the folder where the new program was installed.

8. Locate the file that runs the program (the documentation should tell you its name), and select it to run the program.

   If you see a file that ends in .PIF, as shown in Figure 2.22, use that file to run the program. The file name listing itself may not contain "pif" but if you highlight the file, as in Figure 2.22, you can see to the left of the display that the file name has a "pif" extension.

   If you do not see a .PIF file but there is a .BAT file, use it. (The Rtz.bat file in Figure 2.22 would have been my next choice had there not been a .PIF file.)

   If there are no .PIF or .BAT files, look for a .COM or .EXE file with a name similar to the program itself (for example, Rtz for a program called Return to Zork).

NOTE .PIF files are shortcuts to DOS applications that include special running instructions that help them run better under Windows. If the DOS program comes with a .PIF file, you should try using it. Even if it was developed for an earlier version of Windows, it might still work.

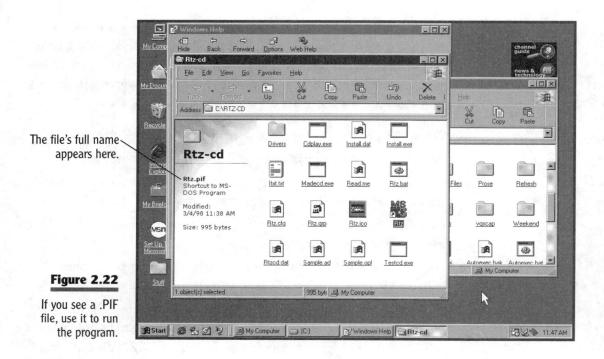

The file's full name appears here.

If it runs—great! In the ideal situation, the DOS program runs perfectly, and when you exit from it, you return to Windows. If that's the case, skip to "Setting Up Shortcuts for DOS Programs" later in this session.

Troubleshooting MS-DOS Programs

If you're reading this section, your DOS program probably isn't working right. I'm sorry. Fortunately, Windows offers lots of troubleshooting advice. Here's what to do:

1. Choose Start, Help. The Windows Help window opens.

2. Click on the Index tab. If this is the first time you've used the Index, it takes a moment or two to come up.

3. Type MS-DOS programs in the text box to jump to that part of the index.

4. Find and click on troubleshooting. In the panel to the right, click on Click here to start the MS-DOS troubleshooter.

5. Choose the appropriate category of problem you're having (see Figure 2.23), and then click on Next. Keep going until Windows Help has narrowed down the problem enough to offer you a suggestion.

6. Follow the instructions to implement the suggestion, and then try your program again.

You may have to visit the troubleshooter a few times if there are multiple problems that are preventing your DOS-based program from working.

Some Basic Troubleshooting Tips

There are far too many scenarios of why a DOS program won't run to explore them all here. (Besides, that's what the troubleshooter is for!) But here's a look at how a DOS program runs from within Windows, and how you can tweak its operation.

MS-DOS Prompt

When you create a shortcut icon to run a DOS-based program from within Windows, Windows creates a .PIF file for it if the program didn't already have one. It's sort of like a shortcut with some special properties,

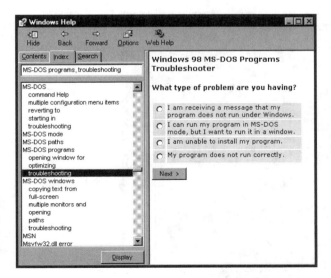

Figure 2.23

Use the Troubleshooter to pinpoint and solve your problem.

and it has a special MS-DOS icon, like the one in Figure 2.22. To modify how a DOS program runs, you modify the properties for this file.

Right-click on the file and choose Properties to open up its Properties. Figure 2.24 shows the one for the icon in Figure 2.22.

Here's a rundown on the most common changes to make to the Properties.

✿ Some older programs require you to type special parameters after the command to run a program at the DOS prompt. Obviously, you can't do this in Windows 98—you're running the program from an icon rather than by typing. You can include these extra commands on the Cmd line field on the Program tab. For example, if you are supposed to run the program at the DOS prompt by typing **rtz -nosound /cd:on**, you would make sure that this is what you enter in the Cmd line field. (By default, only the name of the program to run appears there.)

✿ The Close on exit check box on the Program tab determines whether the DOS window closes when you close down the program. Usually this is a good thing, but if you are trying to troubleshoot why the program isn't working under Windows, you may

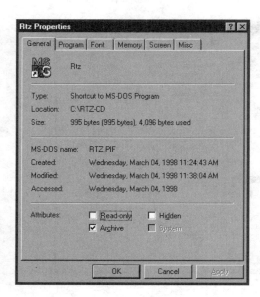

Figure 2.24

DOS-based programs have extra properties that you can set.

want to read any error messages that appear before the program terminates. In such cases, you could deselect this check box so that the DOS window with the error messages remains onscreen until you type **exit**.

⚙ If the program will not run from Windows, and you have tried everything, you may have to run it in MS-DOS mode. This essentially restarts the PC each time you run the program, so that the Windows graphical user interface isn't even loaded. When you exit the program, the PC restarts again and reloads Windows 98. To set this up, click on the Advanced button on the Program tab, to see the Advanced Program Settings dialog box, as shown in Figure 2.25. Click on the MS-DOS Mode check box to turn it on.

⚙ Some programs running in MS-DOS mode require special additions or subtractions to the computer's startup files. You can set these up by choosing Specify a New MS-DOS configuration in the Advanced Program Settings dialog box, and entering custom Autoexec.bat and Config.sys files in the boxes provided.

◆◆

CAUTION Creating a new MS-DOS configuration is for advanced users only, unless a technical support person has told you exactly what to put here.

◆◆

Figure 2.25

You can turn on MS-DOS mode as a last-ditch effort to make a DOS program run under Windows 98.

✿ If the program starts with the window squashed (that is, not full screen), you can switch it to full-screen size by pressing Alt+Enter, but if you set the Usage to Full Screen on the Screen tab, it will always start full-screen, so you can skip that extra step each time.

✿ If your DOS program locks up every time your screen saver kicks in, deselect the Allow Screen Saver check box on the Misc tab.

✿ Some DOS programs have their own shortcut key combinations that you may be accustomed to using. For example, Microsoft Word 5.0 (for DOS) uses Alt+Space to clear formatting. However, if a DOS program's shortcut keys conflict with those for Windows, Windows takes precedence. To make the DOS application take precedence, deselect any of the check boxes in the Windows Short-cut Keys area on the Misc tab.

Setting Up Shortcuts for DOS Programs

Once you get your DOS-based program running just the way you like it, you'll want to create shortcuts to the file that starts the program, so you can run the program easily without searching for it each time through My Computer. You can put the shortcut on the desktop, on the Start menu, or in both places.

To put a shortcut for a DOS program on the desktop, follow these steps:

1. Locate the file that you use to start the program in My Computer, and select it. This could be a .PIF file, a .BAT file, or an .EXE or .COM file.

2. Right-drag the file's icon from the My Computer window and drop it on the Windows 98 desktop. When you drop, a menu appears (see Figure 2.26).

3. Choose Create Shortcut Here from the menu. A shortcut to the file appears.

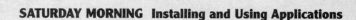

4. (Optional) Right-click on the new shortcut, choose Rename from the shortcut menu, and type a new name for it. Press Enter when you finish. You may want to rename the shortcut to remove the words "Shortcut to" from its title, for example.

One way to put a shortcut on the Start menu is to use the special utility designed for this. To use it, right-click on the taskbar and choose Properties. Then click on the Start Menu Programs tab and click on the Add button, and follow the prompts. However, this method has always seemed unnecessarily roundabout to me. Here is a quicker method.

1. Create a shortcut on the desktop for the program, as in the preceding steps.

2. Right-click on the Start button and choose Open. An Explorer window opens showing the items on the Start menu.

3. Open the Programs folder icon, displaying a list of the contents of the Programs menu (see Figure 2.27).

From here... ...to here.

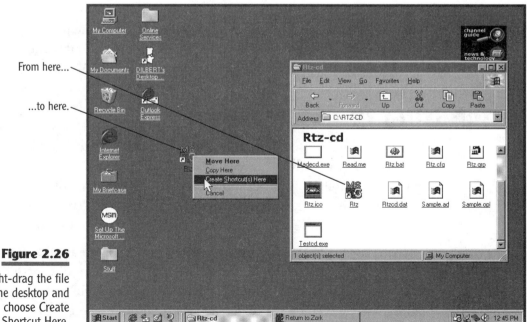

Figure 2.26

Right-drag the file to the desktop and choose Create Shortcut Here.

From here...

...to here.

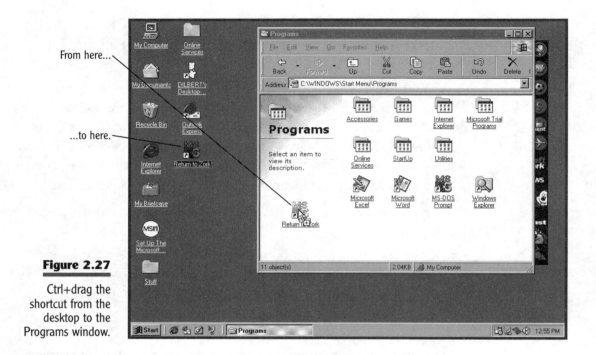

Figure 2.27

Ctrl+drag the
shortcut from the
desktop to the
Programs window.

4. Hold down the Ctrl key and drag the icon from the desktop to the
Programs window. To place the icon in one of the submenus, drag
it on top of one of the folder icons (for example, Accessories).

Customizing the Start Menu

Last night, you learned how to work with files in Windows 98, moving
and copying them from place to place. As you saw in Figure 2.27, the
Start menu itself is nothing more than an arrangement of folders that
contains shortcuts to various programs. You can add, remove, and reorganize the programs on it the same as you do with any other files.

In the preceding steps, you opened the start menu with a right-click and
then the Open command. But if you want to spend a lot of time moving
and rearranging things on the Start menu, you ought to open it in
Windows Explorer, by right-clicking and choosing Explore instead. When
you do so, the Start Menu folder opens, as in Figure 2.28.

Figure 2.28

You can move program shortcuts around on the Start menu from Windows Explorer.

Another way to add shortcuts to the Start menu is simply to drag a program's icon from an Explorer window and drop it on the Start button. That adds the program to the top of the Start menu. Then you can drag-and-drop on the Start menu to move it to another location on the Start menu. This can be kind of tricky. If you click on something on the Start menu, it starts a program. But if you click-and-hold, you can drag it from place to place. You may have a few false starts with this method, but after you master it, you may find it easier.

What's Next?

In this jam-packed morning, you learned about installing, running, and removing programs from your system. You also found out what freebies Windows offers, and found out how to set up DOS-based programs and how to customize the Start menu. Go grab some lunch and hurry back, because this afternoon you're going to learn how to customize Windows to look and act exactly the way you want. This is the cool stuff, like changing colors and displaying desktop pictures, so don't be late.

SATURDAY AFTERNOON

Customizing Windows 98

- Customizing the Taskbar
- Changing the Look of Your Windows Desktop
- Managing Your Multimedia Devices
- Fonts, Fonts, and More Fonts
- Managing Passwords

'll let you in on a little secret: almost nobody uses Windows 98 exactly as it arrives. Most people like to tinker with the program settings until Windows is the easiest, prettiest, and most fun that it can be. In this session, you'll create your own Windows 98 customization masterpiece. By the time you finish this session, nobody will ever mistake your Windows 98 desktop for a standard one.

Customizing the Taskbar

The taskbar is only a little strip of screen real estate, but it's important. Without it, you couldn't access the Start menu or switch between running programs (well, at least not very easily).

The taskbar consists of four areas. From left to right, they are:

- The Start button, which you already learned about this morning.
- Any toolbars that are set up to appear there. By default, the Quick Launch toolbar appears.
- The Programs toolbar—an open area where buttons for any running programs and open windows appear.
- The System Tray area, where you see the clock and perhaps some other icons too, depending on your system.

You can customize some of these areas, and also the entire taskbar itself. The following sections explain how.

Changing the Taskbar Position

The fact that the taskbar sits at the bottom of the screen is actually just convention—it can sit on any of the four sides of the screen you want.

To move the taskbar, just drag it where you want it to go. "Grab" any empty spot on the taskbar and drag your mouse up, to the right, or to the left. At first, nothing seems to be happening, but if you drag a bit further, the taskbar pops into the new location. Figure 3.1 shows it on the right side of the screen.

TIP

The taskbar is kind of big and ugly when it's on the sides, but you can set it to AutoHide, which I'll explain momentarily, to keep it from taking up too much space all the time.

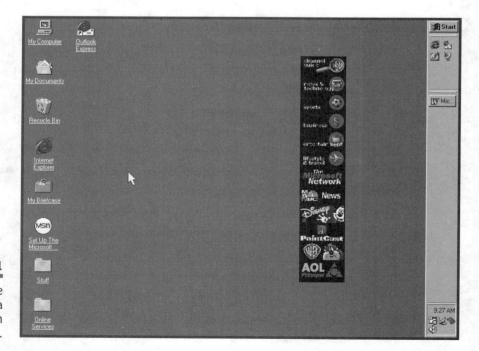

Figure 3.1

You can drag the taskbar to a different position onscreen.

There are a few drawbacks to placing the taskbar on the sides. One, as you can see in Figure 3.1, is that the buttons for open applications are harder to read. The one in Figure 3.1 is for Microsoft Word, but you can't really tell from the button unless you recognize the icon.

AutoHiding the Taskbar

The taskbar is absolutely useful, but sometimes you might wish that you could use the space that it takes up on the screen for something else. To solve this problem, Windows 98 enables you to AutoHide the taskbar. When you do so, the taskbar shrinks to a very thin gray bar until you move your mouse pointer over the area where it should be. Then it springs back into view.

To AutoHide the taskbar, follow these steps:

1. Right-click on an empty area of the taskbar and choose Properties from the menu that appears. The Taskbar Properties dialog box opens (Figure 3.2).

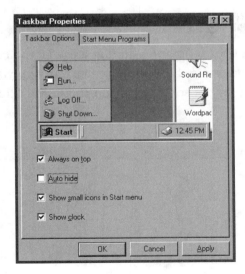

Figure 3.2

You can control the taskbar's appearance here.

2. Click to place a check mark next to Auto Hide.

   While you're here, change any of the other taskbar options as desired:

   ○ **Always on Top:** If you deselect this, application windows can cover up the taskbar. (I don't recommend this.)

   ○ **Show Small Icons in Start Menu:** Reduces the size of the icons that appear next to each command on the Start menu, thereby reducing the overall size of each menu. This is useful if you have a small monitor and a large Start menu with lots of installed programs.

   ○ **Show Clock:** This removes the clock from the system tray area in the bottom right corner of the screen.

3. Click on OK. Your changes are applied.

Now test the taskbar. If the taskbar is still visible, move your mouse to the desktop and click. The taskbar disappears. To make it reappear, move the mouse to the bottom of the screen (or the edge on which you have the taskbar positioned). It pops back into view again.

Changing the Taskbar Size

When you have lots of programs running at once, the taskbar can seem pretty small. In Figure 3.3, for example, there are ten windows and programs open, and they are so squashed on the taskbar that you can't tell what each one is.

Figure 3.3

The taskbar can fill up with running programs to the point where you can't even tell them apart.

TIP

If a program button on the taskbar isn't big enough to display the entire name of the program or file, you don't have to guess what's connected to that button. Simply point to the button (don't click on it) and Windows will display the program or file name in a pop-up box.

A quick fix is to make the taskbar larger (or, more precisely, taller). To do so, position the mouse pointer over the edge of the taskbar, so the mouse pointer turns into a double-headed arrow. Then drag toward the center of the screen. The taskbar grows, and all its pieces shift around to fill the available space (see Figure 3.4).

When you have closed most of the windows, you may want to go back to a normal-sized taskbar. To do so, just drag again on the border, this time dragging it toward the outside of the screen until it is back to normal size.

CAUTION

Sometimes beginners accidentally drag the taskbar to resize it so that it is just a tiny thin line. They then think that the taskbar has disappeared. Not so. It is only sized too small. If this happens to you, position the mouse pointer over the thin line and drag to make the taskbar normal size again.

Managing the System Tray

The System Tray is the area on the right end of the taskbar where the clock sits, perhaps with some other icons, depending on your system. These other icons in the System Tray represent programs that run "in the background" in Windows 98, ready to spring to action whenever you need them.

Figure 3.4

Drag the taskbar's border to make it large enough to see all the programs you have running.

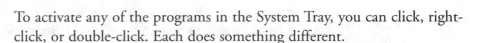

To activate any of the programs in the System Tray, you can click, right-click, or double-click. Each does something different.

- Right-clicking opens a menu, as shown in Figure 3.5.
- Clicking may do nothing, or may open a different menu, depending on the program.
- Double-clicking opens some sort of dialog box with full controls for the program.

Incidentally, the clock in the System Tray is a program. You can point to it to see the current date, right-click on it to get a menu, or double-click on it to open a dialog box where you can change the date and time.

Working with Toolbars

A new feature in Windows 98 lets you place an assortment of toolbars on the taskbar in addition to the Programs toolbar that contains buttons for all of your running programs. Windows 98 starts you out with the Quick Launch toolbar with four buttons installed. From left to right:

- Launch Internet Explorer Browser
- Launch Outlook Express
- Show Desktop
- View Channels

The handiest of these is Show Desktop. If you have several programs open and suddenly realize you need to start another program from a shortcut on the desktop, you can simply click on this button to minimize all windows immediately so that the desktop comes into view. A great time-saver!

Figure 3.5

Right-clicking on a
System Tray icon
opens a menu.

Three other toolbars come with Windows 98, and you can display any or all of them with a simple mouse action or two. To display or hide toolbars:

1. Right-click on the taskbar. A menu appears.

2. On that menu, point to Toolbars. A submenu appears listing the available toolbars. The ones that are already displayed have a check mark next to them (see Figure 3.6).

3. Click on a toolbar name to switch it between being hidden and being displayed. Here are the other toolbars:

   ❖ **Address:** Presents a text box where you can type the path of a folder or an Internet address on your system. Then it opens a window to display your selection.

   ❖ **Links:** Displays the same toolbar as the Links toolbar in Internet Explorer, which you'll learn more about tomorrow.

   ❖ **Desktop:** Displays a toolbar containing all the icons on your desktop. This is useful when you want to run a shortcut from your desktop without minimizing all the open windows.

◆◆◆

CAUTION If you display more than one taskbar toolbar, it can eat up a lot of the space on the taskbar where running programs and open windows appear. If you regularly use several toolbars, consider making the taskbar taller, as explained in "Changing the Taskbar Size" earlier in this session.

◆◆◆

These toolbars are not locked into the taskbar; you can drag them out into the desktop, where they become *floating toolbars*. Just drag the toolbar by the ridged tab on its left edge. A floating toolbar has its own title bar so you can drag it around, and its own Close button so you can get rid of it. Figure 3.7 shows the Quick Launch toolbar in floating mode. (You can resize its window by dragging the corner so that it takes up less space.)

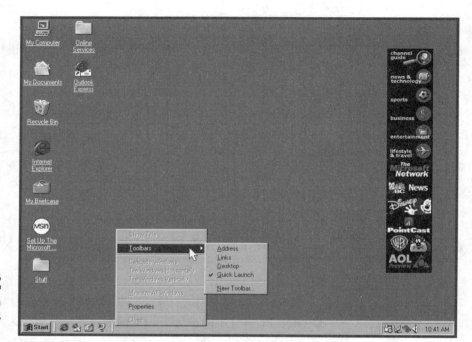

Figure 3.6

Choose which taskbar toolbars you want to show.

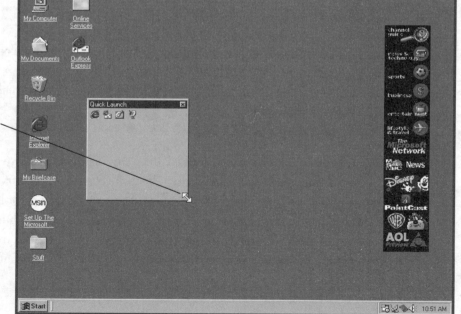

Drag the corner to change the box's size.

Figure 3.7

Toolbars can appear in their own floating windows.

NOTE   Toolbars on the taskbar can be moved and resized. To move a toolbar (for example, from the left to the right end of the taskbar), just drag it by the tab on its left side. To resize a toolbar (for example, to make it shorter or longer), drag its right side. The Programs toolbar—the area of the taskbar where open windows and programs appear— can be dragged off the taskbar to become a floating toolbar.

You can add icons to the Quick Launch toolbar (and to other toolbars as well) by simply dragging a program's icon or shortcut and dropping it on the toolbar. Similarly, you can remove a button from a toolbar by dragging it off of the toolbar and dropping it on the desktop or the recycle bin.

Changing the Look of Your Windows Desktop

Now comes everybody's favorite activity—playing with the way the desktop looks. You can experiment with wild combinations of fonts, colors, patterns, pictures, and other stuff that you haven't even imagined yet.

Changing the Display Resolution

The default display resolution on most systems is 640×480, or standard VGA. This resolution works well on very small monitors (14" and below) and for people who have poor eyesight.

If you have at least a 15" monitor and no vision problems, you may prefer an 800×600 display, or even higher. The resolution of the screen controls the size of the text and icons. The desktop itself expands to fill the entire space, so it looks like you have more empty space on the desktop at higher screen resolutions. In the applications that you work with, there will also be more space at higher resolutions—for example, more cells will appear on the screen at once in Excel.

A closely related factor is the number of colors that can be displayed simultaneously in a particular video mode. The lowest is 16 colors, which is ordinary VGA. Photos do not look good in this resolution, and some games

you play may look funny too. The usual number of colors is 256. Most games and other programs are written to take advantage of 256 colors.

Higher color resolutions may be available too, depending on your monitor and video card, such as 16-bit (sometimes called High Color) or 24-bit (sometimes called True Color). These color resolutions are a big help if you are going to be working closely with photos or other artwork where precise color is an issue. Compare the screens in Figure 3.8 and Figure 3.9, which show the same set of icons at 640×480 and 800×600.

CAUTION You may not always want to use the highest number of colors that your system can display. Higher screen resolutions and numbers of colors can cause a drop in system performance on older systems (like 386 and 486). That's because the monitor and video card have to work harder. (This happens on newer systems too, but you don't notice it as much because the systems are more powerful.)

To change the display resolution, follow these steps:

1. Right-click on the desktop and choose Properties from the menu that appears. The Display Properties dialog box opens.

2. Click on the Settings tab in the dialog box.

3. Drag the Screen Area slider to the left or right to decrease or increase the resolution (see Figure 3.10).

4. (Optional) If you want to change the number of colors used, open the Colors drop-down list and pick a different setting.

5. To test the new setting, click on OK.

6. At this point, you need to deal with one of two things:

   If you are changing only the resolution, A box appears explaining that Windows will resize the desktop on a trial basis. Click on OK again. The new setting appears, along with a box asking "Do you want to keep this setting?" Click on Yes to accept the new setting or on No to reverse it.

If you are changing the number of colors, a Compatibility Warning dialog box appears. Choose Restart the Computer with the New Color Settings and then click on OK.

Figure 3.8

This screen is displayed at 640×480, or Standard VGA.

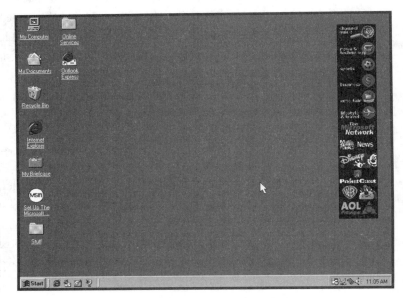

Figure 3.9

This screen is displayed at 800×600.

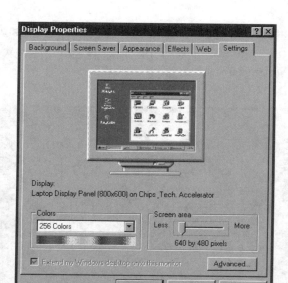

Figure 3.10

Move the Screen
Area slider to
change the
resolution.

NOTE   The higher the resolution, the more of your video card's memory is used. Ditto for colors: the more you use, the more load on the video card. If you have a video card with a minimal amount of memory (say, 1MB), you may have to choose between super-high resolutions and super-high numbers of colors; you may not be able to do both at once. The Display Properties dialog box protects you by not allowing you to set the controls to exceed your video card's memory. For example, on my laptop, I can use 16-bit (High Color) only with 640x480 resolution. If I set Colors to 16-bit and then drag the Screen Area slider to 800x600, the Colors setting automatically sets itself back to 256 colors.

You may have noticed that you can change the font size as well as the resolution. Depending on the resolution, you may be able to choose between Small Fonts and Large Fonts. Small is the default. Large can make the onscreen text more readable while still allowing you to use a higher resolution. Beware, however. Many programs are specifically designed for the default small fonts, and their dialog boxes and controls will look strange and may not work right with a large font display. (QuickBooks is one example of this.)

Hanging New Wallpaper

With Windows 98, you aren't stuck with a plain, ordinary desktop. You can place any of a variety of pictures or patterns on the desktop to create different effects.

Windows 98 comes with many bitmap (.bmp) images that you can use as wallpaper, and you can also create your own or use scanned images. Whatever images you place in the Windows folder on your hard disk will appear on the list of available wallpaper.

When defining wallpaper for your desktop, you have your choice of three placements: centered, tiled, or stretched. If the image is less than full-screen size, Center places it in the middle, in its actual size. Tiled repeats the image over and over, filling up the whole desktop. Stretch enlarges the image so that one copy of it exactly fits. Figure 3.11 shows the difference.

To set up or change wallpaper, follow these steps:

1. Right-click on the desktop and choose Properties from the menu that appears. The Display Properties dialog box opens (see Figure 3.12).
2. On the Wallpaper list, click on a picture. A sample of it appears above the list.
3. Open the Display drop-down list and choose Center, Tile, or Stretch.
4. Click on OK.

If you don't have wallpaper covering the entire desktop (for example, if you chose Center or if you are not using any wallpaper), you can place a pattern on the desktop itself. A *pattern* is sort of an overlay over the desktop that allows the color behind it to peek through. (In contrast, wallpaper covers up the desktop color entirely.) To choose a pattern, click on the Pattern button in the Display Properties dialog box (see Figure 3.12). A Pattern dialog box opens. Choose the pattern you want to use, and click on OK. Figure 3.13 shows the Buttons pattern in use (with no wallpaper).

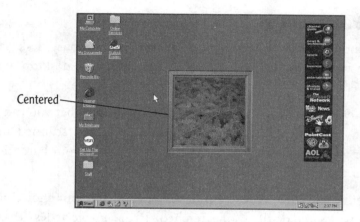

Centered

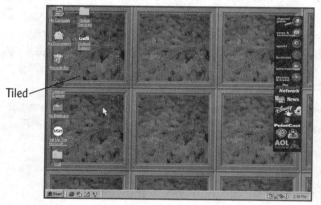

Tiled

Stretched

Figure 3.11

The same image can look very different depending on the Display choice you make.

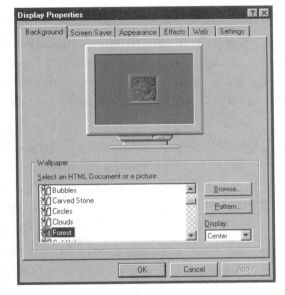

Figure 3.12

Choose your wallpaper and how to display it.

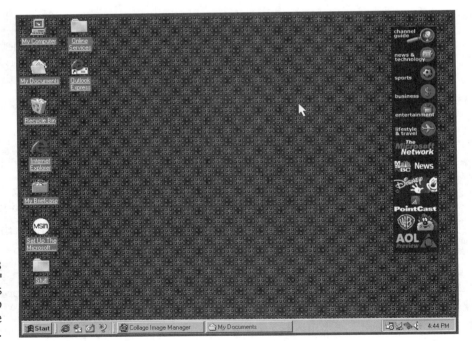

Figure 3.13

Patterns can dress up your desktop too, but in a more subtle way.

Changing the Screen Saver

A long time ago (back in the 1980s), monitors weren't very good, and if you left the same image displayed on them for a long time, that image *burned in*—left a ghost that you could see no matter what else was on the screen. You can still see traces of this on ATM machines and old video games.

Because people were concerned about ruining their monitors, there was a market for screen savers. These programs kicked in when a computer remained idle for more than a few minutes and displayed a constantly changing image to prevent any one image from burning in. Some of the images the screen savers displayed were quite amusing.

Today, monitors are much better, and burn-in is no longer much of a threat, but screen savers are still very popular simply because they're fun. Windows 98 comes with several screen savers.

TIP

You might not have all of the Windows 98 screen savers installed. Turn back to this morning's session and use Add/Remove Programs to add more screen savers (in the Accessories category) to your system.

To choose which screen saver to use, follow these steps:

1. Right-click on the desktop and choose Properties. The Display Properties dialog box appears.

2. Click on the Screen Saver tab. The Screen Saver controls appear.

3. Open the Screen Saver drop-down list and choose the screen saver you want. I like 3D Pipes. Additional controls appear, as shown in Figure 3.14.

4. If you are not sure what a particular screen saver looks like, choose it and then click on the Preview button to see it. Move the mouse or press a key to return to the Display Properties dialog box.

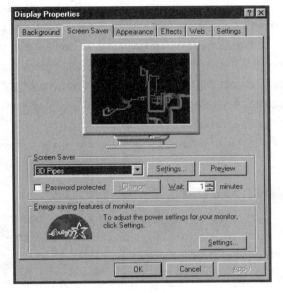

Figure 3.14

Change the screen saver and choose its settings here.

5. (Optional) Click on the Settings button and use the controls in the dialog box that appears to fine-tune your screen saver. The controls are different for each screen saver. Click on OK when you finish to return.

6. In the Wait text box, enter the number of minutes the machine must be idle (no keyboard or mouse use) before the screen saver kicks in. The default is 1, but that will dump you into the screen saver almost every time you stop to think. Try 5 or 10, which work well for most people.

7. Click on OK. You've got yourself a screen saver.

Also on the Screen Saver tab, you'll find controls for your monitor's energy-saving features. You can click on the Settings button in that section to open controls that specify how long your computer must be idle before the monitor shuts itself off to save electricity.

TIP You can use screen savers for a sort of security system. If you are away from your desk and you don't want anyone else playing with your PC while you're gone, set a password for your screen saver by selecting the Password Protected check box and clicking on the Change button to change the password. Then whenever you go to "wake up" the computer from its screen saver sleep, you are prompted for a password. If you don't type it correctly, the PC won't leave screen saver mode.

Experimenting with Colors and Fonts

The colors you see on the screen by default (probably a greenish background and blue window title bars) are merely a suggestion; you can paint any on-screen elements any colors you want.

Windows 98 comes with several *schemes*—combinations of colors and fonts that some programmer thought might be attractive, interesting, or bizarre. The default scheme is called Windows Standard, but you can choose any of the others by following these steps:

1. Right-click on the desktop and choose Properties. The Display Properties dialog box appears.

2. Click on the Appearance tab. The Appearance controls appear (see Figure 3.15).

3. Open the Scheme drop-down list and choose a color scheme. A sample of it appears.

4. Experiment with the various schemes until you find one you like, and then click on OK.

Once you become familiar with the existing color schemes, you might want to create your own. Here's how:

1. From the Appearance tab, choose a color scheme that is somewhat like the one you want to create. (This helps because you do not have to customize every single element.)

Figure 3.15

Choose one of the preset color schemes, or create your own.

2. Click on the item on the sample that you want to change, or choose it from the Item drop-down list. For example, to change the desktop color, choose Desktop.

3. Do any or all of the following, depending on what element you are customizing:

   ✿ Click on the Color button and choose a different color for the screen element.

   ✿ Use the Size and Color 2 controls for the item if they are available to control the size and the secondary color. (Not all screen elements have these.)

   ✿ If the element you are customizing contains text, the Font drop-down list will be available. Choose a different Font, Size, and Color if you want.

4. To save your scheme, click on Save As. Enter a name for the scheme and click on OK to save it.

5. Make sure that your new scheme is selected on the Scheme drop-down list, and click on OK.

> **NOTE** •
>
> To delete a scheme, select it and then click on the Delete button.
> •

Making Mouse Adjustments

Few things are more frustrating than a sluggish mouse pointer that you have trouble controlling. The mouse is the input device that you probably use the most, so it makes sense to get the mouse set up exactly the way you like it.

In Windows 98, you can access all of the mouse controls from the Mouse icon in the Control Panel. To display the Mouse Properties dialog box, choose Start, Settings, Control Panel, and then open the Mouse icon.

The basic Mouse Properties dialog box has three tabs. (You may see more tabs if you have specialized mouse software like IntelliPoint on your system.) The first one, Buttons, appears in Figure 3.16. It controls the mouse button's behavior.

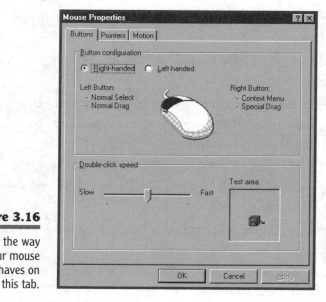

Figure 3.16

Change the way your mouse behaves on this tab.

On the Mouse tab, you have these two settings:

⚙ **Button Configuration**. Right-handed is the default. Left-handed switches the buttons, so the right button functions like the left and vice versa.

⚙ **Double-click Speed**. Adjust this slider to change how fast you have to move for Windows to view two clicks as a double-click. Use the jack-in-the-box to test it; when you double-click successfully on it, it opens or closes.

The second tab, Pointers, lets you choose what the mouse pointer is going to look like (see Figure 3.17). You can choose one of the pointer schemes from the Scheme drop-down list, or click on an individual pointer and click on Browse to find a cursor file (they end in .cur) to use for it. (There are multiple pointers for each scheme because, as you probably already know, the mouse pointer looks different when different things are happening, like waiting, pointing, selecting, and so on.)

Figure 3.17

Pointer schemes let you change the look of your mouse pointers.

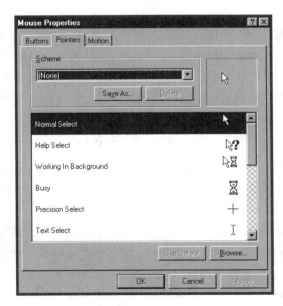

TIP

Windows comes with additional pointer schemes that you might not have installed yet. Refer to this morning's session to recall how to use Add/Remove Programs to install extra Windows components.

The final tab in the Mouse Properties dialog box is Motion. On this tab, you drag the slider to control the Pointer Speed. This is the sensitivity setting for the mouse; it controls how far on the screen the pointer moves when you move the mouse a certain amount. You'll probably have to play with this to find the setting that is most comfortable for you.

Making Noise with Sounds

Sounds

If you have a sound card and speakers, you have probably noticed that Windows makes little sounds when you do certain things (like start the computer or shut it down). These sounds are controlled by the Sounds Properties, which you can access from Start, Programs, Control Panel, Sounds.

In the Sounds Properties dialog box, you can choose a sound scheme from the Schemes drop-down list (see Figure 3.18). If there are no schemes on the list, or only one or two, you can install others with Add/Remove Programs, as you learned in the morning session.

Choose an interesting sound scheme (for example, I like Jungle and Musica). Then check out each sound in it by following these steps:

1. In the Sounds Properties dialog box, click on an event on the Events list that has a speaker icon next to it. (The speaker indicates that there is an associated sound.)

2. Click on the Play Sound button to hear the sound. If you like it, try a different event, until you have heard and approved all the sounds in the scheme.

3. If you don't like the sound associated with an event, open the Name drop-down list and choose a different sound. You can mix and match sounds from all the installed sound schemes this way.

Play Sound button

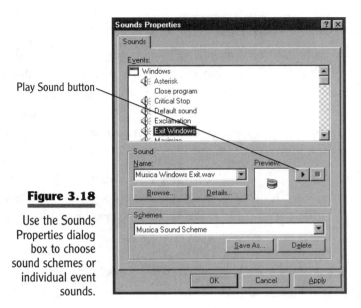

Figure 3.18

Use the Sounds
Properties dialog
box to choose
sound schemes or
individual event
sounds.

NOTE

To use a sound that doesn't appear on the Name list, click on the Browse button to
locate it elsewhere on your hard disk. To remove a sound from an event, choose None
from the Name drop-down list.

4. Click on OK to accept the sound changes.

You will probably find favorite sounds from several sound schemes. I particularly like the Utopia sound scheme's sounds for opening and closing
windows, for example. It sounds like the shutter of a camera clicking. I
also like the Start Windows sound from Musica, and the Critical Stop
from Robotz. You can build your own sound schemes like this:

1. In the Sounds Properties dialog box, start with the sound scheme
   that contains more of the sounds you want than any of the others.

2. Change individual sounds as needed.

3. Click on the Save As button to save your scheme.

4. Enter a name for it, and click on OK. Then click on OK again to
   close the dialog box.

Exploring the Windows Themes

Windows Themes were an extra that you had to buy separately with Windows 95 (in the Plus Pack), but they're absolutely free with Windows 98. Themes are combinations of wallpaper, sound schemes, mouse pointers, desktop colors, and fonts that work together to create an overall atmosphere. There are themes called Dangerous Creatures, Baseball, and Inside Your Computer, among others.

Desktop
Themes

There should be a Desktop Themes icon in your Control Panel (Start, Settings, Control Panel). If there is not, you need to install Desktop Themes with the Add/Remove Programs utility, as explained in this morning's session.

◆◆

CAUTION When you apply a theme, it overrides the settings you have specified in other areas. For example, if you have custom sounds assigned to events, it replaces them with its own. Make sure you have saved your sound, color, mouse pointer, and other schemes if you want to preserve them for later use.

◆◆

To set up a theme, follow these steps:

Desktop
Themes

1. Choose Start, Settings, Control Panel, and then open the Desktop Themes icon. The Desktop Themes dialog box opens.

2. Open the Themes drop-down list and choose a theme. A preview of the theme appears, as in Figure 3.19.

3. If there is any part of the theme that you don't like, deselect its check box in the Settings area to return that aspect to the current Windows settings. For example, in Figure 3.19, I find the font hard to see, so I might deselect the Font Names and Styles check box.

4. To preview the screen saver for the theme, click on the Screen Saver button. Move the mouse to cancel the preview.

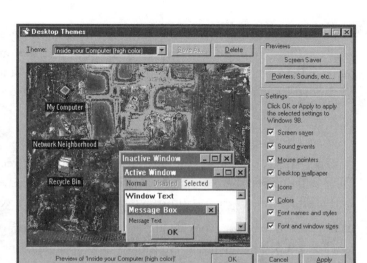

Figure 3.19

You can preview each part of the theme here.

5. To customize the mouse pointers and sounds for the scheme, click on the Pointers, Sounds etc. button. Controls appear that are identical to the controls you've worked with earlier in this session for these items. Use them to make any changes, and then click on OK.

6. Click on OK to apply the theme.

Just as with pointer and sound schemes, you can save your own themes. Just customize the settings and then click on the Save As button in the Desktop Themes box (see Figure 3.19). Enter a name for your new theme and click on OK to save it.

Managing Your Multimedia Devices

On most home systems (like the one you probably have), there is not much need to manage multimedia settings. You probably have one sound card, which handles all of the sound tasks. On more sophisticated systems, you might have more doodads, like a video capture board or special recording equipment.

Multimedia

The Multimedia controls are found under Start, Settings, Control Panel, Multimedia. Go ahead and display them now, just so you'll know what's there. There are five tabs in the dialog box: Audio, Video, MIDI, CD Music, and Devices. Here are some things you can set on each.

Audio

On this tab, you choose your preferred playback and recording devices. (The defaults for these are probably fine.) Click on the Advanced Properties button under each drop-down list for a few extra tweaks.

In the Advanced Properties dialog box for playback, you can choose your speaker setup. The default is Desktop Stereo Speakers, but you can choose something different if appropriate, such as Laptop Mono Speaker or Quadraphonic. Figure 3.20 shows the Advanced Properties for playback. It doesn't matter too much if you have the wrong kind chosen, but choosing correctly can improve the sound quality of your system in small ways.

On the Advanced Properties for both playback and recording, you can set a sampling rate (from Good to Best). This controls the quality of the recording you do. The higher the quality, the more disk space it will take

Figure 3.20

Choose the type of speaker system you have for a modest improvement in sound performance.

to store your recording. Leave it set to Good for most systems. However, you may want to select a higher-quality setting if you plan to use a voice recognition/dictation program.

Video

The Video tab lets you choose the size of the window that videos will play in. The default is Original Size, which gives the best quality. You can choose a different window size, or set it for Full Screen. Be aware, however, that if you use a size larger than the original, the quality of the image may suffer.

MIDI

Here's where you manage the configuration of any MIDI instruments or devices you have on your system. Usually the defaults are fine. You can add new MIDI instruments by clicking on Add Instrument and following the prompts.

CD Music

When you put an audio CD in your drive, it plays automatically by default. If you have more than one CD-ROM drive, this tab lets you specify one of them as the "autoplay" drive. (The default is probably correct.)

Why can't you play audio from all the CD drives on your system? Well, in theory you could, with the right equipment. However, in most cases, you need a special audio cable running between the sound card and the CD-ROM drive (inside the computer) to be able to hear audio CDs through your speakers, and in most systems that cable runs between the sound card and only one of the CD-ROM drives. If you can't play audio CDs on your system but everything else seems right, make sure you have such a cable installed—and then make sure that this tab is set for the drive with the cable.

You can also control audio CD volume here, although most people leave this set for full volume and control the CD audio sound with the master volume control on the taskbar.

Devices

This final tab shows a tree of all the multimedia devices installed on your system. It is somewhat like the System Properties information you get when you choose the System icon in the Control Panel (which you'll learn about this evening). You can choose any device from this tree and double-click on it to display its properties. (Most people will never need to do this.)

Fonts, Fonts, and More Fonts

Windows comes with several fonts, and other fonts come with various software packages you buy (like Microsoft Office). Fonts are typefaces. You can use any font installed on your system with any program that produces formatted text (like word processors). You can also use different fonts to change the way things look onscreen, as you saw with the Desktop Themes earlier in this session.

Fonts

To see what fonts you have, and possibly install others, open the Fonts window (Start, Settings, Control Panel, Fonts). A window appears with an icon for each font on your system (see Figure 3.21).

To see a sample of a font, just open its icon. A sample window appears, as in Figure 3.22. You can print the sample by clicking on the Print button. Close the window by clicking on Done when you finish looking.

When you install software, it sometimes installs extra fonts for you automatically. (That's the case with Microsoft Word, for example.) You can also buy CDs full of fonts that you can install on your system manually. If you have such a CD of fonts, or fonts from some other source, you'll need to install them yourself. Here's how.

1. From the Fonts window (Figure 3.21), choose File, Install New Font. The Add Fonts dialog box appears (see Figure 3.23).

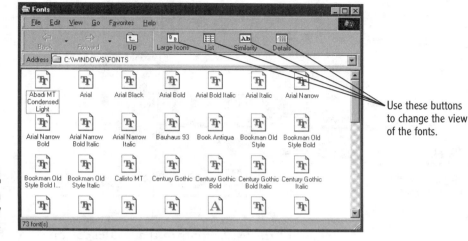

Use these buttons to change the view of the fonts.

Figure 3.21

Here's an overview of my font situation.

Figure 3.22

A sample of the Arial font.

2. Open the Drives drop-down list and choose the one with the disc containing the fonts.

3. If needed, change the folder in the Folders list to point to the folder where the fonts are. (See the documentation that came with the CD if needed.)

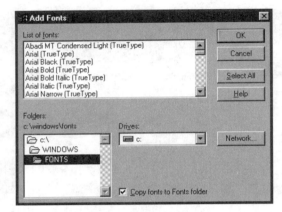

Figure 3.23

Use this dialog box
to install new fonts.

4. Wait for the list of fonts in that folder to appear. It may take several seconds.

5. Click on a font to select it from the list. To select multiple fonts, hold down Ctrl as you click.

6. Make sure the Copy Fonts To Fonts Folder check box is selected.

7. Click on OK to install the selected fonts.

NOTE When you install new fonts, two things happen. The first is that the font files are copied to the Fonts folder on your hard disk (or Windows makes a record of some other location for them). The second is that the availability of those fonts is recorded in your Windows configuration files. Both steps are necessary. That's why you can't just copy font files to your Fonts folder directly.

Date and Time Adjustments

Computers have built-in clocks that are notorious for not keeping very good time. I have one computer that keeps perfect time, but another computer's clock loses about 15 seconds a day, so every few weeks it is seriously behind. You can change the time (and date too, if needed) from the comfort of your own desktop.

To change the time, double-click on the clock on the taskbar. The Date/Time Properties dialog box appears. From there, change the date by clicking on the appropriate day on the calendar. To change the time, type a new time in the digital display under the picture of the clock (see Figure 3.24).

TIP

You can download shareware programs from the Internet that automatically check your computer's time against a very precise clock on the Internet and adjust your system clock automatically.

If you let Windows 98 know what region you're located in (a.k.a. time zone), it can also adjust for Daylight Savings Time. Just click on the Time Zone tab in the Date/Time Properties dialog box and choose your time zone, and then make sure the Automatically Adjust Clock for Daylight Saving Changes option is enabled.

Power Management

Power Management isn't just for laptops, although laptops benefit the most from it. Power Management is useful whenever you want or need to

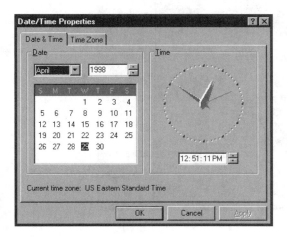

Figure 3.24

Change the date and time if either are incorrect.

conserve power (that is, electricity or batteries). It shuts off certain power-gobbling functions of the computer after a period of inactivity, but fixes it so that those components can spring back into action quickly when you are ready to go again.

Power
Management

Open the Power Management controls from Start, Settings, Control Panel, Power Management. On a desktop machine, you'll find two tabs there: Power Schemes and Advanced. Laptops may have two other tabs: Alarms and Power Meter.

On the Power Schemes tab (Figure 3.25), you choose the primary role for the machine—either Home/Office Desktop or Portable/Laptop. Generally, the former runs on electricity full time, while the latter may often run on batteries.

You can also choose a specific amount of inactive time before the two biggest power-hogging components shut off: the monitor and the hard disk. Open the respective drop-down lists (see Figure 3.25) and make your selections.

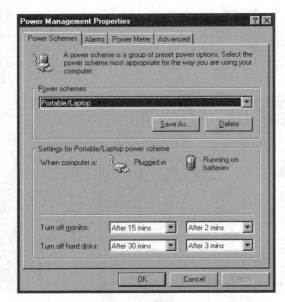

Figure 3.25

Choose your power management scheme.

> **NOTE** The controls in Figure 3.25 are the same as the ones you get if you click on the Settings button on the Screen Saver tab in the Desktop Properties (covered earlier in this chapter). Your monitor will not shut off automatically unless it is "Energy Star Compliant." This is a power-management specification that almost all monitors made in the last five years adhere to.

The controls on the other tabs depend on the specific model of computer and its power management capabilities. You may see check boxes that let you display or hide a power meter on the taskbar, that let you prompt for a password when the computer wakes up from being in Standby mode (a power-saving mode on some laptops), and how low the battery power needs to be before an audible alarm sounds warning you to save your work.

Personalizing User Settings

You can set up Windows 98 so that everyone who uses the computer has their own preferences, including menu contents, desktop colors and fonts, mouse pointers, sounds, and so on. If you enable the feature, Windows will ask you to identify yourself by entering a username and password in a Welcome to Windows dialog box that appears when you start Windows. Then Windows will continue to load using the preferences associated with your username. This makes it easier for folks to share a computer who may have very different ideas of what is cool. (Parents and children shouldn't have to put up with each other's color schemes, in my opinion.)

You might want to enable multiple-user settings even if you're the only one who ever touches your computer. Conceivably, you might want to establish different preferences for different ways that you use the computer. You can log on as a different user, and thus activate a different set of preferences, depending on what you plan to do.

To set this up, you must enable the Multiple Users feature. Here's what to do:

1. Choose Start, Settings, Control Panel, Users. This starts the Multi-User Settings Wizard.

2. Work through the Wizard, clicking on Next to move from screen to screen, and entering information as prompted. At some point in the process you will be asked to choose one of these:

   ✿ Create copies of the current items and their contents. Choose this if you want the new user profile to use all the existing settings. Recommended for most people.

   ✿ Create new items to save disk space. Choose this to start with a blank Start menu that you can manually add program shortcuts to. (Not recommended for beginners, or experienced people either for that matter, unless they have a lot of time on their hands.)

3. When you finish with the Wizard, click on Finish. Windows restarts, and when it does, you can log on as the new user you just created.

Users

Once that's done, you can add new users at any time. To manage the list of users, just visit Start, Settings, Control Panel, Users again. This time, a dialog box opens, as shown in Figure 3.26. From here, you can:

✿ Delete a user by selecting the one you want and clicking on Delete.

✿ Create a new user by clicking on the New User button and then working through the Wizard again. (They're the same fields that you saw when you set up your first user in the steps above.)

✿ Change the user's password by selecting the one you want and then clicking on Set Password.

✿ Click on the Change Settings button to reevaluate the settings you chose when you set up the user initially.

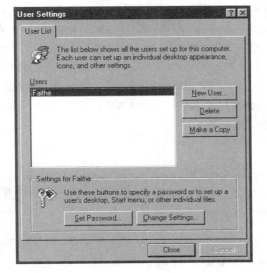

Figure 3.26

Manage your user list from here, or change people's settings.

When you finish, click on Close. You can switch users without shutting Windows down. When the system is set up for multiple users, there is an extra command on the Start menu called Log Off. Use it to log off the current user so someone else can log on.

Managing Passwords

If you are working in a networked office environment, you probably have a network user ID and password that enables you to connect to the company LAN. You probably also have a user ID and password that lets you connect to the Internet. Passwords verify that you are who you say you are. Similarly, in Windows 98, user names and passwords distinguish one user from another if you've activated the multiple-user options described in the previous section.

 NOTE

In addition to the username and password you use to log onto your Windows computer, Windows keeps track of other user names and passwords that you use to access things like networks and your Internet account. After you identify yourself to Windows, Windows will be able to fill in the other user names and passwords automatically so you don't have to type them each time. You'll see how this works with an Internet access account in the Sunday Morning session.

Each time you start your PC, you might be prompted for a user name and password. If both of the following are true, Windows will not prompt for a password at startup:

✿ You have set it up so that all users use the same settings.

✿ You have assigned a "blank" password to the default user (that is, no password at all).

Otherwise, you're prompted for a user ID and password.

 NOTE

Forgetting a password will not lock you out of Windows 98. If you don't know your user name and password, you can just make up a new user name and log on as a new user on the fly. However, you won't have access to your customized user preferences and you'll have to re-enter user names and passwords to access other resources, such as a network or an Internet account.

When you change the Windows password, you change it for whatever user is logged on (if you use multiple users on your system). Make sure you are logged on as yourself before you change it if more than one person uses your system. To change the Windows password, follow these steps:

Passwords

1. Choose Start, Settings, Control Panel, Passwords. The Passwords Properties dialog box opens.

2. Click on the Change Windows Password button. The Change Windows Password dialog box appears (see Figure 3.27).

Figure 3.27

You can change the Windows password here.

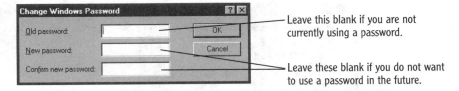

Leave this blank if you are not currently using a password.

Leave these blank if you do not want to use a password in the future.

3. In the Old Password box, type your old password. If you are not currently using a password, leave it blank.

4. In the New Password and Confirm New Password boxes, type the new password you want to use. To remove the password so that you do not have to log on to Windows, leave both of these blank.

5. Click on OK.

Oddly enough, the Passwords Properties dialog box is also where you tell Windows whether you want to use the multiple user settings feature. You might expect to find this option somewhere in the User Settings dialog box, but it's really on the User Profiles tab of the Passwords Properties dialog box, as shown in Figure 3.28. Adjusting this setting is pretty straightforward. To disable the multiple user feature, select the All Users of This Computer option. To enable it, select the Users Can Customize option. If you enable the option, you can also specify what preferences will be included in the User Profile Settings.

What's Next?

Well, now your Windows desktop is truly your own. You've probably got some wild colors and wallpaper going on, and maybe some different sounds and pointers too. Go have some dinner, because in this evening's session, you'll learn about installing hardware (no, not hammers and screws—sound cards, modems, that sort of thing.) Trust me, it'll be fun.

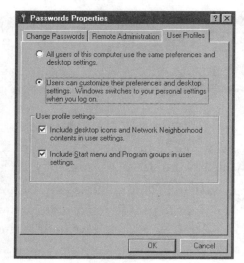

Figure 3.28

This is where you can turn the multiple user profile feature on or off.

SATURDAY EVENING

Adding and Configuring Hardware

- ✿ Taking Inventory of Your System
- ✿ Installing New Hardware
- ✿ Configuring New Hardware
- ✿ Installing the Extra Software
- ✿ General Troubleshooting

You don't have to be a certified technician to add simple components to your system like printers, modems, and scanners. What you do need, however, is a basic understanding of how Windows 98 automatically detects (or fails to detect) your new hardware, and how to troubleshoot the most common problems that beginners encounter when installing computer components on a Windows 98 system.

This session is broken down into two parts. In the first part, you'll learn about add-on components and how to install and configure them. If all goes well for you—great! Go to bed early. The second part of this session provides troubleshooting guidance for those who run into problems. You may not need this troubleshooting information this evening, but you (or a friend) will probably need it in the future.

Understanding the Hardware Installation Process

You might think that installing new hardware is as simple as plugging it in and turning on your PC. A few upgrades are like that, but most involve a bit more effort. Here's a quick rundown:

1. Assess your system and figure out what you need to buy. Then buy it, trying to get the best price possible.

2. Physically install it.

3. Configure your system BIOS if needed. (You'll probably want to get help with this one. Fortunately, it's not necessary when installing most peripheral devices.)

4. Let Windows autodetect the device.

5. Troubleshoot problems if Windows does not do it right (a very real possibility).

I'll try to help you a bit with each of these in this chapter, with an emphasis on the latter two items. If you're interested in diving into the first three in detail, I suggest *Upgrade Your PC In a Weekend*, also published by Prima.

Taking Inventory of Your System

Before you buy and install new components, you should familiarize yourself with what you already have. You should know, for example, how much memory your computer has installed. If you are going to be installing some sort of internal device (like an internal modem or a sound card), you should also know which IRQs are free.

Windows offers a couple of great tools for checking out your current system contents. Device Manager is the more basic of the two, displaying all the installed hardware in a tree fashion. To take a look at it, follow these steps:

System

1. Choose Start, Settings, Control Panel, System. The System Properties dialog box appears.

2. On the General tab, take note of the amount of memory your system has and the type of processor (see Figure 4.1).

3. Click on the Device Manager tab. The Device Manager appears.

4. Double-click on the little PC next to Computer at the top of the tree. A Computer Properties dialog box appears, showing which IRQs are in use for which devices (see Figure 4.2). Click on OK to close the dialog box when you finish looking.

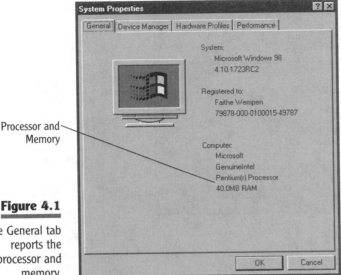

Processor and Memory

Figure 4.1

The General tab reports the processor and memory.

ADDRESSES AND IRQS

Each device that communicates directly with the processor has a base address and an IRQ number. The base address is a hexadecimal code that refers to the location in memory that holds the device's information. For example, COM1's base address is usually 2F8H. Each device must have its own unique base address. There are many addresses available, so you are not likely to run out of them.

IRQ stands for Interrupt Request. These are communication lines between the device and the processor, and most systems have 15 of them. Generally speaking, each device has its own. Systems work best that way. However, sometimes devices are forced to share. This works all right unless both devices try to use the IRQ at the same time. If that happens, your computer usually locks up or one of the two devices malfunctions.

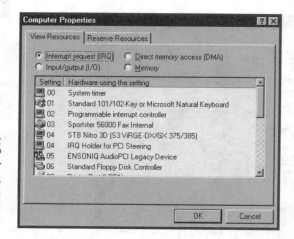

Figure 4.2

The Computer Properties reports which IRQs are in use, among other things.

5. Click on the plus sign next to a hardware category you are curious about (for example, Display adapters). A list of the installed devices in that category appears (see Figure 4.3).

6. Double-click on the device to see its Properties dialog box. (These are the techie details about the device.)

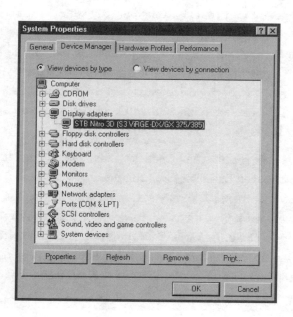

Figure 4.3

Device Manager shows you what you currently have installed.

7. Click on the Resources tab. This shows the system resources that the device is using. (This will be important to you later, when you install new devices.) Note that the Conflicting Device List reads "No Conflicts." This is good (see Figure 4.4).

8. Click on any of the other tabs that look interesting. Different devices have different tabs. Don't worry if you don't understand them. Just look. Don't make any changes.

9. Click on OK to close the Properties dialog box.

10. Repeat Steps 5 through 9 to explore the other devices on your system. When you finish, click on OK to close the System Properties dialog box.

Another way to take stock of your system is with the System Information utility. This is a brand-new affair with the 98 version of Windows, and it provides very in-depth information about not only the hardware but the software too. It may be a bit of overkill for simply figuring out what hardware you've got, but you really should take a look at it once, so you'll be able to find it again if you need it. Follow these steps:

1. Choose Start, Programs, Accessories, System Tools, System Information. The System Information window opens.

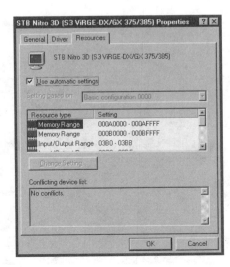

Figure 4.4

Each device uses a unique set of system resources, including an Address and an IRQ. More about these later.

2. Click on the plus sign next to Components to see a list of the hardware you can peruse.

3. Click on one of the categories, just to see what's there. For example, Figure 4.5 shows the Display. Compare it to Figure 4.4 to see the difference in details provided by System Information versus Device Manager.

4. Check out the Problem Devices category. This lists any device problems or conflicts you currently have on your system, making them easy to track down and fix. (More on that later in this session.)

5. Now click on Hardware Resources in the left-hand pane and check out the categories there. The I/O category is particularly useful, listing all of your system's IRQs and which devices are using them. (It's basically the same information that you saw in Figure 4.2, in Computer Properties.)

6. Explore your system using System Information. When you finish, choose File, Exit.

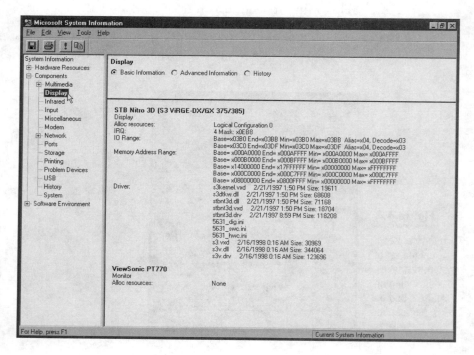

Figure 4.5

Here is the video display through the eyes of System Information.

Figuring Out What You Need

Sometimes it is hard to know what hardware to buy for your PC. There are so many models of everything, with confusing specifications! In general, you should try to follow the recommendations from the computer's manufacturer. Here are some hints for the average home system.

- **Memory**: Check your system's manual to find out what kind you need. You'll need to know the type (SIMM or DIMM), the minimum speed (probably 70ns or 60ns), the size (30-pin, 72-pin, or 168-pin), and the denomination (4MB, 8MB, 16MB, 32MB, or 64MB).

- **Hard Disk**: You can probably buy and install an additional hard disk, unless your old one is broken. Look for one with an IDE interface (or EIDE, or ATA-2, they're all approximately the same), with at least twice the capacity that you think you need.

- **Video Card**: Make sure that you get one that takes advantage of your PC's local bus, a special, high-speed card slot. Check the manual to find out what type you need: VLB, PCI, or AGP. If you are a game enthusiast, consider a card with 3-D capabilities, which makes programs with fancy 3-D graphics run more smoothly.

- **Sound Card**: Look for a SoundBlaster-compatible card, or a genuine SoundBlaster if you don't mind spending a few extra dollars. Look for at least 16-bit (more bits are better). If you have a PCI motherboard (most Pentium systems do), you can look for a PCI sound card; otherwise look for an ISA model.

- **CD-ROM Drive**: Look for at least 16X, and an IDE interface. If you have an SCSI card in your PC already, you could use an SCSI model instead, but don't buy an SCSI card just to use an SCSI CD-ROM drive. If you can afford it, you might consider a DVD-ROM drive, which can play the new DVD format discs. (These drives play standard CDs too.)

NOTE   SCSI stands for Small Computer System Interface. It is a fast kind of interface, but more expensive than the IDE that is already built into your motherboard. Home users do not need it.

☼   **Modem**: Look for a 56K model, or if price is an issue, a 33.6K will do. There are two 56K standards: Kflex and X2. Make sure you get the kind that your Internet service provider supports. (Check before buying.) When the new standard is in place, you may be able to download an update file that will upgrade your modem to the new standard.

Making a Boot Disk

Before you try to install any new components, make sure you have an emergency boot disk. If you didn't make one when you installed Windows 98, do it now.

An emergency boot disk is a disk you can insert in your floppy drive that will start the computer if something happens to your hard disk so that it won't boot anymore. It's a simple thing, and it only takes a few minutes to make, but it can mean the difference between fixing a problem yourself later and paying some technician $75 to do it.

Follow these steps:

1. Find an empty disk, or one that contains nothing that you want to keep.
2. Label it "Windows 98 Startup Disk."
3. Choose Start, Settings, Control Panel.
4. Open Add/Remove Programs.
5. Click on the Startup Disk tab (see Figure 4.6).

Add/Remove
Programs

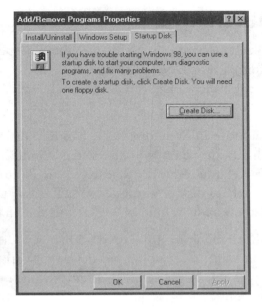

Figure 4.6

The Create Disk
command on the
Startup Disk tab
automates the
process of creating
a startup disk.

6. Click on the Create Disk button.

7. If prompted, insert the Windows 98 CD-ROM into your CD-ROM drive and click on OK to continue.

8. When prompted, insert your disk into the disk drive and click on OK to continue.

9. Wait for the appropriate files to be copied to the disk. It may take several minutes.

10. Wait for the progress bar to disappear and the Startup Disk tab to return to view.

11. Shut down the computer (Start, Shut Down, Restart) and test the disk to make sure the computer starts correctly with it.

12. Remove the boot disk from your disk drive and turn the power off. You are ready to install new hardware.

Installing New Hardware

This isn't a book about hardware, so I won't go too deeply into this topic in the space allotted, but here are some basics. For more information, check out the book I mentioned earlier in this chapter, *Upgrade Your PC In a Weekend.*

Configuring hardware in Windows 98 is basically the same no matter what kind of hardware you're working with. Windows 98 provides a generic Add New Hardware utility that works for all kinds of hardware, whether it's a new hard disk or a scanner. (You'll learn about it in "Configuring New Hardware in Windows 98" later in this chapter.)

However, if you're itching to get started with a new device you've just bought, or if you want to set up an old device to work with your new system, you may be able to get up to speed quickly just by reading one of the following sections.

General Installation Hints

✿ Read the directions that come with the new device, and follow them to the letter. Check your PC's user manual to get hints about how to work on your specific model.

✿ Turn off your PC before you do any work inside it.

✿ If you need to remove the screws that hold the case cover in place, put the screws somewhere safe.

✿ Before touching any electronics inside the computer, ground yourself by touching the power supply (the big metal box inside your PC's case.) Do this often while working inside the PC. For extra safety, buy a grounding strap that you attach to your wrist and to the PC case to prevent static electricity discharges.

✿ Do not use magnetized screwdrivers or other tools to work on a PC. Try picking up a screw with the tip of your screwdriver. If you can, it's magnetic, and you shouldn't use it.

Installing Printers

1. Turn off both the old printer and the PC before disconnecting them.

2. Install the ink or toner cartridge in the new printer according to the instructions provided. Run the printer's self-test before you hook up the printer to your PC.

3. Turn off the printer and the computer and then connect the two machines using a printer cable. The plugs on each end of the printer cable are different and there's usually only one place on the computer and one on the printer for those plugs, so it's usually easy to get it hooked up right.

4. Read the instructions carefully regarding printer driver installation. (The printer driver is a set of software instructions that tells Windows about the special features of the printer and how to access them.) For some printers, you can't just let Windows take over; you must run a special installation program from a disk that came with the printer.

The first time you turn your PC on after connecting the printer, Windows may detect the printer automatically. (See "Scenario #1" later in this session.) This happens if you are using a newer printer that supports "Plug and Play."

If Windows does not automatically recognize your printer, you must run setup software. If you have a disk that came with the printer, run the setup software on it, as explained in "Scenario #3" later in this chapter. If you do not have a disk, or if you have a disk but it does not contain a recognizable setup program, follow these steps to let Windows set up the printer using its own drivers:

1. Choose Start, Settings, Printers. The Printers folder opens.

Add Printer

2. Open the Add Printer icon. The Add Printer Wizard dialog box appears. Click on Next to continue.

3. Choose Local Printer (assuming you are not on a network), and click on Next.

4. If you do not have a setup disk for your printer, choose the printer manufacturer and model from the lists that appear (see Figure 4.7). If you have a setup disk, insert it in your floppy drive and click on Have Disk.

5. When prompted for the port to use, choose LPT1: and click on Next.

6. Enter a name for the printer (for your own information only).

7. You're asked whether you want the printer to be the default printer. Click on Yes or No.

8. Click on Next.

9. You're prompted to print a test page. Click on Yes or No as desired. (Yes is recommended if you are not sure the printer will work with Windows 98.)

10. Click on Finish. If prompted for the Windows 98 CD, insert it and click on OK.

See "Troubleshooting Printer Problems" at the end of this session if your printer does not work as expected.

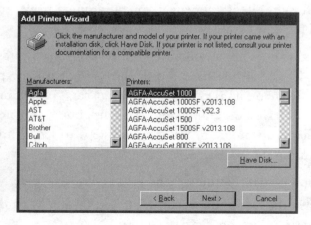

Figure 4.7

Choose your printer's make and model to use the drivers supplied by Windows 98.

NOTE After you have installed a printer, an icon for it appears in the Printers folder (Start, Settings, Printers). You can select this icon to view a print queue for the printer, listing all the documents waiting to be printed. From this window you can also pause the printer, set printer properties, and purge jobs from the queue. When a printer is printing, an icon for it appears in the system tray. You can double-click on this icon to open the printer's print queue window too, as a shortcut.

Installing Modems

Modems can be tough to configure in Windows 98! The most important thing when installing a modem is to read the directions that come with it, and follow them to the letter.

If you have a free COM port (also called a serial port) on the back of your PC, do yourself a favor and buy an external modem. They are much easier than internal models for beginners to set up.

If you are installing an internal modem, but you have an available built-in COM port too, you may want to disable the built-in COM port in the BIOS setup program so that the modem will not have to share its IRQ with the unused COM port. (That's kind of a complicated thing to do; ask a friend for help if needed.)

After you've installed your modem, Windows 98 may detect it automatically. (See "Scenario #1" later in this chapter.) If it doesn't, or if it detects the modem but the modem still doesn't work, try running the installation software that came with the modem, as described in "Scenario #3". If that fails, try "Scenario #4."

 TIP You can add a modem using the Control Panel's Modems icon. Choose Start, Settings, Control Panel, Modems, to open the Modems Properties dialog box. Then click on the Add button to open the Install New Modem wizard. You can also get here from the Add New Hardware Wizard (described in Scenario #4 later in this chapter), but this is a shortcut.

If you have an older modem, you may not have the installation software for it. If that's the case, try using "Scenario #4" and selecting the manufacturer and model from the list that Windows 98 provides. Windows 98 may be able to provide generic driver software for the modem that will make it work at least at a basic level. You may also be able to download updated drivers from the manufacturer's Web site (if you have another modem you can use, that is, while you're trying to get this one to work!)

Modems

The way a modem works is controlled by its Properties settings. You can check out a modem's properties by choosing Start, Settings, Control Panel, Modems, and then double-clicking on the modem you want to check out. The settings you can change here include the modem speaker's volume, the maximum speed, and a host of techie details such as stop bits and error correction. (Don't worry about what these mean; chances are good that you will never need to fuss with them.) If you are having trouble with your modem, see "Troubleshooting Modem Problems" later in this session to learn how to change some of these modem property settings to clear up the problem.

You'll also need to tell Windows something about where you are calling from so it can properly dial phone numbers using your modem. To do so, follow these steps:

1. Click on the Dialing Properties button on the General tab of the Modem Properties dialog box to open the Dialing Properties dialog box, as shown in Figure 4.8.

2. Select the country you're calling from and fill in your area code. If you need to dial 9 or some other number to get an outside line before dialing a phone number, fill in that information along with the codes to disable call waiting if that applies to you. Select Tone or Pulse dialing.

3. Click on OK to record this information for future use and close the dialog box.

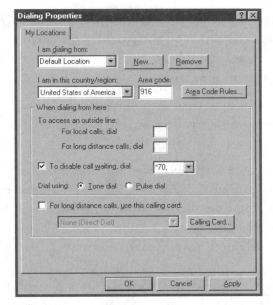

Figure 4.8

Windows uses this information to dial outgoing calls using your modem.

To make a connection to an Internet service provider, set up a Dial-Up Networking connection, as you will learn on Sunday morning. You can set properties for each connection, such as the phone number to dial and details about the system you are connecting to. These are features of individual connections, not of the modem.

Installing Scanners

There are two ways to hook up a scanner to your computer: some scanners require a special circuit card that you plug into your motherboard inside the computer, and others connect to your parallel printer port (and share it with your printer). For home use, the latter is better.

To share a parallel printer port with a scanner, unplug your printer from the PC's port. Then plug the scanner into the port, and plug the printer into the extra outlet on the scanner cord. This should all be thoroughly explained in your scanner installation instructions.

On some scanners, you need to go into your system BIOS setup and tell it to use a particular mode on the parallel port (such as Bidirectional or ECP/EPP). Have a techie friend help you do this, or follow the instructions that come with the scanner.

Scanners vary widely in their setup procedure. Almost all of them come with setup software that you must run. (See "Scenario #3" later in this session.)

Some scanners come with their own interface cards that plug into a socket inside of your computer. Windows 98 may automatically detect such scanners when you start the PC for the first time with the card inserted (see "Scenario #1" later in this session). However, the scanner may still not work correctly until you install its software.

TIP   Many scanners are "TWAIN-compatible." TWAIN is a standard for image acquisition that many graphics programs support, so if your scanner is TWAIN-compatible, you can operate the scanner from within your favorite graphics program, such as PhotoShop or Paint Shop Pro. After you have installed the scanner and its software, try it out in a graphics program to see for yourself.

Installing Monitors

Monitors are easily installed. Just plug one into your PC. If it is as good as (or better than) the monitor you were previously using, it should work fine. You can fine-tune its performance in Windows 98 by changing the refresh rate and adjusting the monitor controls, covered in "Troubleshooting Video Problems".

If you plug in a new monitor and you see nothing but a blank screen, refer to the section "Blank Screen, Single Beep" later in this chapter to figure out why the monitor might not be working.

If you plug in a monitor that is not as good as the one that you had previously used with Windows 98, you might have to adjust Windows 98's setup. For example, suppose you were using a whiz-bang super-VGA monitor in a very high resolution. You then gave that monitor to your brother, and plugged in an old regular VGA monitor. Windows 98 is set up to operate at the high resolution, and your poor old VGA monitor doesn't understand the signals being sent to it. In this situation, Windows 98 will start in "Safe Mode." This is a troubleshooting mode that uses only generic settings so you can troubleshoot problems. (You can tell you're in Safe Mode because the words "Safe Mode" appear in all four corners of the desktop.) In Safe Mode, change the monitor type, as explained in the section "Display Flickers Noticeably" later in this chapter.

NOTE You may also want to adjust the display resolution to take best advantage of the different monitor. See the Saturday Afternoon session for details.

Installing PC Cards

A PC card is a credit-card sized device that you plug into a PCMCIA slot on a laptop. In Windows 98, using such devices is easy. Just plug them into your laptop's slot, and Windows 98 automatically detects the device. The first time you insert a new device, it prompts you for software (see "Scenario #2"). Subsequent times, it merely recognizes the device.

PC Card
(PCMCIA)

Whenever a PC Card is inserted, you'll see a special PC Card Status icon in the system tray (down by the clock). Double-click on this icon to open the PC Card Properties dialog box, which lists the PC Card devices that are currently plugged into the laptop.

Windows 98 lets you "hot swap" devices in PC Card slots. That means you can remove one device and plug in another in the same slot without shutting down the computer. To do so, however, you must first stop the device that you are removing. To do so, follow these steps:

1. Double-click on the PC Card icon in the system tray, opening the PC Card (PCMCIA) Properties dialog box (see Figure 4.9).

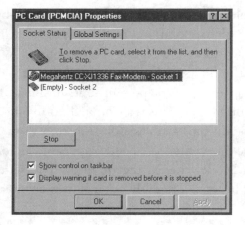

Figure 4.9

Manage your PC
Card devices,
including shutting
one down so you
can remove it and
insert another, from
this dialog box.

2. Click on the device on the list that you want to remove.

3. Click on the Stop button.

4. Remove the card from your laptop.

5. If needed, plug another device in that slot.

Installing Networks

Home users probably won't have much occasion to install a network, but a small business might benefit from one. In a perfect world, Windows 98 detects a newly-installed network card perfectly, and prompts for the needed drivers (Scenario #2). In a less-perfect world, you might need to run a special installation program that came with the network card (Scenario #3), and configure the network server to recognize the new device. It all depends on several factors, including the network type, the network card, and the type of server. That's a lot of variables!

If all this sounds complicated—well, it is. Beginners should not attempt to install networks; rely on a techie friend or rent a professional for the afternoon.

Configuring New Hardware

After you have the physical installation taken care of—and the BIOS setup has been changed if it needs it—you are ready for the big test: Will Windows see the new device? To find out, power up your PC.

 TIP

When I am installing a new device that requires poking around inside the computer, I usually don't put the PC's cover back on until I am sure the new device is working. That way I have to struggle with replacing the cover only once.

Theoretically, Windows should detect your new hardware automatically and install the right drivers for you. (A driver is the software that tells Windows about the special features of a particular device and how to access those features.) It works that way if you have a Plug and Play-compatible BIOS and your new device supports Plug and Play. Unfortunately, Plug and Play doesn't always work. Sometimes it works imperfectly; sometimes not at all. First, I'll go over the ideal situation; then I'll tell you how to overcome some common stumbling blocks.

Scenario #1: Everything Works Fine

Try these steps first. They cover the way Plug and Play is supposed to work:

1. Turn on the computer. Windows starts. Windows detects the new device and installs drivers for it, possibly prompting for the Windows 98 CD-ROM.

2. Test the new device to make sure it works. (If it doesn't work properly, try Scenario #3. Some sound cards and modems, in particular, may not work right until you run their own setup software, even though Windows appears to detect them.)

Scenario #2: Windows Prompts for a Setup Disk

Sometimes Windows detects something new, but needs a little help deciding whether to install a driver for it or not:

1. Turn on the computer. Windows starts. Windows detects the new device and asks you if you want to install a driver for it. The dialog box includes a Have Disk button.

2. Insert the floppy disk or CD-ROM that came with the device and click on the Have Disk button. Windows reads the driver from the disk and installs the device.

3. Test the new device to make sure it works. (If it doesn't work, try Scenario #3.)

Scenario #3: You Need a Setup Program

If Windows didn't detect the device at startup, or it detected it but the device doesn't work, now would be a good time to run any setup software that came with the device. Follow these steps:

1. Place the disk or CD-ROM into the appropriate drive on your computer.

2. Open the My Computer window from the desktop, and then open the icon for the drive containing the disk you just inserted.

3. Look on the screen for a file that is likely to be the setup program. Look for names like INSTALL.EXE, INSTALL.COM, INSTALL.BAT, SETUP.EXE, SETUP.COM, SETUP.BAT.

4. Open the file that runs the setup program. The setup program runs.

5. Follow the on-screen instructions to complete the setup program's work. If asked if you want to restart the computer, click on Yes (or Restart, or whatever the button is called).

6. Test the new device to make sure it works. (If it doesn't, try Scenario #4.)

Scenario #4: Windows Must Be Told to Detect the Device

Sometimes, for whatever reason, Windows doesn't immediately notice that there's something new. If you don't have a setup program, or if you have one and running it didn't make the device work, here's how to prompt Windows into noticing the new device. (If you ran the setup program in Scenario #3 and it still isn't working, this is not likely to do any good, but it's worth a try.)

NOTE There is a special wizard for printers called Add New Printer. If you know that it's a printer that you need to set up, choose the Add New Printer icon from the Printers folder (Start, Settings, Printers) rather than going through the Add New Hardware wizard in the Control Panel.

Add New
Hardware

1. Turn on the computer. Windows starts. Nothing unusual happens. The new hardware is not detected.

2. Choose Start, Settings, Control Panel.

3. Open the Add New Hardware icon. The New Hardware Wizard opens.

4. Click on Next to continue. Windows looks for Plug-and-Play devices. If it finds any, it reports them to you and asks whether they are the ones you want to install. If yes, click on Yes, the device is on the list. If no, click on No, the device isn't on the list.

5. If you choose Yes, follow the prompts to install the drivers, skipping the rest of the steps here.

   If you choose No, or if Windows didn't find any Plug-and-Play devices, you're asked if you want Windows to detect the new hardware. Select Yes (see Figure 4.10) and click on Next.

Figure 4.10

Let Windows try to detect the hardware before you resort to manual configuration.

6. A message appears telling you that Windows will now look for the new hardware. Click on Next to begin the search.

7. Wait for the progress indicator to reach 100% and another dialog box to appear. It may take several minutes. If Windows finds the new hardware, you see a dialog box like the one in Figure 4.11; if it doesn't find it, you see the dialog box in Figure 4.12.

8. If Windows detected the hardware (Figure 4.11), continue to Step 10. If not, skip to the following scenario.

9. Click on the Details button to see what Windows found.

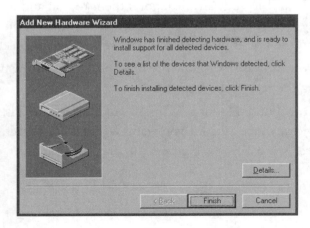

Figure 4.11

This is what you see if Windows was successful in identifying the new hardware.

Figure 4.12

You'll see this if Windows didn't detect any new hardware.

10. Do one of the following:

   ♦ If the device on the list is the device you are installing—great. Click on Finish to finish the installation.

   ♦ If the device on the list is not the device you installed, Windows did not detect it correctly. Click on Cancel. Then redo Steps 1 through 5 of this procedure. When you get to Step 6, click on No, and then jump to Step 2 of Scenario #5.

Scenario #5: Windows Fails to Detect the Device

If you're reading this, you've just completed Scenario #3 or #4 and Windows wasn't able to find your device. Follow these steps to install the device's driver manually.

1. From Figure 4.12 (the screen where Windows reports that it couldn't find your hardware), click on Next. A list of hardware types appears, as shown in Figure 4.13.

2. Click on the device type you are installing (for example, Modem), and then click on Next.

3. If you are installing a modem, a box appears offering to search for the modem. (You won't see this box with any other device type.)

Click on the Don't Select my {device type}; I will select it from a list check box, and then click on Next. A list of manufacturers and models appears for that device type. The one for modems is shown in Figure 4.14.

NOTE

In step 3, why are you bypassing the automatic detection? Because you came here from Scenario #3 or #4, where detection failed. There's no reason to think that detection will work now when it failed earlier.

Figure 4.13

Choose the type of hardware you are trying to install from this list.

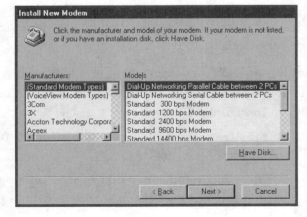

Figure 4.14

You can choose your device's make and model from a list of devices that Windows supports.

4. Do one of the following:

   ✿ If you have a setup disk that came with the device, place it in your floppy drive and click on Have Disk. In the Install from Disk dialog box, confirm the drive letter for the floppy (A:\ is the default) and click on OK. Windows finds the driver and installs it. If there are drivers for more than one model on that disk, you see a list of them; double-click on the name of the model you have.

   ✿ If you do not have a setup disk, or you have one but it does not contain the right files (perhaps you have tried the previous suggestion and it didn't work), select the device's manufacturer from the list. Then on the right-hand list, select the model number. Click on Next to continue.

5. If you are installing a device that requires you to select a port, a dialog box appears asking you to do so. For example, Figure 4.15 shows one for a modem. If you see such a box, do one of the following:

   ✿ If the port that the device is connected to appears on the list, click on it and then click on Next to continue.

   ✿ If the port that the device is connected to does not appear (for example, if you have a new internal modem set for COM3 but COM3 does not appear), click on Cancel and go to the appropriate Troubleshooting section later in this session for the device you're having problems with.

   ✿ If you see an information request other than port, click on whatever setting is appropriate and click on Next to continue.

6. When you see a message that your device has been set up successfully, click on Finish. If asked to restart the computer, click on Yes (or Restart, or whatever the button says).

7. Test the device to make sure it works. If it doesn't, check the Troubleshooting sections later in this session.

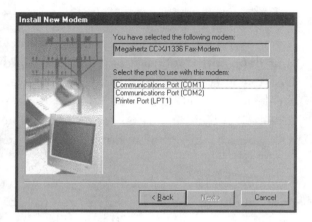

Figure 4.15

For some devices
such as modems,
you must
specify a port.

Installing the Extra Software

Once you get the device set up, you may want to run the setup programs
for any extra software that came with the device. For example, if your
new modem came with a communication program, you might want to
install it.

This is strictly your call. Personally, I seldom install the software that
comes with a new modem because it duplicates the capability already
built into Windows. On the other hand, I almost always install the software that comes with a sound card, because it usually includes a cool
audio CD player with fancy controls and a sound or video editing
program that is fun to play with.

More Fine-Tuning and Configuration

Most hardware devices have lots of settings. You can use them to fine-
tune or customize the device's operation. To see any of them, locate the
device in the Device Manager and click on Properties to display its properties. Each Properties dialog box has one or more tabs of settings you can
change. For example, a printer can be set for Portrait or Landscape printing or to print a specific number of copies of every print job. A modem

can be set to always dial an area code, regardless of the area code being called. A video card can be set to always use a certain refresh rate. You get the idea. Experiment!

Take a Break

If you aren't having any problems with your PC, you can hit the hay early tonight. The rest of this session is dedicated to the unlucky individuals for whom everything did not go smoothly when setting up new hardware. It's extensive because PC troubleshooting is not a simple matter, even in Windows 98.

If you have to go through the troubleshooting gauntlet, take a moment first to catch your breath, make a sandwich, and get ready to ride the "what's wrong with my computer?" roller coaster.

General Troubleshooting

I wish things always worked right the first time, but unfortunately they don't. I have been installing computer hardware for years, and yet it seems like every time there is at least one problem to be stamped out, even with Windows and its supposedly foolproof hardware installation. But you know what? It's usually due to my own carelessness. Perhaps I didn't firmly seat a card in a slot, or I forgot to set a jumper. Or maybe the new device is trying to use the same IRQ as an existing one.

If you are having video, modem, or sound problems, skip to the specific troubleshooting sections later in this session for those issues. Otherwise, start your troubleshooting journey here.

Turning on the computer is your first test. If the computer starts normally and Windows appears as usual, you've done something right. Use the following troubleshooting information to determine what the problem is.

Blank Screen

The hardest problems to troubleshoot are those where you don't see any information onscreen. With these, it's hard to know where to start. Here are some hints.

Blank Screen, No Fan

SYMPTOM: The screen is blank, and you hear absolutely nothing from the PC, not even a fan.

EXPLANATION: The computer is not getting power, or the power supply is defective.

SOLUTION: Check the following:

- ❏ Is the computer plugged into an electrical outlet?
- ❏ If the computer is plugged into a surge protector or power strip, is its power switch on?
- ❏ Is the power cable plugged firmly into the back of the computer?

If all of these things check out, you may have a bad power supply or fan, or the processor may not be inserted correctly on the motherboard (if you recently have messed with it).

Blank Screen, Fan Only

SYMPTOM: The screen is blank, and you hear nothing except the power supply fan. There is no disk activity.

EXPLANATION: Assuming you did nothing to the motherboard or the processor, you probably do not have the video card installed correctly.

SOLUTION: Check the following:

- ❏ Is the card firmly seated in its slot?
- ❏ Is the card in the right kind of slot?

If you are still having a problem, the new video card may be defective.

Blank Screen, Constant Beeping

SYMPTOM: You see a blank screen and hear a series of beeps.

EXPLANATION: If you just installed more memory in your PC, either it is not installed correctly or it is defective.

SOLUTION: If you installed memory, check these things:

❏ Have you installed the memory in the correct banks?

❏ Have you set any needed switches or jumpers?

If you have another computer available that uses the same kind of memory, swap out the SIMMs or DIMMs one at a time to see if you can determine whether one of them is faulty.

Blank Screen, Single Beep

SYMPTOM: You see a blank screen and you hear a single beep. The floppy disk light flashes briefly, and you hear the hard disk spinning.

EXPLANATION: The computer is starting normally but the monitor isn't displaying the startup messages.

SOLUTION: Try to figure out where the disconnect is between the monitor and the computer, or why the monitor isn't working:

❏ Is the monitor getting power? Check to make sure it is plugged in and turned on. A light should illuminate on its front when it has power.

❏ Is the light on the front of the monitor solid green? If so, that's good. If it's amber or blinking, this could indicate one of two things: Either the monitor is working fine but not receiving any signal from the computer, or the monitor is in stand-by mode. Some monitors have a stand-by button on the front; try pressing all the buttons on the front to see if any of them change the light to solid green.

❏ Are the monitor contrast and brightness controls set appropriately? If the brightness is turned all the way down, it can look like the screen is blank.

❏ Is the monitor firmly plugged into the video card?

❏ If you changed video cards, did you get the card firmly seated in the right type of slot?

If all of these things check out, you may have a defective monitor, monitor cable, or video card.

BIOS Info Followed by Error Message

If the system passes its basic startup tests, you see a BIOS message on the screen. It reports the brand and serial number of the BIOS, how much memory the computer has, and perhaps some other information too. After that, if all goes well, Windows loads. If all doesn't go well, you see an error message instead.

Floppy Drive Failure

SYMPTOM: You see the BIOS identification onscreen, followed by a message that the floppy disk drive has failed. The light on the floppy drive stays on constantly.

EXPLANATION: Your floppy drive cable is plugged in backwards at one or both ends. Did you unplug it when you were installing your new component?

SOLUTION: Unplug the ribbon cable from the floppy drive and plug it in the other direction, so the stripe on the cable aligns with Pin #1.

If you are sure it is already correctly oriented, check the other end of the ribbon cable, where it plugs into the motherboard or the I/O controller card. On the motherboard or card, there should be a tiny "1" next to one end of the socket. Make sure the stripe on the ribbon cable plugs into that end.

SYMPTOM: You see the BIOS identification onscreen, followed by a message that the floppy disk drive has failed. The floppy drive does not light at all.

EXPLANATION: You may have a defective floppy drive, or your floppy drive cable may be bad, or not completely plugged in. Or the floppy drive cable may be plugged in backwards at one or both ends. Did you bump one of the connectors while you were rattling around inside your PC?

SOLUTION: Check to make sure the stripe on the ribbon cable is aligned with Pin #1 on both ends, as explained in the preceding symptom and solution.

Also make sure that you got the connector on the ribbon cable connected to all the pins on the motherboard or I/O card, not just one row of them. Sometimes it is hard to see this because of all the other cables in the way.

If you are sure that the cable is on correctly, you may have a bad floppy drive or a bad cable.

Hard Drive Failure

SYMPTOM: You see the BIOS identification onscreen, followed by the message Hard Disk Fail.

EXPLANATION: You probably just installed a new hard disk, and it is not working. There is probably a mechanical failure with the drive or it is not connected correctly.

SOLUTION: Check the following:

❏ Is the hard disk correctly connected with the stripe on its ribbon cable plugged into Pin #1 at both ends?

❏ If there are two IDE controller sockets on the motherboard or I/O card, is it plugged into the one labeled Primary? In many cases, a system won't work if there is only one hard disk and it is plugged into the Secondary socket.

❏ Is the power supply cable firmly plugged into the back of the hard disk?

❏ If you are using the Cable Select method of establishing a drive's slave or master status, is the drive using the correct connector on the ribbon cable for its status?

If all these things check out, your drive probably has a mechanical problem, which you can't repair yourself. Return it for a refund or exchange.

Operating System Failure

SYMPTOM: You see the BIOS startup screen, and then a message about No Operating System or No Command Processor, or perhaps a message prompting you to insert a disk with startup files.

EXPLANATION: Your hard disk does not contain the startup files needed to start the computer. Perhaps you just installed a new hard drive?

SOLUTION: Pull out your Windows 98 Startup disk (aren't you glad you took care of it earlier in this session?) and put it in your floppy drive. Then restart the computer and follow the directions on the screen. Make sure you have your Windows 98 CD-ROM handy; you'll need it to reinstall Windows.

Memory Error

SYMPTOM: You see the BIOS identification message onscreen, followed by a memory error message.

EXPLANATION: If this is the first time you have started your PC after installing the new memory, this may be a normal message asking you to enter and exit the BIOS setup program. Press whatever key it tells you to press to enter the BIOS setup, and then exit from it, saving the changes. Strange as it may sound, that's all it takes on most systems to configure new memory.

If you have entered and exited the BIOS setup program once already since installing the new memory, your system's memory is faulty or improperly installed, or you have jumpers or DIP switches on the motherboard set incorrectly for the amount of memory on your system.

SOLUTION: Assuming you have already done the in-and-out of BIOS setup once, you need to figure out why the system is rejecting the memory. Older systems can be extremely finicky about the memory they will accept and the way it must be installed.

Check the following:

❏ Have you chosen the correct type of memory, as indicated in the computer's manual?

❏ Have you installed it in the right bank or banks, according to the chart in the manual?

❏ Is the memory firmly locked into the bank and held in place with clips at both ends?

❏ Have you set any DIP switches or jumpers on the motherboard necessary for the new memory?

If you are still getting a memory error at startup, perhaps the memory itself is bad; contact the vendor and see if you can get a replacement.

Windows Starts but New Device Doesn't Work

If the PC appears to work okay but your new upgrade doesn't function, maybe you have installed it wrong or forgotten to install the drivers. Maybe it has an address or IRQ conflict, or maybe it's just plain broken. You never know until you check it out.

Check the following things first:

❏ Did you read and carefully follow the installation instructions that came with the device? Read them again to make sure you didn't miss something.

❏ Is the hardware physically installed correctly? Check all cable connections and make sure all circuit boards are pressed completely into their slots.

❏ Did you remember to run the installation software that came with the device?

If all that looks right, jump to the appropriate troubleshooting section that follows, depending on your operating system and the type of device you are installing.

Troubleshooting Video Problems

If you've recently installed a new video card or monitor, getting optimal results can be a real challenge.

With Windows 98, you don't have a scrambled video problem like you might have seen in DOS or Windows 3.1, because Windows 98 has Plug-and-Play capability, so it detects when the old video card is no longer there and removes its drivers. If it can determine what type of video card you have, it automatically installs drivers for it; otherwise it installs a generic VGA video driver for the new card.

So instead, the video problems you'll see are more a matter of quality. If Windows can't detect your new video card's type, it uses a generic VGA driver, and you won't get the image quality or system performance with it that you would with the video drivers designed specifically for your video card. The following sections explain some problems you might encounter and how to correct them.

Image Doesn't Fill Entire Monitor, or Is Off-Center

SYMPTOM: The startup text looks okay, but when Windows starts, there is a noticeable black ring around the edge on at least one side, or the image appears off-center or cut off on one side.

EXPLANTION: Your monitor's image controls need to be adjusted.

SOLUTION: Refer to your monitor's manual to find out how to adjust it.

TIP

In Windows 98, you can change the refresh rate for your display, which you'll learn to do under "Display Flickers Noticeably" later in this session. Changing the refresh rate often throws off your carefully set image size and position adjustments, so if you are planning to change the refresh rate, do it before you spend a lot of time adjusting the monitor controls.

Windows Fails to Detect New Card

SYMPTOM: Windows detects your new video card as "Generic VGA."

EXPLANATION: Windows cannot figure out what kind of video card you have just installed. Perhaps your PC's BIOS does not support Plug and Play, or perhaps the new card does not.

If possible, you should install drivers for your specific video card, even if the system appears to be working okay with the generic drivers. You will get maximum video performance by using drivers designed specifically for your video card.

SOLUTION: Install a driver specific to your new card. Follow these steps:

1. Right-click on the desktop and choose Properties from the shortcut menu that appears.

2. Click on the Settings tab.

3. Click on the Advanced button. The display properties box for your video card appears.

4. Click on the Adapter tab if it is not already on top.

5. Note the adapter type on the first line. If it does not match your actual video card, click on the Change button. The Update Device Wizard dialog box appears.

6. Click on Next to begin, and then choose Display a list of all the drivers in a specific location, so you can select the driver you want. Click on Next to continue.

7. Click on the Show All Hardware option button.

8. Do one of the following:

   ✿ If you have a disk that came with your video card, put it in your floppy drive and click on the Have Disk button. The Install from Disk dialog box opens. Click on OK to accept the A drive. Windows locates the driver. If there is more than one driver on the disk, it opens an extra box where you can choose among them. Choose the one that matches your video card, and click on OK.

⚙ If you do not have the disk, locate your video card's manufacturer on the left-hand list, and then the model on the right-hand list (see Figure 4.16). Then click on OK.

CAUTION In Step 7, if your model does not appear on the list, do *not* use an alternate model. Even though the names may be similar, the drivers may be very different. Instead, click on Cancel. Then visit the video card manufacturer's Web site and download the driver you need, or telephone them and ask them to send you a driver disk.

Display Flickers Noticeably

SYMPTOM: Ever since you installed the new video card or monitor, the video display flickers, causing eyestrain.

EXPLANATION: The refresh rate is not set as high as it should be. The refresh rate is jointly determined by the maximum capability of the video card and the monitor. If either is set for "generic" in Windows, the refresh rate used will be low.

SOLUTION: Make sure Windows knows what model of video card and monitor you have. To do so, follow these steps:

1. Right-click on the desktop and choose Properties from the shortcut menu that appears.
2. Click on the Settings tab.
3. Click on the Advanced button. The Advanced Display Properties dialog box appears.
4. Click on the Adapter tab if it is not already on top.
5. If your correct adapter is not listed, click on the Change button and install a new driver for it, as explained in the preceding section.
6. Click on the Monitor tab.
7. If your correct monitor is not listed, click on the Change button and specify it, just like you did for the video driver (see Figure 4.17).

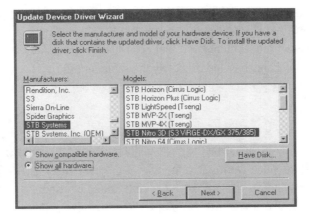

Figure 4.16

Choose your video card manufacturer and model from the list if you do not have an installation disk for it.

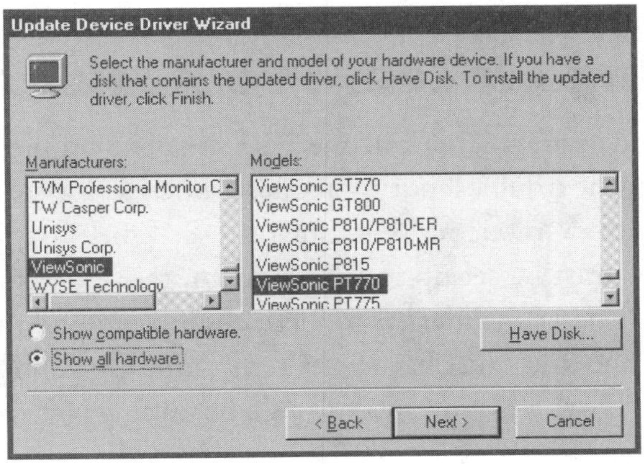

Figure 4.17

Choose your monitor from the list, or the closest model available if yours is not listed.

8. Return to the Adapter tab and make sure that Optimal is chosen on the Refresh Rate drop-down list.

9. Click on Close to close the dialog box. A dialog box appears informing you that Windows is going to change your refresh rate. Click on OK.

10. Windows displays a dialog box asking if you want to keep the new refresh rate. If you click on Yes, the change takes effect. If you click on No, or do nothing for 10 seconds, it goes back to your old refresh rate. (This is to prevent a new refresh rate from taking hold that scrambles your display.)

NOTE The monitor you choose determines the refresh rate used, but little else. If you do not see your exact model number on the list, it is usually okay to choose a similar model, because it probably has approximately the same refresh rate.

TIP Some video cards come with their own utility programs for Windows. For example, I have an STB Nitro video card that came with a program called STB Vision. I can use this program in Windows to set a specific refresh rate to be used.

Troubleshooting Modem Problems

I have had more clients call me with modem problems than with any other kind of troubleshooting request. There's just so much that can go wrong with a modem! Not only must it be installed properly, but Windows must be set up for the modem, the address and IRQ must be set right (if it is an internal model), the phone line must be connected properly, and you must have your communication software set up to recognize it. That's a lot to expect from a beginning computer user. Here are some places to start.

Windows Doesn't See the Modem

SYMPTOM: Windows did not detect the modem, and does not know it is there.

EXPLANATION: Perhaps either the modem or your BIOS is not Plug and Play compatible, or perhaps you need to run an installation program that came with the modem.

SOLUTION: Look through the disks that came with the modem, and see if there is an installation program that you have failed to run. If there is, read the part of the instructions that pertains to Windows 98, and then run it. (If the directions don't have anything about Windows 98, look under Windows 95.)

If there is no installation program, manually install the modem in Windows, as you learned earlier in this session.

The Modem Doesn't Work

SYMPTOM: Windows detected the modem when you installed it, but the modem doesn't seem to work.

EXPLANATION: The modem probably has an address or IRQ conflict with another device.

SOLUTION: Use the Device Manager to troubleshoot the modem problem:

1. In Windows, open the Control Panel and select the System icon.

2. Click on the Device Manager tab.

3. Click on the plus sign next to Modem to display the list of modems installed. Your modem should appear on the list. It may have a yellow circle with an exclamation point, indicating there is a problem with it. (If your modem is not on the list, or if there is no Modem entry, look for an Other Device entry. If your modem appears under that category, see "Windows Sees Modem as Other Device later in this session.)

4. Click on the modem and then click on Properties. A Properties dialog box appears for the modem.

5. In the Device Status area, if it does not say "The Device is Working Properly," click on the Resources tab.

6. In the Conflicting Device List, if there is a conflict listed, note whether it is an Input/Output Range conflict or an IRQ conflict.

7. Click on the Use Automatic Settings check box to deselect it.

8. Open the Setting Based On drop-down list and choose a different configuration. Keep trying different configurations until you find one that says No Conflicts in the Conflicting Device List.

9. Click on OK to close the dialog box.

10. Now try using your modem again. It should work now.

NOTE In rare cases, all of the configurations on the list (in Step 8) have a conflict. If this is the case, you can try changing the Interrupt Request (IRQ) and the Input/Output Range separately. Choose the configuration from the Setting Based On list until you find one with only one conflict. Make a note of what it is (Interrupt Request or Input/Output Range.) Then click on the matching line in the Resource Settings list. Next, click on the Change Setting button. One of two things may happen: you may see a message that the setting cannot be modified, or you may see a box containing alternate settings. If you see the latter, try a different setting. Repeat this until you find a setting that produces No Conflicts.

If you see the message that the setting cannot be modified, there is one last thing you can try. In the Conflicting Device list, note the device that is the other half of the conflict. Then try modifying the settings for that device so that it no longer conflicts with your sound card.

Windows Sees Modem as Other Device

SYMPTOM: When you look for your modem in the Device Manager list, it is listed under Other Devices rather than under Modem.

EXPLANATION: Windows partially detected the new device, but it couldn't figure out that it was a modem.

SOLUTION: This usually happens when the modem comes with its own drivers that need to be installed. Assuming you have a driver disk from the modem manufacturer, follow these steps:

1. From the Device Manager, click on your modem and then click on Properties to display its Properties dialog box.

2. Click on the Driver tab.

3. Click on the Update Driver button. The Update Device Driver Wizard dialog box appears.

4. Place the disk containing the modem driver in your floppy drive, and then click on the Next button.

5. Click on Search for a better driver than the one your device is using now, and click on Next again.

6. On the screen that appears (see Figure 4.18), choose which drives on which you want to search for the driver. Then click on Next.

NOTE If you include Microsoft Update in the list of locations to check, the wizard will log onto the Internet and check the Microsoft Web site for the latest drivers.

7. When the wizard reports that it has found the new driver, click on Finish. The new driver is installed and your modem moves to the Modem list in Device Manager.

8. Close the Device Manager dialog box.

9. Try your modem again. It should work now.

No Dial Tone

SYMPTOM: Your modem appears to be installed correctly, but you get a message that there is no dial tone when you try to use it. An attached telephone may or may not work.

Figure 4.18

Windows can search for the driver on all the disks in your system, including the floppy drive.

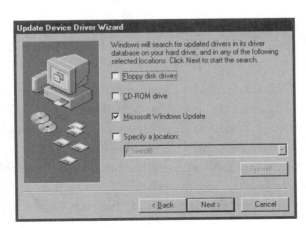

EXPLANATION: You do not have a working telephone line plugged into the correct jack on the modem.

SOLUTION: You do not have to turn off your computer to troubleshoot this. Check the back of the modem. Are there two telephone jacks? One is for the incoming line and the other is for an outgoing phone. Make sure that you have the incoming line plugged into the correct jack. If they are not labeled, switch which one the line is plugged into and try the modem again.

If that doesn't help, try plugging a telephone directly into the line that is feeding into the modem. Do you hear a dial tone? If not, your telephone line is the problem.

If you heard a dial tone through the telephone, unplug the line from the telephone and plug it back into the modem. Then plug the telephone into the other jack in the modem (the outgoing one, probably labeled PHONE). Do you still hear a dial tone? If so, the telephone dial tone is passing through the modem successfully, and should be detected.

Modem Makes Endless Connection Noises

SYMPTOM: The modem appears to dial and connect with the remote site, but instead of connecting, it keeps making static noises and beeping, over and over, until the remote modem finally gives up and hangs up on it.

EXPLANATION: Your modem string is not set correctly in your communication program or your phone line is very staticky.

SOLUTION: First, check to see if this happens in every communication program. For example, if it's happening with America Online, use the CompuServe or Prodigy startup kit included in the Online Services folder in Windows and try connecting to one of those services. (Most offer one month free, so it doesn't cost anything to try.) If the problem is occurring only with the one service, then the modem setup string is wrong. Call the online service's technical support line for help.

If the problem is happening with all connections, your phone line is probably extremely bad. This happens when a household has bad phone service to begin with and then installs a second line that runs over the same wires. The already-weak phone line, when split in two, becomes unsuitable for modem connections. Modems require much clearer phone lines than humans. If you have a second phone line in your house, try the modem on the other phone line. If that clears up the problem, call the phone company and have them look at the line that is causing the problems.

Modem Won't Stay Connected

SYMPTOM: The modem dials and connects, but then hangs up after a few seconds. Repeated attempts almost always have the same result.

EXPLANATION: The setup string that the program is sending to the modem is inappropriate for that modem. Different modems require different setup strings, in the form of "Hayes commands." Each setup string begins with AT for attention, followed by a series of two-character codes that turn on or off certain modem features.

When you install a communication program such as the America Online software, it asks what kind of modem you have. This is important because it knows what strings to send to what modems. If you tell it the wrong type, it will send the wrong string. Even though it may be able to briefly connect, it won't be able to stay connected.

The setup string sent to the modem with Windows 98's Dial-Up Networking depends on the modem driver in use.

SOLUTION: Make sure you have chosen the correct modem type in the communication program. If it is right, check the modem manual; the modem manufacturer may suggest certain setup strings to use for certain online services.

The procedure for checking the setup string varies from program to program. For example, in America Online, you choose Setup from the sign-on screen and then click on the Modem Commands button. Call the technical support phone number for the online service you are using if you cannot figure out how to access its setup string.

Since Dial-Up Networking takes its setup string from the modem driver, if you have this problem with dial-up networking, you may not have the right driver installed for your modem. See "The Modem Doesn't Work" earlier in this section to learn how to change the driver.

NOTE It could be your Internet Service Provider's fault if your dial-up Internet connection hangs up on you. At times of peak usage, I sometimes have to dial my provider 10 times or more before Dial-Up Networking will connect and stay connected. If the modem works at least some of the time, chances are good that you have Windows set up correctly and the problem is on the other end.

Troubleshooting Sound Problems

Lack of sound isn't usually critical to a program—but it's annoying to pay good money for a sound card and have it not work, or work with only some of your programs.

If you aren't getting sound, you need to figure out whether the sound card isn't working at all or just in certain programs. Narrow it down, and then see the appropriate section among the ones that follow.

❑ Have you run the setup software that came with the sound card? Most sound cards won't work unless you do so, even if Windows autodetects them.

❑ Do you have speakers plugged into the sound card? If the speakers have a power switch, is it on? Are the speakers plugged into an electrical outlet (if they're the kind that run on AC current rather than batteries)? Or do they have the appropriate batteries installed?

❑ Is there a DOS-based diagnostic program that came with the sound card? Such a program can tell you whether the sound card is working at all. If you can get sound from it, you know that the problem is the way the sound card is set up in Windows.

No Sound, Diagnostic Program Reports Failure

SYMPTOM: The sound card does not work at all, even in its own diagnostic program. The diagnostic program reports that the sound card is not functioning.

EXPLANATION: The sound card is either defective or improperly installed.

SOLUTION: Check the installation instructions that came with the sound card to make sure you performed the installation as directed. Make sure you ran the installation software, and that you restarted your computer afterwards.

The sound card diagnostic program should check the IRQ that it is using to make sure that it doesn't conflict with any other devices. Pay attention to this test, and specify a different IRQ and base address if needed. Some older sound cards may need to have jumpers set on the card itself to change the address and IRQ.

Finally, check that the sound card is completely seated in its socket.

Still no luck? The sound card may be defective. Return it for an exchange or refund.

No Sound, Diagnostic Program Thinks It's Fine

SYMPTOM: The diagnostic program acts like everything is fine, but you don't hear any sound.

EXPLANATION: Something is probably wrong with your speakers.

SOLUTION: Check the following:

❏ Are your speakers plugged into an electrical outlet if they require it?

❏ Are the speakers plugged into the correct socket on the sound card? Is the connection firm?

❏ Are they turned on if they have a power switch?

❏ Is their volume turned up?

If all of the above checks out, you may have a defective speaker. (One speaker is usually the "leader" and the other one just plugs into it, so if the lead speaker is the faulty one, neither may work.)

Sound Doesn't Work in Specific Program

SYMPTOM: You hear sound in Windows, but in one particular DOS-based program (perhaps a game) the sound does not work.

EXPLANATION: Today's DOS-based games are typically very sophisticated, with lots of sound and music. But unlike Windows-based programs, DOS-based programs cannot rely on the operating system handling the sound, so they must provide their own special drivers. Most games support at least three or four different sound cards, but if you don't have one of the supported cards, you're out of luck.

The most popular brand of sound card is SoundBlaster (and its variants, SoundBlaster Pro and SoundBlaster 16), so most off-brand cards try to offer SoundBlaster compatibility. They do so, however, with varying degrees of success. Even though your sound card is supposed to be completely SoundBlaster compatible, it may have a few little quirks in it that prevent it from working in all situations where a true SoundBlaster card would work.

SOLUTION: If you still have the installation disks for the program, reinstall it. You may be given a choice of sound cards during installation.

If that doesn't work, look in the same directory as the program's files for a configuration program. (Hint: there is probably something about "CONFIG" in the name, and it probably ends in EXE, COM, or BAT.) If you find such a program, run it; maybe it will let you specify what sound card you have.

Still no luck? Check the manual that came with the sound card. Perhaps there are tips in it for making your sound card perform in SoundBlaster-compatible mode.

Your last recourse is to contact the game's manufacturer to see if there is a patch available that will make the game work with your sound card.

If you strike out on all counts, and this game is really important to you, consider buying a different sound card. A genuine SoundBlaster card can be had for less than $100 if you get a no-frills model. (The SoundBlaster 16 Basic is a good choice.)

Windows Doesn't See Sound Card

SYMPTOM: When you install a sound card and then start Windows, it does not detect any new hardware.

EXPLANATION: Maybe your PC doesn't support Plug and Play, or maybe the sound card doesn't.

SOLUTION: There are two ways to install sound card drivers in Windows: use Windows 98's Add New Hardware wizard or run an installation program that came with the sound card. If the sound card's own installation program is Windows 98–sensitive, it's the better of the two options. Generally speaking, you would use the Add New Hardware Wizard method only if the sound card is old (pre-1995).

Running the installation program that came with the sound card is easy—just pop the disk in your floppy drive and run the setup program. You can browse for the file name in My Computer, or you can do the following to have Windows detect and run the setup program:

1. Place the floppy disk in the drive.

2. Open the Control Panel and choose Add/Remove Programs.

3. Click on the Install button. Windows looks for the installation program, finds it on the floppy, and begins the installation.

If you don't have a setup program on disk for the sound card, you can use Windows 98's Add New Hardware wizard to install a driver for the card. Follow the procedure outlined earlier in this chapter for doing so.

Windows Sees Card but There's No Sound

SYMPTOM: Windows detected your sound card and put it on the Device Manager list, but you can't hear any sound.

EXPLANATION: Perhaps your speakers are not working or your volume is turned down too low. If there is a yellow circle next to the sound card on the Device Manager list, perhaps there is an address conflict.

SOLUTION: Check the easy things first:

❏ Are the speakers turned on and working?

❏ Is the volume turned up in Windows? If you're not sure, double-click on the speaker icon in the bottom right corner of the Windows screen to open a dialog box where you can adjust the volume.

TIP

If you do not have a speaker icon (or some other volume control icon) next to the clock in the System Tray (in the bottom right corner of the Windows screen), you can turn on its display like this: from the Control Panel, double-click on the Multimedia icon. The Multimedia Properties dialog box appears. Click to place an X in the Show Volume Control on the taskbar check box, and then click on OK.

If you still do not have sound, follow these steps:

1. From the Control Panel, choose the System icon.

2. Click on the Device Manager tab.

3. Select the entry for your sound card. (Click on the plus sign next to Sound, Video, and Game Controllers if needed.)

4. Click on the Properties button. A Properties dialog box for the sound card appears.

5. In the Device Status area, if it does not say "The Device is Working Properly," click on the Resources tab.

6. In the Conflicting Device List, if there is a conflict listed, note whether it is an Input/Output Range conflict or an IRQ conflict.

7. Click on the Use Automatic Settings check box to deselect it.

8. Open the Setting Based On drop-down list and choose a different configuration. Keep trying different configurations until you find one that says No Conflicts in the Conflicting Device List.

9. Click on OK to close the dialog box.

10. Try using your sound card again. It should work now.

 NOTE

In rare cases, all of the configurations on the list (in Step 8) have a conflict. If this is the case, you can try changing the Interrupt Request (IRQ) and the Input/Output Range separately. Choose the configuration from the Setting Based On list until you find one with only one conflict. Make a note of what it is (Interrupt Request or Input/Output Range.) Then click on the matching line in the Resource Settings list. Next, click on the Change Setting button. One of two things may happen: you may see a message that the setting cannot be modified, or you may see a box containing alternate settings. If you see the latter, try a different setting. Repeat this until you find a setting that produces No Conflicts.

If you see the message that the setting cannot be modified, there is one last thing you can try. In the Conflicting Device list, note the device that is the other half of the conflict. Then try modifying the settings for that device so that it no longer conflicts with your sound card.

Windows Sees Card as Other Device

SYMPTOM: Windows automatically detects your sound card, but it doesn't work, and on the Device Manager list it appears in the Other Device category.

EXPLANATION: Your sound card requires that you run its own software to set it up, and you have not done this yet. Some sound cards do not work correctly when merely detected by Plug and Play; they need their own special drivers to operate.

SOLUTION: Run the installation program that came with the sound card.

In some cases, the sound card may not have come with a full-fledged installation program. Instead it may simply have a disk with a driver on it (perhaps a file with a DRV or a DLL extension, and maybe a file called OEMSETUP.INF.) To install the driver for your sound card from such a disk, follow these steps:

1. From the Control Panel, choose the System icon.
2. Click on the Device Manager tab.
3. Locate and double-click on the line for your sound card, opening its Properties dialog box.
4. Click on the Driver tab.
5. Click on the Update Driver button. The Update Driver wizard opens.
6. Place the floppy disk in your floppy drive, and follow the instructions onscreen to update the driver. (It's the same procedure outlined in the Modem Troubleshooting section earlier in this session.)
7. If prompted, click on Yes to restart your system with the new driver in place.

Troubleshooting Printer Problems

Printers are easy to install (just plug them into the PC's parallel port), but there are an amazing array of things that can go wrong with them.

Windows Doesn't Detect Printer

SYMPTOM: You hook up a new printer, but Windows doesn't notice it.

EXPLANATION: The printer may not be Plug and Play compatible.

SOLUTION: Set up the printer using the Add Printer Wizard. Choose Start, Settings, Printers, and choose Add Printer to start the wizard. Follow the on-screen prompts.

Printer Won't Print

SYMPTOM: You issue the Print command in an application, but nothing comes out of the printer.

EXPLANATION: The print job is not reaching the printer; there is a break in the communications somewhere along the line.

SOLUTION: Trace the following route, noting where it breaks down:

1. Look in the System Tray (by the clock) in Windows. Do you see a printer icon?

   YES: Go on to Step 2.

   NO: Go back to the application and try printing again using File, Print. Check the printer name at the top of the dialog box to make sure you are using the right printer. If not, open the drop-down list and choose the correct one.

2. Double-click on the Printer icon in the System Tray to open the printer's status window. Does the print job appear there?

   YES: Go on to Step 3.

   NO: Are you sure it didn't already print? Check the printer output tray. Are you sure you are sending it to the right printer, if you have more than one available?

3. Does the print job say ERROR in the Status column?

   YES: Highlight the print job and press Delete to delete it. Turn the printer off and back on again, and try printing again from the application.

   NO: Go on to Step 4.

4. Does the title bar of the printer status window say Paused?

   YES: Open the Printer menu and choose Pause Printing to take the printer off Pause.

   NO: Go on to Step 5.

5. Look at the printer. Is there a red light lit or flashing on it?

   YES: Check the printer. Does it have paper? Is the paper jammed? Is the ink cartridge or ribbon still good?

   NO: Go on to Step 6.

6. Are there any other flashing lights on the printer (amber or green, for example)?

   YES: The print job is in the process of printing. Be patient and wait.

   NO: Go on to Step 7.

7. Are there any lights at all lit on the printer? In particular, is the Online light lit?

   YES: Is the printer connected to your PC with a cable? Are the ends snugly attached?

   NO: Look for an Online button on the printer and press it. The Online light should illuminate. If not, check to see that the printer has power.

If none of these things solve your problem, look in the manual that came with the printer for more ideas.

Printer Prints with Type Scrunched on Half the Page

SYMPTOM: In most or all programs, the printer's output appears tiny and squashed, covering only about half of the page.

EXPLANATION: The ink cartridge is not installed properly (on an inkjet), or Windows has assigned the wrong driver.

SOLUTION: Check the ink cartridge to make sure it is firmly and correctly seated. If that's okay, check to make sure you are using the right driver for your printer.

Printer Prints Garbage Characters

SYMPTOM: The printer's output is not formatted correctly, and extraneous letters or characters appear.

EXPLANATION: The printer does not understand the commands coming to it from Windows.

SOLUTION: Reinstall the printer driver. To do this, delete the printer's icon from the Printers folder (Start, Settings, Printers) and reinstall it with Add Printer.

If that doesn't work, see if there was an installation program that came with the printer. You may have to run it to get the printer to work correctly, even if Windows autodetects the printer.

If it still doesn't work, check with the printer manufacturer to see if an updated driver is available for Windows 98.

Printout Has Black Streaks or Faint Areas

SYMPTOM: The quality of the printout is bad.

EXPLANATION: There is something wrong with the printer. This is not a Windows problem.

SOLUTION: Check to make sure the ink or toner is installed correctly and is not running low. Your printer may need professional servicing or cleaning.

New Device Works but System Crashes Frequently

Now let's look at a slightly different problem: your new device is installed, and it works like a charm, but other odd things have started to happen. Perhaps your system locks up for no reason more often now, or perhaps some other device doesn't work anymore. These are the thorniest problems to troubleshoot, because the cause of the problem is not obvious. Is it the new device, or is it an old device's reaction to it? Here are some things to check:

- If the system locks up when you try to use two devices at the same time (for example, if it locks up when you move your mouse, but only when the modem is in use), you probably have a device conflict. Turn back to the sections on modems and sound cards if you need help tracking down a conflict.

- Perhaps the driver for one or more devices has gotten corrupted. Try reinstalling all your drivers (by running the setup programs that came with the devices).

- Check manufacturer Web sites for driver updates. Not all devices come with Windows 98 drivers; some of them have only Windows 95 drivers, and those don't always work well. Perhaps there is a known problem with a certain driver under Windows 98 that can be fixed by downloading an update.

- If all else fails, reinstall all your software. This sounds extreme, and it may take you several hours, but compared to how many hours you will probably waste in the future trying fruitlessly to track down the reason for the problem, it may be the best solution in the long run. To do this, back up everything important (and make sure you get everything, every data file that you ever may want again, every custom template in every application—everything. Consider backing up your *entire* hard drive contents. Then reformat your hard disk and start over, reloading Windows 98, and then all your drivers and applications and backed up data files. Ask a techie friend to help you if you're a beginner.

- If you still have crashes after a complete reinstall, suspect the hardware itself. Perhaps you need to install a *firmware* update (a BIOS update that affects only a single device) for a particular device, or maybe you have some bad memory. (A memory chip with a tiny flaw in it can sometimes cause system problems, although it appears to work normally most of the time.) The best thing to do in this case is to contact the PC manufacturer and ask for ideas. Be persistent. If you bug the makers enough, they will eventually figure out your problem, arrange service, or even send you a replacement computer.

What's Next?

After reading this chapter, you should be fairly comfortable with adding a new device to your system and configuring it in Windows 98. Congratulations—your newfound knowledge may save you hundreds of dollars in installation charges in the future! You can go off to bed feeling pretty good about yourself. Tomorrow morning's session will dive into the topic that everybody seems to be talking about these days—the Internet.

Getting Connected to the Internet and Browsing the Web

- ⚙ Getting Windows Ready for an Internet Connection
- ⚙ Browsing the Web with Internet Explorer

Good morning! If you're following the *In a Weekend* schedule, it's Sunday morning and you've probably finished brunch and read the important parts of the Sunday paper. Now, you've reluctantly decided to forego reading the rest of the paper in order to devote your time to learning more about Windows 98. So turn on the computer and go fill up your coffee cup—Windows will be ready for you by the time you get back.

So far, you've covered a lot of ground learning about the features of the Windows desktop, how to install and run programs, how to customize Windows settings, and how to install and configure hardware. Today, you get to explore some of the fun stuff—Windows 98's connections to the Internet. In this morning's session, you'll learn about the following:

- ✪ Selecting an Internet service provider
- ✪ Configuring Windows to communicate over the Internet
- ✪ Using Internet Explorer to browse the World Wide Web
- ✪ Finding information on the Internet

In the afternoon and evening sessions today, you'll learn about features that support e-mail and newsgroups, creating your own Web page, and taking advantage of Active Desktop to automatically update and display information from the Internet on your computer.

Getting Windows Ready for an Internet Connection

The goal of this first half of this morning's session is to get your computer system connected to the Internet. Setting up an Internet connection isn't terribly difficult, but there is more to it than just plugging in a modem. Before you can successfully connect your system to the Internet, you'll need to do the following:

- Choose an Internet connection service (called an *Internet Service Provider*, or *ISP*) and establish an account with it.
- Install and configure the network software you'll need to connect to the Internet.
- Set up Windows to use your modem to connect to the ISP (unless you will be connecting to the Internet via a local area network).
- Set up your Internet software, such as Internet Explorer and Outlook Express, to use the Internet connection and accounts you established.

 NOTE Most Windows users will need to use the services of an Internet service provider to connect to the Internet, and will make that connection with a modem plugged into a telephone line. If you're one of the lucky few with a full-time connection to the Internet via your local area network, you can skip the section called "Establishing a Connection with a Modem." You can probably skip the "Installing the Network Software" section as well, because your network system administrator will almost certainly take care of that for you. Even though the "Choosing an Internet Service Provider" section won't apply to you directly, you may want to skim it; your local area network and its system administrator will be providing you with similar services, and it may be interesting to see how they compare with commercial offerings.

Windows 98 includes a special program, the Internet Connection Wizard, that will take you through the entire process, step by step.

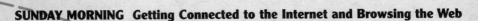

However, the options offered by the wizard are somewhat limited, and it isn't very thorough when it comes to configuring your system. So I'll show you how to set up an Internet connection manually. It's really no more difficult to do it manually than it is to use the wizard. Except for the convenience of leading you from one step to another automatically, the only advantage to using the Internet Connection Wizard is that it can suggest a list of ISPs (which you probably won't need).

Choosing an Internet Service Provider

You can't just connect your personal computer directly to the main backbone of the Internet—at least it's not practical to do so. After all, the Internet isn't just one big network, but a worldwide network composed of many smaller networks. The way to get connected to the Internet is to become a part of one of those smaller networks.

Typically, a large corporation or an educational institution connects all the computers on its campus to a network so they communicate with each other. Then it connects one or more of its powerful central server computers to the Internet. These servers can relay messages and data from any computer on the local network to any other computer connected to the Internet.

So how can you get connected to the Internet if you're not part of a corporate or university network? That's where ISPs come in. An Internet Service Provider is a business that sets up a computer network with servers connected to the Internet. It also connects these servers to a bank of modems and phone lines that allows customers to call in and connect to the network as needed.

In addition to access to the Internet, the ISP provides services such as e-mail accounts, newsgroup servers, and Web site hosting. The ISP then sells network access accounts to individuals and small businesses who want to use the ISP's network to access the Internet and use the other services.

The whole arrangement is similar to getting telephone service. Large companies, hospitals, universities, and the like all have their own private phone systems that are set up to handle internal communications but are also connected to the main telephone system to allow calls between any extension and any outside number. Individual telephone subscribers, on the other hand, are connected to a local telephone exchange, which then connects to the main telephone network to allow calls from any phone in the exchange to any other phone number anywhere.

The big difference between telephone service and Internet service is that telephone service is usually a monopoly with the main telephone network and all the local telephone exchanges in a given area owned by the same company. But you don't find the same kind of monopolies in the ISP business. You can buy Internet access service from a number of different local, regional, and national providers who are all competing for your business. And, in most cases, the local access point and the main transmission lines are owned and operated by separate companies.

ISPs can be grouped into two general categories: online services and plain Internet service providers. The plain Internet service providers do just that—they provide access to the Internet. An ISP might set up a special Web page with some members-only news and announcements or something of that sort, but the main focus is on providing access to the Internet and Internet-related services such as e-mail and perhaps a Web home page. An online service, on the other hand, tries to be more.

In the old days before the Internet got to be so popular, the online services each sought to provide a network and a set of services such as e-mail and discussion groups for their subscribers. But those services were for the exclusive use of members of the same service. Members of one online service couldn't communicate with members of another service—at least not easily. The various online services each tried to provide a unique set of services (emphasizing features such as chat rooms or forums), aiming to develop a sense of community that would attract customers to their own proprietary network. Today, all the major online services also provide access to the Internet as well as to their own services, and members of an online service can communicate with anyone on the Internet, including

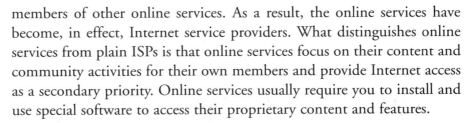

members of other online services. As a result, the online services have become, in effect, Internet service providers. What distinguishes online services from plain ISPs is that online services focus on their content and community activities for their own members and provide Internet access as a secondary priority. Online services usually require you to install and use special software to access their proprietary content and features.

So, which is best—an online service or a plain Internet service provider? It depends. If you are interested in the special features of a particular online service, subscribe to that service. If you do, you'll be able to get access to the Internet from the same source. However, if you just want efficient access to the Internet and an e-mail address, you'll probably be better off with a plain ISP.

The Microsoft Network

Microsoft tries to make it easier for Windows users to get signed up with a few of the more popular online services and Internet service providers. There is a shortcut icon on the desktop for Microsoft's own Microsoft Network (MSN) online service. Selecting and opening that icon will automatically take you through all the steps necessary to install the MSN software, establish a connection to the network, and gather all the information (such as name, address, and credit card number) needed to sign you up for an MSN account. To get you started, MSN offers a free trial period, during which you can try out the service before they begin charging a regular monthly fee. (The terms and conditions are all explained by the setup program before you are committed to subscribing to the service.)

NOTE You'll need to have your modem properly installed, configured, and connected to the phone line before you can use any of the signup programs for online services or ISPs. If necessary, refer to the Saturday Evening session for instructions on how to set up your modem.

In addition to the MSN icon on the Windows desktop, you'll probably find an icon for the Online Services folder. This folder contains icons for setup programs similar to the one for MSN that will help you get signed up with other online services and Internet service providers. To use one of these automated signup programs, simply open the Online Services folder and then select and open the icon for the service you want to join. Typically, the Online Services folder will contain icons for the following services:

The Microsoft Network

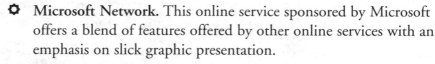
- **Microsoft Network.** This online service sponsored by Microsoft offers a blend of features offered by other online services with an emphasis on slick graphic presentation.

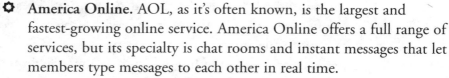
- **America Online.** AOL, as it's often known, is the largest and fastest-growing online service. America Online offers a full range of services, but its specialty is chat rooms and instant messages that let members type messages to each other in real time.

America Online

CompuServe

- **CompuServe.** This full-service online service is known for the quality of its discussion groups, known as forums, which cover a variety of topics, professions, and special interests.

Prodigy Internet

- **Prodigy Internet.** This is a former online service that has dropped most of its proprietary facilities and now concentrates on providing Internet access for a nationwide user base.

AT&T WorldNet Service

- **AT&T WorldNet.** The dominant force in the long distance telephone market is also an Internet service provider offering basic service nationwide.

Of course, you're not restricted to the service providers with icons in the Online Services folder. You have many other options as well. Table 5.1 shows just a few of the possibilities.

- **Regional ISPs.** Most of the regional telephone operating companies offer Internet access service in addition to regular telephone services. You may find other ISPs serving your region as well.

- **Local ISPs.** Check your local telephone book, newspaper ads, bulletins posted at local computer stores, and recommendations from friends and co-workers to find out about local Internet service providers. Although a few local ISPs are not much more than hobbyists and may deliver poor service and support, many local ISPs offer excellent service at very good prices for the customers in their area.

TABLE 5.1 OTHER SERVICE PROVIDERS

Service Provider	Phone Number	Web Address
Concentric Network	800-939-4262	www.concentric.net
EarthLink	800-395-8425	www.earthlink.com
FlashNet	800-352-7420	www.flash.net
IBM Internet Connection	800-722-1425	www.ibm.net
NETCOM	800-NETCOM1	www.netcom.com
MindSpring	888-677-4764	www.mindspring.com
NTR.net	800-962-3750	www.ntr.net
Sprint Internet Passport	800-545-5040	www.sprint.com/sip/
SpryNet	800-777-9638	www.sprynet.com

Getting set up with an ISP that doesn't have an icon in the Online Services folder is only a little less convenient. The ISP's setup program isn't preinstalled on your hard drive along with Windows. That means you'll need to call the ISP on the phone (or visit its Web site using a computer that already has Internet access) to request information and an Internet access account. The ISP's customer service representative can probably set up your account by asking you a few questions on the phone and will then give you all the information you need to manually configure Windows to access your new account.

If you're willing to wait a few days, most ISPs will send you a disk in the mail that contains a setup program similar to the ones in the Online Services folder. Just run the setup program and fill in the blanks on some on-screen forms, and the setup program will install the software and adjust the Windows settings that are necessary for you to access the Internet through that ISP. When you set up an Internet access account, the ISP should provide you with the following items:

- An assortment of Internet software and instructions on how to install and use it. (This isn't really necessary because Windows includes all the Internet software you're likely to need.)

- Instructions for setting up Windows to connect to its network and access the Internet (including the Internet addresses for the network servers that Windows and your Internet software will need to access).

- The user ID and password you will need to access the ISP's network.

- Your e-mail address and the account name (user ID) and password you'll need to access your e-mail account.

- The Internet address for the ISP's newsgroup server and also the addresses of servers that supply things like chat and directory services (if the ISP provides such extra services).

- If the ISP provides you with a Web page, you'll also get a Web page address and probably a separate address, user ID, and password to use when you publish your Web page.

Don't let this list overwhelm you. It's not really as complicated as it looks. Besides, you won't have to commit all the various addresses, user IDs, and passwords to memory. The only ones you'll need to remember are the user ID and password that give you access to the ISP's network, and perhaps your e-mail and Web site addresses (so you can tell other people how to send you e-mail and where to find your Web page). Windows keeps track of all the other addresses and information after you enter it the first time. In fact, the ISP's setup program will probably enter most of the information for you automatically.

After running the setup program you get from your ISP, you may find that Windows is fully configured and ready to access the Internet. There's a good chance that the setup program will have installed all the necessary software and adjusted the required Windows settings and options. If so, you can just skim over the remaining sections before the break in the middle of this session. (I suggest that you skim rather than skip the material so that you will at least be familiar with the various Internet-related settings in case you need to change or troubleshoot them in the future.) If you need to proceed with manually configuring your Internet settings, read on.

Installing the Network Software

Windows 98 needs two components, one hardware and one software, in order to connect to any network—including the Internet. The hardware component is called a *network adapter* and provides the physical connection between your computer and the network. Windows must be configured to work with the specific network adapter that is installed in your computer. (If you connect to the Internet over your phone line, your modem will serve as a virtual network adapter. In that case, you configure Windows to use the Dial-Up Adapter as your network adapter.)

The software component is called a *network protocol*. You can think of the network protocol as being the set of rules that govern communication on the network.

Again, Windows needs the appropriate network protocol installed before it can communicate with other computers on the network. The network protocol used on the Internet is *TCP/IP*. (The formal name is Transmission Control Protocol/Internet Protocol, but everybody just calls it TCP/IP.)

Network

You can quickly check to see if these two essential components are installed in your copy of Windows. Just open the Control Panel (click on Start, Settings, Control Panel) and then open the Network applet. When the Network dialog box appears, click on the Configuration tab (see Figure 5.1) and examine the entries in the list box. You should see an entry for your network adapter and a separate entry for the TCP/IP protocol on that adapter. If you will be using a modem to connect to the Internet, the adapter you're looking for is Dial-Up Adapter and the protocol line should read `TCP/IP -> Dial-Up Adapter`. (See the second and fifth lines in the list box shown in Figure 5.1.) If you connect the Internet over a real, hard-wired network, the adapter might have a name such as EtherExpress or NE2000 and the protocol line would read TCP/IP -> EtherExpress or TCP/IP -> NE2000.

If both of these components are installed, you're all set. You don't have to worry about any configuration settings for them and you can simply close the Network dialog box and go on to the next topic, learning how to establish a network connection with a modem. However, if support for the adapter or the TCP/IP protocol is lacking, you'll need to install the missing component before you proceed any further.

Installing the Network Adapter

To install support for your network adapter (or the virtual Dial-Up Adapter if you're connecting to the Internet using a modem), follow these steps:

Network

1. Open Control Panel and then open the Network applet. When the Network dialog box appears, click on the Configuration tab. (If you were checking to see if the network adapter and protocol are installed, this step is already done.)

2. Click on Add to open the Select Network Component Type dialog box, as shown in Figure 5.2.

3. Select Adapter from the list and click on Add. This will open the Select Network Adapters dialog box, as shown in Figure 5.3.

4. Select Microsoft in the Manufacturers list box and Dial-Up Adapter in the Network Adapters list box (if you will be connecting to the Internet via modem) or select the manufacturer and model of the network adapter card installed in your computer. Then click on OK. Windows adds the adapter to the list of installed network components.

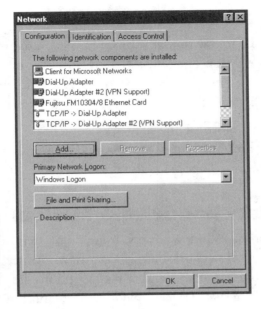

Figure 5.1

You need to have both a network adapter and the TCP/IP protocol installed.

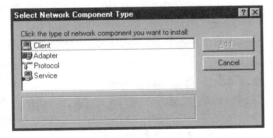

Figure 5.2

What kind of network component do you want to install?

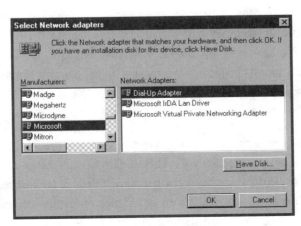

Figure 5.3

Select the manufacturer first, and then the model of the adapter you want to install.

Installing the TCP/IP Protocol

To install TCP/IP, follow the same procedure you used to install support for the network adapter. The only differences are that in Step 3, you select Protocol instead of Adapter; and in Step 4, you select Microsoft from the Manufacturers list and TCP/IP from the Network Protocols list.

After installing support for the network adapter and protocol, close the Network dialog box. You'll need to reboot your computer for the changes in installed network components to take effect.

Establishing a Connection with a Modem

If you're like most Windows users, your computer isn't permanently hooked up to a local network that is, in turn, connected to the Internet. Instead, you'll use a modem and a regular phone line to call in to a modem at your Internet service provider and establish a temporary connection to the Internet as needed. To do that, you're going to need a way to control your modem. You have to get it to dial the ISP, establish a connection, and log on to the ISP's network—once that's done, Windows can use that connection to handle messages traveling between your Internet software and other Internet addresses. The Windows feature that handles this connection is called Dial-Up Networking.

NOTE I'm assuming that the Dial-Up Networking component of Windows is already present on your system. (It's typically part the default installation.) If Dial-Up Networking isn't installed, you can add it by using Add/Remove Programs on the Control Panel. (You learned how to install Windows components in the Saturday Morning session.) Dial-Up Networking is one of the options under Communications on the Windows Setup tab.

Dial-Up Networking enables you to enter all the information you need to make a connection to your ISP just one time. After you enter the information, making the connection to your ISP is as simple as opening the connection icon. You can even configure Internet Explorer and Outlook Express to open the connection automatically as needed.

To begin working with Dial-Up Networking, you'll need to open the Dial-Up Networking folder (see Figure 5.4). There are several ways to get there, but the simplest is to start with the My Computer icon on your desktop. Open it, locate the Dial-Up Networking folder in the My Computer window, and open it as well.

Setting up a Dial-Up Networking Connection

To create a dial-up networking connection for your Internet service provider, follow these steps:

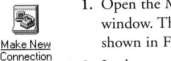

Make New
Connection

1. Open the Make New Connection icon in the Dial-Up Networking window. This will open the Make New Connection dialog box, as shown in Figure 5.5.

2. In the top text box, type a name for this connection. You can enter anything that makes sense to you, but I suggest something descriptive, such as **Personal Internet Account**. (Surely you can do better than the default My Connection.)

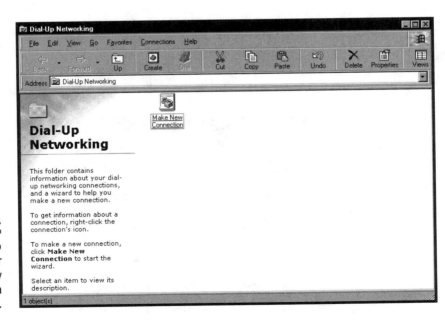

Figure 5.4

The Dial-Up Networking folder starts out empty except for a single icon.

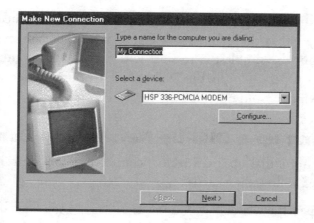

Figure 5.5

Start by giving your connection a name.

3. In the Select a Device drop-down list, select the device you want to use to make this connection. In most cases, there's only one choice: your modem. (If necessary, you can click on Configure to open the Properties dialog box for your modem and adjust the modem settings, and then return to the Make New Connection Wizard.) Click on Next to proceed to the next page of the wizard (see Figure 5.6).

4. Enter the Area Code and Telephone Number for your ISP's modem and, if necessary, select the ISP's country in the Country Code drop-down list. After entering the phone number, click on Next. The final confirmation page of the Make New Connection Wizard appears.

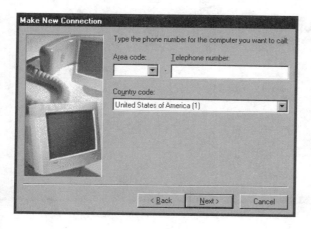

Figure 5.6

Who ya gonna call?

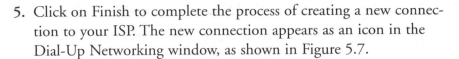

5. Click on Finish to complete the process of creating a new connection to your ISP. The new connection appears as an icon in the Dial-Up Networking window, as shown in Figure 5.7.

Now you have a basic connection to your ISP defined. Dial-Up Networking knows how to dial the number for your ISP's modem. But you're not ready to use the new connection yet. Windows will need more information before you can successfully log on and establish a connection with the ISP's network.

TIP

You can define a number of different dial-up networking connections. For example, you can create separate connections to access an online service, an ISP, and a corporate network. If your ISP has more than one phone number, you can set up a separate connection for each number. If you travel with your computer, you can set up a separate connection with the local telephone number for your ISP in each city you visit.

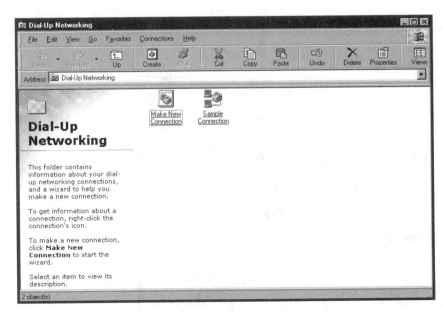

Figure 5.7

Each connection has its own icon on the Dial-Up Networking screen.

TCP/IP Settings and Other Technical Stuff

Once in a while, you might get lucky and stumble across an ISP that can use the default settings in a new Dial-Up Networking connection without modification, but it's rare. Normally, you'll need to adjust the settings in each Dial-Up Networking connection to match the recommended settings supplied by your ISP. It's a little tedious, but you'll only have to do it once. To adjust those settings, follow these steps:

Sample Connection

1. In the Dial-Up Networking window, right-click on the icon for the connection you want to edit and choose Properties from the shortcut menu that appears. This will open a properties dialog box for the connection (see Figure 5.8).

2. Click on the Server Types tab to display the options shown in Figure 5.9.

3. Change the settings on this page of the dialog box to match the recommendations of your ISP. Typical settings might include selecting PPP, Internet, Windows NT Server, Windows 98 in the Type of Dial-Up Server list box; no options checked in the Advanced Options box; and only the TCP/IP option checked in the Allowed Network Protocols box.

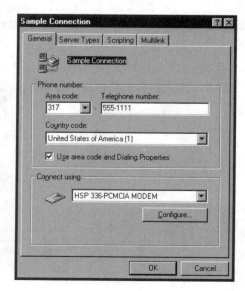

Figure 5.8

The General tab displays the information you defined when you created the new connection.

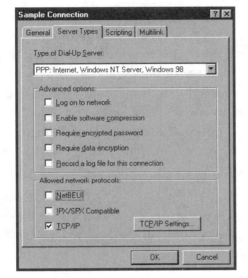

Figure 5.9

These are typical settings, not defaults.

4. Click on TCP/IP Settings to open the TCP/IP Settings dialog box, as shown in Figure 5.10.

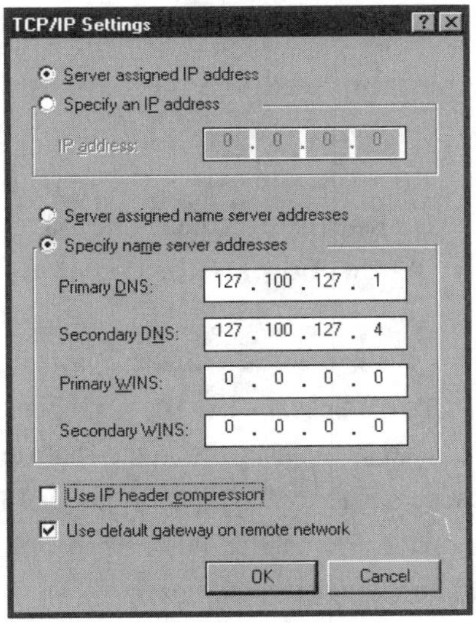

Figure 5.10

Be sure to enter the address numbers very carefully.

5. Again, change the settings on this page to match the recommendations of your ISP. A typical configuration might include checking the Server Assigned IP Address option, checking the Specified Name Server Addresses option, entering addresses for the Primary DNS and Secondary DNS (the Primary WINS and Secondary WINS settings are usually left blank), and checking both of the options on the bottom of the page. After adjusting the settings, click on OK to close the TCP/IP Settings dialog box.

6. If instructed to do so by your ISP, click on the Scripting tab and adjust the settings there.

7. After adjusting all the settings, click on OK to close the properties dialog box for the connection. Now your Dial-Up Networking connection is ready to use.

Logging On

To use your Dial-Up Networking connection, simply click (or double-click) on the icon in the Dial-Up Networking window to open it. Windows will open a Connect To dialog box, as shown in Figure 5.11. Type your user name (also called user ID or account name) and your password in the spaces provided. (The password appears as a series of asterisks to prevent anyone from reading your password off the screen.) If you want Windows to save your password for this connection in an encrypted file on your hard disk and enter it for you automatically the next time you open this connection, check the Save Password option. After you enter your user name and password, click on Connect.

◆ ◆

If the Connect To dialog box does not appear when you first open a Dial-Up Networking connection, you may need to make an adjustment. In the Dial-Up Networking window, pull down the Connections menu and choose Settings. In the Dial-Up Networking dialog box that appears, make sure the Prompt for Information Before Dialing option is checked and then click on OK to close the dialog box.

◆ ◆

Figure 5.11

This is where you enter the user name and password that serve as the key to unlock access to your account with your Internet service provider.

After you click on Connect, Windows will activate your modem to dial the phone number you set up in the connection. (You'll probably be able to hear the modem dialing.) When the ISP's modem answers, the two modems will negotiate a data transfer connection. (The noise and tones you hear are the communication between modems.) Once that's accomplished, Windows will use your username and password to log on to the ISP's network and establish a connection to that network, and from there, to the Internet. During the dialing and logon process, Windows will report the status of the connection in a small message box (see Figure 5.12). After the connection is established, the message box will disappear and an even smaller connection icon will appear in the System Tray portion of the taskbar (see Figure 5.13).

Figure 5.12

Windows keeps you informed of its progress while establishing a Dial-Up Networking connection.

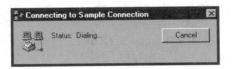

Figure 5.13

This icon indicates an open modem connection.

Dial-Up Networking Connection

At this point, you could go ahead and surf the Web, check your e-mail, or do any of the other things you might want to do on the Internet. However, I haven't shown you how to do any of those things yet. So you might as well just close the connection until you are ready to use it again.

To close your Dial-Up Networking connection to the Internet, right-click on the connection icon in the System Tray and choose Disconnect from the shortcut menu that appears. Windows will break the connection to the Internet and then instruct the modem to hang up the telephone line.

TIP

After you successfully complete a connection with the Save Password option enabled, Windows will automatically enter your username and password in the Connect To dialog box for that connection. As a result, there's no reason to display the dialog box onscreen. To keep it from appearing, choose Settings from the Connections menu in the Dial-Up Networking window, and then disable the Prompt for Information Before Dialing option in the Dial-Up Networking dialog box.

Establishing a Connection over a Local Network

As stated earlier, most Windows users will probably connect to the Internet via a telephone line and modem. A lucky few will be working on computers that are connected to local area networks that also provide connections to the Internet. If you are connected to such a network, the system administrator for the network will probably take care of configuring Windows to access the Internet in the course of connecting your system to the network in the first place.

Once an Internet connection is set up to make use of a local area network, it's even easier to use than accessing the Internet with a Dial-Up Networking connection.

Normally, if you use a local area network, you will log on to the network when you start Windows and log off of the network when you shut down

Windows and turn off your computer. Any time you are connected to the network, you are also connected to the Internet—at least indirectly. So you don't have to do anything to establish an Internet connection or log on to another network to access the Internet.

Take a Break

Finally! That gets the tedious technical stuff out of the way. By now, your coffee cup is probably empty and your bladder needs to be. So take a break and get away from the computer for a few minutes. (Just don't put too much Irish in your Irish coffee or you won't be able to blame the leprechauns when your computer won't work.) When you get back, you'll learn how to put your new Internet connection to good use surfing the World Wide Web.

Browsing the Web with Internet Explorer

Before the break, you learned how to get your Windows 98 computer connected to the Internet. Enabling your computer to exchange bits and bytes with other computers on a big network does not, in itself, do you much good. It's the information and communications available on the Internet that make it worthwhile to get connected. To take advantage of your Internet connection, you'll need to use some special software that enables you to find and view Internet documents and to send and receive Internet messages.

Internet Explorer is the centerpiece of Windows 98's suite of Internet software programs. (The other major Internet software programs supplied with Windows are Outlook Express for e-mail and newsgroups, NetMeeting for online conferencing, and FrontPage Express for creating Web pages.) Internet Explorer is Microsoft's popular *Web browser*—that is, it's a viewer program designed to display specially formatted documents called Web pages.

THE WEB IN A NUTSHELL

Web pages are electronic documents that can contain not only text but also graphics and multimedia content such as sounds, animations, video clips, and interactive elements. To view a Web page, you use a special software program called a Web browser that automatically reformats each Web page for optimum on-screen display within the Web browser window.

One of the distinctive characteristics of the World Wide Web is that Web pages can contain *hyperlinks*—highlighted text or areas of the page that, when clicked on, instruct the Web browser to locate and display another Web page. You can click on a hyperlink in a table of contents page to go to the referenced page or click on a hyperlinked term in some text to bring up a page of background information. And that's just the beginning. The interactive possibilities of hyperlinks are almost unlimited.

A *Web site* is a collection of Web pages that is posted on a special computer server connected to a network so that anyone on the network can access and view the Web pages. Often, the Web server is located on the Internet so anyone with a Web browser and an Internet connection can reach it, but many Web sites are located on local networks and are accessible only to users connected to the same network.

The Web has, in a few short years, evolved into a powerful and immensely popular publishing medium. The diversity of information available on the Web is truly astounding. Web sites range from simple home pages published by individuals to online brochures published by businesses, and from academic papers to online catalogs and electronic commerce shopping sites. You can find information on the Web on everything from aardvarks and astronomy to zebras and zydeco music. It seems like there are Web sites for every hobby, religion, organization, political party, sport, fan club, and special interest imaginable. The Web is full of business and financial information and educational opportunities abound. (And yes, you can also find sex, violence, and hate-group materials on the Web, just as you can in society.)

Internet Explorer will let you view it all—the good, the bad, and the ugly. Internet Explorer can help you search for the good stuff on the Web and filter out the bad. As for the ugly, you're on your own there. (Your best defense against unattractive, poorly designed Web pages is to just move on to a more attractive site as quickly as possible.)

NOTE Despite all the publicity and hype about the World Wide Web and the Internet that might lead you to think otherwise, the World Wide Web and the Internet are not the same thing! It's true that the two are closely linked. However, the Internet is a communications network that facilitates many different activities in addition to the World Wide Web, including e-mail, newsgroups, file transfers, conferencing, telephony, and much more. The Web, on the other hand, is an electronic publishing medium that is not confined to the Internet. You'll find Web pages everywhere from your local hard drive and CDs to every level of network, intranet, and extranet, in addition to the Internet.

Introducing Internet Explorer

Internet Explorer

Now it's time to learn to use Internet Explorer. The first step is starting the program. If you're the meticulous sort, you may want to open your Dial-Up Networking connection to the Internet before launching Internet Explorer. However, it isn't really necessary because Internet Explorer will prompt you to initiate a connection to the Internet when necessary. To open the Internet Explorer window, you can either choose Programs, Internet Explorer, Internet Explorer from the Start menu, or simply open the Internet Explorer shortcut icon on your Windows desktop.

TIP

Another handy way to start Internet Explorer is to click on the Internet Explorer icon in the QuickLaunch toolbar on the taskbar.

NOTE

The Internet Connection Wizard may appear automatically the first time you attempt to start Internet Explorer. If it does, simply follow the wizard's prompts to specify the Dial-Up Networking connection or other Internet connection you want Internet Explorer to use.

When you open Internet Explorer, it will automatically attempt to display a default Web page known as the *home page*. If that home page is located on a remote Web server (and it usually is), the program will attempt to connect to the Internet before it even displays the Internet Explorer window onscreen. If you have a full-time Internet connection through your local area network, or a Dial-Up Networking connection to the Internet is already open, the Internet Explorer window will open and the home page will begin loading. If there isn't a connection to the Internet already available, Internet Explorer will display the URL Not Found in Offline Mode message, as shown in Figure 5.14. Click on Connect to instruct Internet Explorer to go ahead and initiate an Internet connection. (If you click on Stay Offline, Internet Explorer will attempt to load the most recent version of the home page that it can find saved on your hard drive.)

Next, a Dial-Up Connection dialog box appears, as shown in Figure 5.15. It looks a little different from the Connect To dialog box you see when you open a Dial-Up Networking connection manually, but it works the

Figure 5.14

Internet Explorer lets you know if it's not connected to the Internet.

same way. Enter your username and password and then click on Connect. When you do, the dialog box changes to report on Dialing Progress. Again, it looks a little different from the message box you see when establishing a Dial-Up Networking connection manually, but the function is the same. Once the connection is established, the Dialing Progress dialog box disappears and the Internet Explorer window opens and begins loading the home page.

When the Internet Explorer window opens, it looks something like the one in Figure 5.16. Most of the window is devoted to displaying the Web page you are viewing, surrounded by the usual window border and other elements. In addition to the familiar title bar, menu bar, and scroll bar, the Internet Explorer window normally sports three toolbars. The Standard Buttons toolbar (shown just below the menu bar) is a collection of buttons that nearly eliminates the need to use the menus by providing one-click access to most commonly used commands. Below the Standard Buttons toolbar, you see the Address bar and the Links bar. The Address bar contains a single feature—a text box where you can type in the address of a Web page you want to load. The Links bar contains a set of buttons that provides ready access to selected Web sites. (If there isn't room for all the Links buttons to appear in the space allotted to the Links bar, you can use the small arrows at the ends of the toolbar to scroll other buttons into view.)

Figure 5.15

Track the progress of the dial-up connection

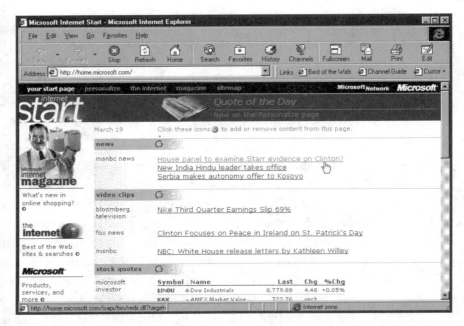

Figure 5.16

Welcome to the
Internet Explorer
window—your
window to the Web.

The buttons on the Standard Button toolbar provide easy access to most
of the features of Internet Explorer that you'll need to use while surfing
the Web. Here's a brief listing of the buttons and their functions:

- ✿ **Back.** Click on this button to return to the previous page you were
  viewing in Internet Explorer. Clicking on the little arrowhead on
  the Back button displays a drop-down list box showing the last
  several pages you viewed in this Internet Explorer session. Selecting
  a page from the list is a faster way to go back to one of those pages
  than clicking on Back a number of times.

- ✿ **Forward.** Just as the Back button allows you to go back to a previously viewed page, the Forward button allows you to go forward
  again through the list of viewed pages. Click on the button once to
  go to the next page in sequence or click on the arrowhead to
  display a drop-down list box and select a page to go to.

❖ **Stop.** Stop loading the current page. Click on this button when you've seen enough to know you're not interested in the rest of the page that Internet Explorer is in the process of loading. It also comes in handy to halt the downloading of huge graphics.

 ❖ **Refresh.** Clicking on this button instructs Internet Explorer to reload the current page. Occasionally, some of the components of the page won't load properly, in which case clicking on Refresh gives the page another chance. You'll also click on Refresh when you want to make sure you are viewing the latest, up-to-the-minute information on a page that is constantly being updated.

 ❖ **Home.** Click on Home to display the default home page—the one that loads automatically when you start Internet Explorer, not necessarily the home page you, or someone else, might have posted on the Web. (You can set Internet Explorer to display any Web page as the home page. You'll learn how later in this session.)

 ❖ **Search.** Click on Search to display, or close, Internet Explorer's Search bar. You use the Search bar to search the Web for interesting sites.

 ❖ **Favorites.** The Favorites button displays the Favorites bar—a listing of Web pages for which you have saved the addresses so you can easily find and view them again.

 ❖ **History.** Click on this button to display the History bar, which keeps track of the Web pages you visited over the last couple of weeks. The History bar enables you to go back to that page you remember seeing a few days past.

 ❖ **Channels.** Clicking on this button displays the Channels bar— a listing of specially formatted Web sites. You'll learn more about Channels in the Sunday Evening session.

 ❖ **Fullscreen.** This is Internet Explorer's super Maximize button. Clicking on it causes Internet Explorer to take over the entire computer screen and even hides some of Internet Explorer's own menus and toolbars to make more room for Web page content.

- ✪ **Mail.** Clicking on Mail will open your Internet e-mail program (normally, that's Outlook Express).

- ✪ **Print.** Click on Print to print a copy of the Web page you're viewing. When you print a Web page, you get the whole page, not just the part that is visible in the Internet Explorer window when you click on the button.

- ✪ **Edit.** Clicking on Edit opens your Web page editing program (usually FrontPage Express) and automatically loads a copy of the page you're viewing in Internet Explorer into the editor so you can edit it (or just study it to see how the Web page author constructed the page).

Of course, the most important part of surfing the Web is following hyperlinks on the Web pages displayed in the Internet Explorer window. Usually, text hyperlinks will be underlined and colored blue. Hyperlinked graphics will usually look like buttons or icons or will give you some other visual clue that something will happen if you click on the graphic object.

 However, the appearance of hyperlinks, like most other things on a Web page, is almost entirely at the discretion of the Web page designer. So, you can't count on hyperlinks always being underlined or marked in any particular way. What you can count on is that Internet Explorer will be able to detect hyperlinks on a Web page and indicate them to you by changing the mouse pointer from its usual arrow shape to a pointing hand shape when you point to a hyperlink. (If you look closely, you'll see the hand pointer pointing to a hyperlink in Figure 5.16.)

To follow a hyperlink on a Web page, simply click on it. Internet Explorer will get the address of the document referred to in the hyperlink, contact the server where the document is stored, and immediately begin downloading the document and displaying it in the Internet Explorer window. Depending on the speed of your Internet connection and the complexity of the Web page, it can take anywhere from a few seconds to a couple of minutes or more for the whole Web page and all of its graphics and other

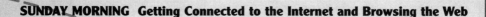
elements to appear in their final form. When the page appears, you can read the text, examine the graphics, and continue your explorations by following more hyperlinks.

No doubt, the default home page (it could be the Microsoft home page or something else) that appears when you open Internet Explorer will include several hyperlinks. Try clicking on one of them to open another page. Then use the Back button to return to the first page and try another hyperlink. Take a few minutes to explore a little bit and get the feel of viewing Web pages in Internet Explorer.

TIP

Unlike some other programs, you can have multiple copies of Internet Explorer open on your desktop at the same time, each displaying a different Web page. This means you can be reading a Web page in one Internet Explorer window while another Internet Explorer window is downloading the information necessary to display a different Web page in another window. If you press and hold Shift when you click on a hyperlink, Internet Explorer will open a new window and load the hyperlinked page into it instead of loading the new page into the current window. You can quickly move through a Web page using the Shift-click technique to open new windows for each hyperlink you want to explore. After you get several Windows open, you can use the taskbar buttons to select which one you want to read. By the time you have Shift-clicked several different hyperlinks, there's a good chance that the first page you selected will probably be downloaded and ready to read—no waiting.

Entering Web Addresses

Every Web page or site has an address called a *URL* (*Uniform Resource Locator*) that serves essentially the same purpose as the address of your house, apartment, or business. Your street address describes a physical location using a standardized format that is understood by mail carriers, couriers, delivery people, and others who need to find your house or send you messages. A Web site address describes a virtual location instead of a physical one and the format of the address is different, but its purpose is really the same. The Web site's URL provides a unique identifier for the Web site and describes the location so Internet Explorer (and other Web browsers) can find it.

With the growing popularity of the World Wide Web and the Internet, more and more businesses and individuals are setting up Web sites and promoting them by publicizing their Web address. Nowadays, you see Web addresses such as **http://www.primapublishing.com** (the Web site for the publisher of this book) everywhere you turn, from business cards and stationery to magazine and television ads.

If you have the address for a Web site you want to visit, viewing that site with Internet Explorer is a piece of cake. Simply type the address into the Address box in the toolbar and press Enter. Internet Explorer will locate the Web server on the Internet, retrieve the Web page, and display it for you. To try it out, type **http://www.whitehouse.gov** in the Address bar and press Enter.

URLs can be kind of long and hard to type, so the Microsoft programmers gave Internet Explorer a couple of features that can help reduce the amount of pounding on the keyboard you have to do. When you start typing a URL in the Address box, Internet Explorer compares what you are typing to other URLs you've entered before. If it finds a possible match, the program displays the complete URL in the Address box. If that's the address you want, you can stop typing and just press Enter. Otherwise, just ignore Internet Explorer's suggestion and keep typing the URL.

Sometimes, you don't have to type the complete URL for a Web site for Internet Explorer to be able to locate it. If you enter only part of a URL, Internet Explorer will try to complete the address using the most common values for the missing parts. For example, if you leave off the service portion of the URL and type in just a server name, Internet Explorer will automatically add http:// to the beginning of the address and will then attempt to load the default Web page available on that server. As a result, you can view the page at **http://www.company.com/ index.html** by typing just **www.company.com** in the Address box. In

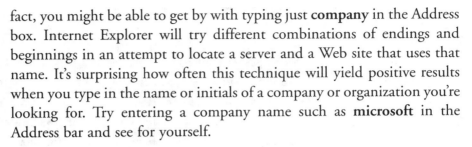

fact, you might be able to get by with typing just **company** in the Address box. Internet Explorer will try different combinations of endings and beginnings in an attempt to locate a server and a Web site that uses that name. It's surprising how often this technique will yield positive results when you type in the name or initials of a company or organization you're looking for. Try entering a company name such as **microsoft** in the Address bar and see for yourself.

The Address box in the Internet Explorer toolbar is also a drop-down list box. Click on the arrow at the right end of the Address box to display the list showing the last several Web addresses you've entered. If you want to revisit one of those Web sites, simply select it from the list. There's no need to retype the URL. Internet Explorer will load the selected Web page just as if you had typed its URL in the Address box.

NOTE Other Explorer windows, such as the one Windows opens to show you the contents of a folder, can also include an Address bar in the window's toolbar, just like Internet Explorer. If you enter a Web address in that Address box, Windows will transform the window into an Internet Explorer window and attempt to load the requested Web page.

TIP A quick and convenient way to open a Web page in Internet Explorer is to choose Run from the Start menu, type the URL for the Web page in the Run dialog box when it appears, and click on OK. Windows automatically launches Internet Explorer and loads the requested Web page.

Going Back to Where You've Been

Internet Explorer keeps track of where you've been so you can go back again. The program keeps a running History list of the Web sites you've visited and the pages you viewed over the last couple of weeks or so. If you

ANATOMY OF A WEB ADDRESS

A Web address is more properly called a URL, which is short for Uniform Resource Locator. Actually, a URL could describe the location of other Internet resources, such as multimedia and graphics files and other kinds of documents in addition to Web pages, but Web page addresses are the most common example of URLs. They're the ones that most people see and use regularly.

A URL such as http://www.company.com/myfolder/document. html may look long and complicated, but it's not so hard to understand once you break it down into its component parts. The first part of the URL—http://—indicates the service, or the kind of handling this resource will need. For Web pages, that's usually http://, which stands for Hypertext Transfer Protocol, but it might be another service, such as ftp:// (File Transfer Protocol), https:// (Hypertext Transfer Protocol Secure), or any one of several others. The next part of the URL—www.company.com— names the computer server where the desired file is located. (Web servers often start with www, but not always.) The rest of the URL—/myfolder/document.html—specifies the file name of the document and the folder where it is stored. This last part of the URL is often omitted from the address for a Web site because, if the file name isn't specified, the Web server will automatically supply a default Web page, and the Web designers can simply make sure the Web page they want you to see first is the one the server will send as the default.

While Web sites often omit the folder and file name portion of the URL, another variation of a URL, called a *relative URL*, often omits the server or folder information, or both. In that case, the missing information in the URL is assumed to be the same as the current page you're viewing. Thus, relative URLs are used to refer to other files and documents within the same Web site.

recall seeing something interesting at a Web site you ran across last week, you don't have to try to remember how you got there and then retrace your steps to return to the site. Instead, you can use the History list to go back to any page you viewed recently—all it takes is a few mouse clicks.

To use the History list, start by clicking on the History button in the Standard Button toolbar. Internet Explorer displays the History bar on the left side of the window, as shown in Figure 5.17. The workspace where the current Web page is displayed shrinks to make room for the History bar.

If you've just begun working with Internet Explorer, there won't be much history of Web page viewing to list in your History bar. You'll probably have a few entries under the Today heading. The History bar shown in Figure 5.17 is more typical of what you'll see after you've been using Internet Explorer for a while. Notice that it has headings for Today, other days in the current week, and three previous weeks.

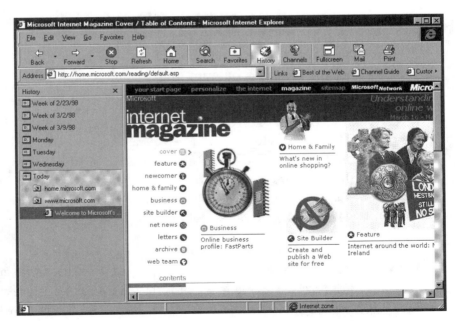

Figure 5.17

The History bar makes it easy to return to sites you've visited recently.

To locate a Web site in the History list, first click on a date heading. Internet Explorer will expand the History list to display the Web sites you visited that day or week. Next, click on the Web site you're interested in to expand the History list again to include the individual Web pages you viewed at that site. Finally, click on the name of the page you want to view. Internet Explorer will begin loading the page and display it for you.

When you no longer need to see the History bar, simply click on the History button in the toolbar again. The History bar disappears and Internet Explorer's full workspace is once again devoted to displaying the current Web page.

 NOTE You can change how many days of Web surfing history Internet Explorer displays in the History bar. You can also erase the history list if you don't want others to be able to see where you've been. I'll show you how to change these settings later in this session.

Keeping a List of Favorite Sites

Sometimes you find a Web site that you know you'll want to return to again and again. You want to make a note of its URL—the Web surfing equivalent of adding a phone number to your Rolodex. That's where the Favorites list comes in.

 The Favorites folder is a place where you can keep shortcuts to Web pages (and to other documents and files as well). Although you'll probably use the Favorites list primarily with Internet Explorer, Windows provides ready access to your Favorites from the Start menu and from the Favorites menu in other Explorer windows as well.

 NOTE You may have heard the term *bookmark* used to describe saving information about a Web page you plan to revisit. Bookmarks is the name of the feature in the popular Netscape Navigator Web browser that is roughly equivalent to Internet Explorer's Favorites.

Using Favorites to quickly access a Web page couldn't be simpler. You just select the page you want from the Favorites menu. To make room for numerous Favorites entries, the Favorites menu is organized into sub-menus, much like those on the Start menu. Internet Explorer ships with some predefined entries on the Favorites menu and you can try some of them to learn how to use the Favorites menu. However, you'll want to add your own entries to the Favorites menu as you begin exploring the Web. After all, the whole point of the Favorites list is that it should be a list of *your* favorite sites.

TIP

Clicking on the Favorites button in the Standard Button toolbar will display the Favorites bar on the left side of the Internet Explorer window. It's the same list of Favorites that is available on the Favorites menu. The difference is that the Favorites bar remains open until you close it by clicking on Favorites again. If you plan to check several sites one after another, the Favorites bar may be more convenient than having to pull down the Favorites menu each time you want to make another selection.

NOTE

The buttons in the Links toolbar are another form of Favorites. You simply click on one of the buttons to open that page in Internet Explorer. Like the items in the Favorites menu, you can customize the buttons in the Links bar to provide access to your own favorite Web sites.

Adding a Web page to your Favorites list is a simple process. Just follow these steps:

1. Start by displaying the Web page that you want to add to your Favorites in the Internet Explorer window.

2. Pull down the Favorites menu and choose Add to Favorites. This will open the Add Favorite dialog box, as shown in Figure 5.18.

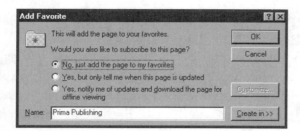

Figure 5.18

Add a Web page
to your list
of Favorites.

3. Make sure the No, Just Add The Page To My Favorites option is selected under the question about subscribing to the page. (You'll learn about subscriptions and how to set them up in the Sunday Evening session.) The Name box already contains the title of the Web page. Normally, that makes a good name for the Favorite entry, but you can edit or replace it if you want.

4. Click on Create In to expand the dialog box, as shown in Figure 5.19. The folders in the Create In list correspond to the submenus in the Favorites menu.

5. Select the folder (submenu) where you want your new Favorite item to appear. If necessary, you can click on New Folder to add another submenu in the Favorites menu.

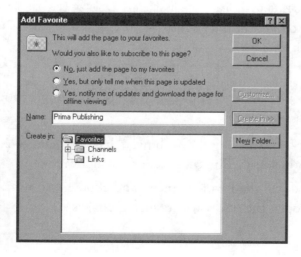

Figure 5.19

This list of folders
corresponds to the
submenus in the
Favorites menu.

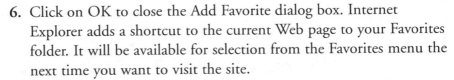
6. Click on OK to close the Add Favorite dialog box. Internet Explorer adds a shortcut to the current Web page to your Favorites folder. It will be available for selection from the Favorites menu the next time you want to visit the site.

Sooner or later, your Favorites list will become overgrown with obsolete and unneeded items. When that happens, you'll need to do some weeding and pruning to get it back into shape. Internet Explorer provides a convenient tool to make managing your Favorites list a relatively painless process.

When you need to clean up your Favorites list, choose Organize Favorites from the Favorites menu in Internet Explorer (or any other Explorer window). Windows will display the Organize Favorites dialog box, as shown in Figure 5.20.

The Organize Favorites dialog box contains a simple list box showing the folders and shortcuts stored in your Favorites folder. The folders appear as submenus in the Favorites menu and the shortcuts appear as menu items.

Using the Organize Favorites dialog box is as simple and straightforward as the dialog box itself. To remove an item from the Favorites menu, select it in the list and click on Delete. To edit the name of an item, select it, click on Rename, and then type in the new name and press Enter. To

Figure 5.20

When Favorites get out of hand, you can reorganize them.

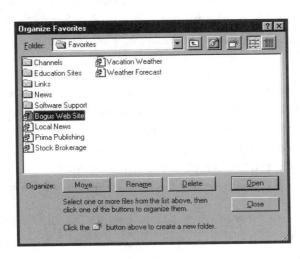

move an item to a folder or submenu, select it and click on Move. This
will open a small Browse for Folder dialog box. Select the folder you want
to move the shortcut to and click on OK. After you get your Favorites
folder whipped into shape, click on Close to close the dialog box.

NOTE Favorites items that you move to the Links folder will appear as buttons on the Links
toolbar as well as items in the Links submenu of the Favorites menu.

Searching for Information and Web Sites

So far, you've learned how to view Web sites by following hyperlinks from
other pages and by entering the URL for the page you want, and you've
learned how to get back to the good stuff later. But how do you find
something on the Web that you know, or suspect, exists, if you don't have
its URL or a page with a hyperlink to it? The World Wide Web is so big
that you would have no hope of finding what you seek with random
prowling.

The answer to this problem is to use a *search engine*, which is a special
Web site that maintains a huge database of other Web sites, Web pages,
and key text from those pages. The search engine allows you to search its
database for a term or a phrase and returns a list of Web pages that contains a match to your search criteria. Then you can click on a hyperlink
to one of the Web pages on the list to check it out for yourself.

NOTE If you want to get technical about it, there are distinct differences between search
engines, directories, spiders, indexes, and other forms of Web page databases. However,
the term *search engine* seems to be gaining in popularity as a general name for the services that allow you to search for information on the Web.

There are a number of these search engines available on the Web. Nearly
everyone has heard of Yahoo, but there are many others, such as Infoseek,

HotBot, Lycos, Switchboard, DejaNews, and more. Some index Web pages while others index resources such as newsgroup articles and e-mail addresses.

Internet Explorer includes some features to make using search engines easier and more convenient. The Microsoft Web site includes a facility that consolidates access to several of the more popular search engines all on one page. That's a big improvement over having to go to each search engine's individual Web site to conduct a search. Internet Explorer goes one better by bringing most of the capabilities of that consolidated search page into the Search bar, which can remain conveniently available at the left side of the Internet Explorer window while you view a Web page in the rest of the window.

To conduct a search with the Internet Explorer Search bar, start by clicking on Search to display the Search bar on the left side of the Explorer window, as shown in Figure 5.21. The Search bar will appear immediately, but there may be a few seconds' delay before the contents of the Search bar appear—Internet Explorer has to connect to the Microsoft Web site and load information from the search page there.

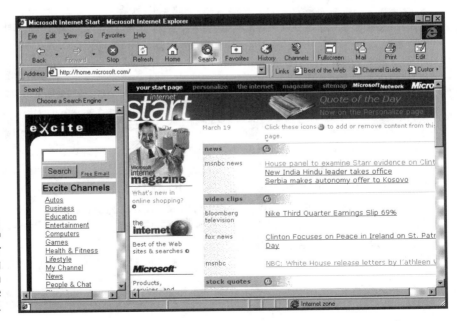

Figure 5.21

The Search bar makes using popular search engines more convenient.

The Search bar displays a simplified entry form for the default search engine selected from the search engines available on the Microsoft site. If you would rather use a different search engine from the one selected by default, click on Choose a Search Engine at the top of the Search bar and select a search engine from the drop-down list. There may be only one search engine listed if you haven't used any other search engines yet, but you can always choose List of All Search Engines to display the full selection of search engines available on the Microsoft site.

The list of search engines will appear on a Web page in the right portion of the Internet Explorer window. Select a different search engine and it will appear in the Search bar after a moment. Henceforth, that search engine will show up as an option on the Choose a Search Engine list.

The search options available in the Search bar will vary depending on which search engine is selected. Typically, you will have the option of clicking on one of an assortment of predefined categories or entering a search term in a text box and then clicking on a button to initiate a search for Web sites in the database that match your search term. Internet Explorer will send your search request to the search engine Web site. When the search engine replies, the results will be displayed within the Search bar, as shown in Figure 5.22, and not in a separate Web page displayed in the main viewing window.

To follow up on your search, scroll down the list of search results in the Search bar, viewing the Web page names and short descriptions displayed there. When you see a link to a Web page that looks interesting, click on it. Internet Explorer loads the selected page in the main viewing window on the right, as shown in Figure 5.23. Notice that the search results remain available in the Search bar and you can easily check out other Web pages by clicking on hyperlinks in the Search bar one by one. When you no longer need the Search bar, you can close it by clicking on the Search button in the toolbar.

SUNDAY MORNING Getting Connected to the Internet and Browsing the Web

Figure 5.22

The results of your search appear in the Search bar.

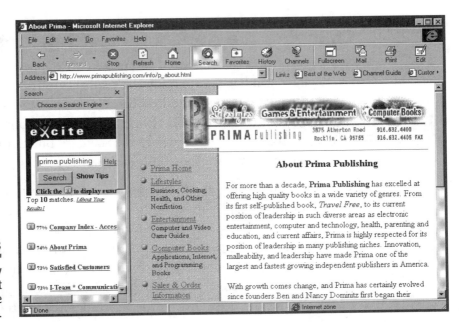

Figure 5.23

Check out a likely item without abandoning the search results.

Just for fun, try searching for a term used in your favorite hobby or pastime. Be sure to use a fairly specific term for your search to boost your chances of getting reasonably focused and relevant results. For example, if you're interested in sailboat racing, the name of a class of racing sail-boats, such as *J-24,* will make a better search term than the word *sailing.* Check out a couple of Web sites suggested by the search results. Then choose another search engine and repeat the search. See how many of the same Web pages show up in both searches.

Customizing Internet Explorer

Internet Explorer offers you lots of options for changing the appearance of the Internet Explorer window and modifying the way the program responds to certain situations and conditions. You'll rarely need to change most of the settings, so I won't try to cover all of them in the limited space of the next few pages. Instead, I'll concentrate on the options you're most likely to use.

Changing the Appearance of Internet Explorer

One of the simplest changes you can make in the appearance of the Internet Explorer window is to modify the toolbars. You can turn each of the toolbars (Standard Buttons, Address Bar, Links) on or off by choosing Toolbars from the View menu and then clicking on the toolbar name in the submenu. (You'll surely want to keep the Standard Buttons and Address Bar toolbars, but you might choose not to display the Links toolbar.)

Another option in the Toolbars submenu allows you to turn Text Labels for the buttons on the Standard Buttons toolbar on or off. By default, text labels are on, meaning that each button is labeled with both an icon and a text label. Turning text labels off leaves just the icon on each button, which has the side effect of making each button much smaller so that the entire Standard Buttons toolbar takes up much less space (see Figure 5.24). The buttons are a little harder to recognize, but the icons provide adequate identification once you get used to them.

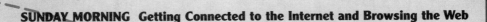

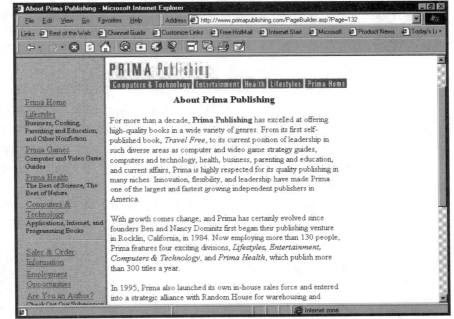

Figure 5.24

You can rearrange Internet Explorer's toolbars.

You can also rearrange the toolbars, changing their order and relative size. However, you can't move them to a different location in the Internet Explorer window—they're trapped in that band below the title bar and above the work area where the Web pages are displayed. Notice how the arrangement of the toolbars in Figure 5.24 differs from the default arrangement in the other figures.

If you look carefully at the Internet Explorer window, you'll see that each toolbar has a small vertical bar at its left end. This is the toolbar's *handle*. To move or resize a toolbar, simply drag its handle to a new position. Resizing a toolbar by dragging its handle left or right in the same row is easy, but attempting to move a toolbar to another position can be a challenge because of the way the toolbars jump into position and displace the other toolbars. (Arrrgh!!!) It may take a few tries to get the effect you had in mind.

The most radical change you're likely to make to the appearance of the Internet Explorer window is when you switch to Fullscreen mode. Simply clicking on the Fullscreen button in the Standard Button toolbar instantly transforms the Internet Explorer window from a normal window to the super-maximized Web page display, as shown in Figure 5.25. Not only does Fullscreen maximize the Internet Explorer window to fill the entire screen, it also eliminates the title bar, menu bar, and other toolbars, leaving only the Standard Buttons toolbar, reduced to the small buttons without text labels. Even the Windows Taskbar disappears behind the Fullscreen Internet Explorer display. Clicking on Fullscreen again returns the Internet Explorer window to its normal condition. (That's assuming that you haven't become so enamored of the Fullscreen mode that you now consider it "normal.")

The whole point of Fullscreen mode is to provide maximum viewing space for Web page content. The Search bar, History bar, Favorites bar, and Channel bar behave differently in Fullscreen mode. Instead of

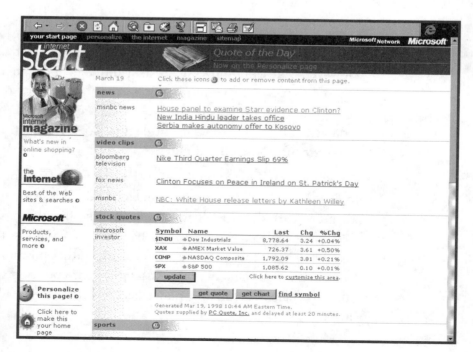

Figure 5.25

Fullscreen mode fills your screen with the Web page.

remaining onscreen until you close them, the Search bar (and others) will slide off to the left after a few seconds of inactivity in the bar. Pointing to the left edge of the screen brings the bar back temporarily.

■■■

If you want the Search bar to stay visible when using Internet Explorer in Fullscreen mode, click on the pushpin icon at top of the Search bar to lock it in place.

■■■

If you want to work with any other program or window while Internet Explorer is in Fullscreen mode, you'll first need to minimize the Internet Explorer window—you can't get to any other Windows or to the Windows Taskbar while Internet Explorer is occupying every pixel of your desktop. To minimize Internet Explorer, click on Minimize—the button is disguised but it's still there. It's the dash between the Internet Explorer icon and the X in the upper right corner of the screen.

Taking Care of Security

Everyone is concerned about security on the Internet these days, and with good reason; there's some nasty stuff out there. There are potentially damaging programs that can be automatically downloaded to your system and run while you are viewing a Web site. There's the risk of personal information that you submit via on-screen forms being intercepted between your computer and its eventual destination and being misused. And there's the risk of younger family members stumbling across adult-oriented materials that are inappropriate for children.

Internet Explorer includes features to help you manage all these risks. In most cases, the real risks are slight, but the potential for problems does exist and it's entirely appropriate to be concerned and to take some measures to protect yourself and your system from harm. Some of Internet Explorer's security features are more effective than others, but at the very least, you'll want to know what security features are available.

Internet Explorer provides a pretty good set of tools for protecting your computer from potentially dangerous programs that you might encounter on the Internet. To see the settings for the security tools, pull down the View menu and choose Internet Options, and then, when the Internet Options dialog box appears, click on the Security tab to display the settings, as shown in Figure 5.26.

You'll need a little background to understand what these settings mean. So here goes. Internet Explorer divides the universe of Web sites into four zones, according to their potential for security risk, and then applies different levels of security measures to Web sites in each zone. The four zones are as follows:

- **Local intranet zone.** These are Web pages published on servers that are part of the same local network as your computer.

- **Trusted sites zone.** These are Web sites that you have specifically identified as sites that can be trusted not to download harmful content onto your computer.

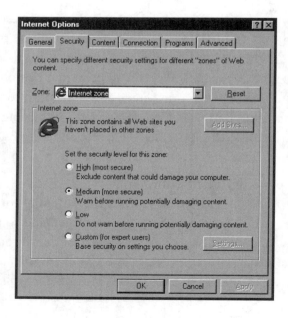

Figure 5.26

Adjust the security settings according to your tolerance for risk.

- **Restricted sites zone.** This is just the opposite of the Trusted sites zone. It's a list of Web sites that you have specifically identified as potential sources of damaging content.

- **Internet zone.** This zone encompasses most Web sites on the Internet—it includes any Web site that isn't assigned to one of the other three zones.

Although there are four zones, Internet Explorer normally uses only two of them—the Local intranet zone and the Internet zone. The other two zones, the Trusted sites zone and the Restricted sites zone, are both lists of specific Web sites that you must define if you want to use them. (It's probably not worth your time and trouble to build those lists unless you are a heavy Web surfer with very specific needs.)

You can assign one of three different security levels to each zone. (Actually, there is a fourth security level—Custom—that allows you to individually adjust a whole list of security settings, but that's best left to the experts.) Here's a brief summary of the security levels:

- **High.** Automatically rejects most forms of Web content that have the potential to do anything harmful to your computer. This is the safest setting, but you'll miss out on a lot of nice features and effects just because they are in the same general class of Web content as potentially damaging programs.

- **Medium.** Displays a warning before running any Web content that has the potential to be harmful. You have the option to accept or reject the content on a case-by-case basis.

- **Low.** Automatically runs most forms of Web content without issuing any warnings. You get all the special effects and fancy programming features of the Web sites you visit shown automatically without the inconvenience of prompts and dialog boxes popping up in the process. However, this setting leaves the door open for potentially harmful content to run automatically, too.

As you might have guessed, the middle road is the way to go in most circumstances. Internet Explorer will prompt you before running any Web content that has the potential to contain instructions that would damage your computer. It's a minor inconvenience to respond to the prompts, but it means you are in control. Of course, you won't be able to tell from the prompt whether you are about to run a harmless special effect or a dangerous virus, but you can make an educated guess based on things like the reputation of the individual or company posting the Web site you are viewing. If something doesn't seem right, you can just say no.

The Medium security level is the default setting for both the Local intranet zone and the Internet zone. If you want to change the security level for a zone, first select the zone you want to change from the Zone drop-down list box, then select the security level setting in the lower portion of the dialog box. Click on Apply to record the new setting.

Protecting your computer from potentially damaging programs is one thing. Protecting your children from Web sites that display adult content is a bigger challenge. Internet Explorer includes a feature called the Content Advisor that attempts to address this challenge. Unfortunately, it's not very successful because it relies on a rating system to determine the suitability of Web sites—and most Web sites, good or bad, are not rated. Still, it has some uses. If you want to use the Content Advisor, you can follow these steps to enable and configure the feature:

1. Open the Internet Options dialog box (choose Internet Options from the View menu) and click on the Content tab to display the options, as shown in Figure 5.27.

2. Click on Enable in the Content Advisor area in the top of the dialog box. Internet Explorer will prompt you for a supervisor password.

3. Enter your Content Advisor password. If this is the first time you have enabled the Content Advisor, you'll need to enter the password twice to create it. Otherwise, you can enter the password once and click on OK. This activates the Content Advisor feature. Internet Explorer will begin screening the Web pages you visit.

Figure 5.27

Content Advisor is Internet Explorer's sex and violence filter.

4. Click on Settings and then enter your password and click on OK when the Supervisor Password Required dialog box appears. This will open the Content Advisor dialog box, as shown in Figure 5.28. (If necessary, click on the Ratings tab.)

5. Click on a content category in the list box and then drag the slider to set the level of filtering you want to impose on that content category. Repeat the process for each of the four categories: Language, Nudity, Sex, and Violence.

6. Click on the General tab of the Content Advisor dialog box (see Figure 5.29) and adjust the settings in the User Options area according to your preferences.

   ○ **Users can see sites that have no rating.** Checking this option weakens the protection provided by Content Advisor because most sites on the Internet are not rated. On the other hand, if you leave this option disabled, Content Advisor will prevent access to many excellent but unrated sites.

Figure 5.28

You can set the Content Advisor for your tolerance level on four different content areas.

> ✿ **Supervisor can type a password.** Checking this option allows you to override Content Advisor's restrictions by typing in your supervisor's password to enable Internet Explorer to display a restricted Web site. Enabling this option gives you a way to deal with the many unrated sites.

7. Click on OK to record the Content Advisor settings. Click on OK again to close the Internet Options dialog box. Internet Explorer will check each Web site's rating against these settings before displaying each Web page.

If you decide that you no longer want to use the Content Advisor feature, you can turn it off by repeating Steps 1, 2, and 3 of the procedure above, except that in Step 2, you click on Disable instead of Enable.

Setting Other Preferences

You can set many other options and preferences in Internet Explorer. Three of the ones you're most likely to use are located on the General tab of the Internet Options dialog box (see Figure 5.30), which you can open by choosing Internet Options from the View menu.

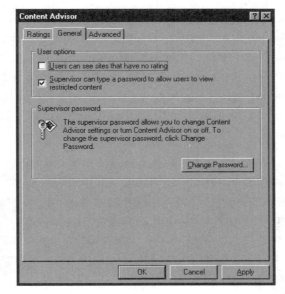

Figure 5.29

These options control how Content Advisor handles unrated sites.

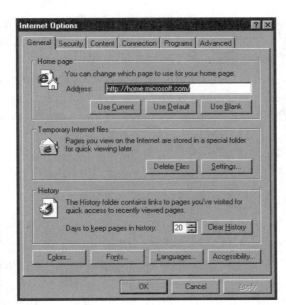

Figure 5.30

Here is an assortment of options you'll probably use.

First, there's the Home Page setting. This is where you can specify the Web page that Internet Explorer will load automatically when you open the program. If you want to change the home page, you can type in the URL of any Web page in the Address box. Alternatively, you can save yourself some typing by displaying the desired page in Internet Explorer before you open the Internet Options dialog box and then clicking on Use Current to enter the current page's URL as the home page address.

Any time you want to go back to the default home page, just click on Use Default. The third button, Use Blank, will display a blank page when you open Internet Explorer. Using a blank page as your home page will enable you to open Internet Explorer without the program attempting to connect to the Internet and load a Web page immediately. Consequently, you may want to use the blank page option on a laptop computer that isn't always connected to a modem and phone line.

The next option on the General tab of the Internet Options dialog box is Temporary Internet Files. Internet Explorer saves copies of recently accessed Web pages, downloaded graphics, and much more in temporary files on your hard disk. To control how much hard disk space Internet Explorer can use for its temporary files, click on Settings to open the Settings dialog box, as shown in Figure 5.31. Move the slider in the Temporary Internet Files Folder area to specify the maximum amount of hard disk space Internet Explorer can use, then click on OK to close the Settings dialog box. If you want to clean out Internet Explorer's storehouse of temporary files, click on Delete Files and then click on OK in the Delete Files dialog box that appears.

The third option area on the General tab of the Internet Options dialog box is History. There you can set the number of days of Web surfing history you want Internet Explorer to keep and display in the History bar. If you want to erase the list of Web pages in the History bar (cover your tracks so no one can tell you were surfing *those* Web sites), just click on Clear History and then confirm the action by clicking on Yes in the message box that appears.

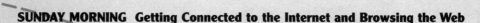

Figure 5.31

You can curb
Internet Explorer's
appetite for hard
disk space.

What's Next?

Next up on the agenda is a lunch break, so close the Internet Explorer window and close your Internet connection too, so your friends can get through on the phone. It's time to get away from the computer for a while. When you start the next session this afternoon, you'll learn that there's more to the Internet than the World Wide Web. You'll learn to use e-mail and more besides. So be sure you return refreshed and ready to go.

Reaching Out with E-mail and News

- ✪ Setting Up Outlook Express
- ✪ Sending and Receiving E-mail with Outlook Express
- ✪ Reading the News
- ✪ Subscribing to Newsgroups
- ✪ Posting Articles You've Written

Good afternoon! I hope you had a pleasant lunch, or tea, or whatever you chose as a break after this morning's session. This morning, you learned how to connect your computer to the Internet and how to use Internet Explorer to display Web pages. But there's more to the Internet than just the World Wide Web. E-mail may not be as flashy and exciting as the Web, but if you're like most people, you'll probably find that e-mail is the Internet application you use the most. And that's just the beginning. There are many different ways to use the Internet as a communications medium. In this session, you'll learn about the Windows features that support Internet e-mail, and do the following:

- Set up Outlook Express to access your e-mail accounts and to read newsgroup articles

- Send and receive e-mail messages and organize your messages in folders

- Read (and write) the news on Internet newsgroups

Setting Up Outlook Express

Outlook Express is the Windows 98 program for handling Internet e-mail messages and newsgroup articles. Don't confuse Outlook Express with its bigger sibling, Outlook 98. Outlook Express is designed just for Internet e-mail and newsgroups and is included free with Windows 98 and Internet Explorer 4. Outlook 98, on the other hand, is designed to handle e-mail on a corporate network as well as the Internet, and includes a full assortment of personal information management features such as a To Do list, contact list, and appointment calendar. Outlook 98 is part of the Microsoft Office suite of business productivity programs and it's also available as a separate program.

You probably know what e-mail is. The term *e-mail* is short for electronic mail, the simple text messages you can send to another computer user. The messages are stored on a network computer (called a mail server) until you use a program such as Outlook Express to download and read the messages addressed to you. E-mail messages are relatively private. They are addressed to specific individuals (or at least to specific e-mail accounts) and you must use an ID and password to access the messages stored in your mailbox on the mail server.

You've probably used e-mail at work or at school (or seen others using it, even if you didn't have an e-mail account of your own). However, a lot of corporate e-mail is set up to allow communications only within the company's own local network, and the e-mail programs used on such networks often send messages using proprietary formats. Outlook Express, on the other hand, is designed to handle e-mail using standards that are common throughout the Internet. Outlook Express will work with almost any e-mail account from a typical Internet Service Provider. However, Outlook Express won't allow you to access the proprietary e-mail systems found on some corporate networks or on the big online services (such as America Online or CompuServe). You can use Outlook Express to send messages from an Internet e-mail account to online service subscribers, and you can read the replies you get from them.

NOTE Increasingly, corporate networks are being converted to intranets—local networks that use the same networking protocols and standards as the Internet. If your corporate e-mail system uses the same protocols as the Internet, you'll be able to use Outlook Express with your corporate e-mail account as well as with your Internet e-mail accounts—provided your corporate network police approve.

In addition to regular e-mail, Outlook Express can handle another set of messages—the ones found in the Internet's public discussion forums, called newsgroups or Usenet news. There are tens of thousands of newsgroups covering almost every imaginable topic ranging from obscure academic and technical subjects to various types of computer software, psychological problems, and the lives and times of TV stars. Newsgroups use a variation of e-mail messaging in which messages go to a special account for the newsgroup rather than to individual addresses. The messages are then duplicated on news servers all over the Internet where they are available to any Internet user with a news reader program and access to one of the news servers. Now that includes you—because Outlook Express is your news reader and just about every ISP maintains a news server for use by subscribers who want to participate in the public discussions on the various newsgroups.

Installing Outlook Express

Add/Remove Programs

You probably won't need to install Outlook Express—it's part of the typical Windows 98 installation. But just to be sure, you can check your system to confirm that Outlook Express is available. Start by opening Control Panel (click on the Start button in the taskbar and choose Settings, Control Panel) and then open Add/Remove Programs. When the Add/Remove Programs dialog box appears, click on the Windows Setup tab. Make sure there is a check mark beside the Microsoft Outlook Express item in the Components list. That will indicate that Outlook Express is installed. If it isn't, you can install it now. (Refer to the Saturday Morning session for detailed instructions on installing Windows components.)

Starting Outlook Express

After you confirm that Outlook Express is installed on your system, you're ready to get started using the program. Actually, Windows gives you a choice of several ways to start Outlook Express. You can use any of the following techniques:

✿ If there is an Outlook Express shortcut icon on your desktop, open it.

 ❖ If the Quick Launch toolbar is visible in the taskbar, click on the Outlook Express button. (This is my favorite technique, because it's always available.)

❖ From the Start menu, choose Programs, Internet Explorer, Outlook Express.

❖ Choose Mail from the Go menu in any Explorer window.

• •

 The Go, Mail command in Explorer and the Mail button in Internet Explorer might open another e-mail program instead of Outlook Express. If you want to use Outlook Express instead of the other program when you click on the Mail button or command, start Outlook Express by using one of the other techniques and then open the Tools menu and choose Options to open the Options dialog box. On the General tab, check the Make Outlook Express My Default E-mail Program option and then click on OK to close the dialog box and record the setting. This will make Outlook Express the program that Explorer or Internet Explorer will open when you choose Mail.

• •

❖ In Internet Explorer, you can click on the Mail button in the Standard Buttons toolbar.

You can use any of these techniques, but the result is the same—Outlook Express opens. The first time you launch Outlook Express, you may see one or more dialog boxes requesting simple configuration information such as the folder you want to use for messages or which Dial-Up Networking connection you want to use to connect to the Internet. (You probably won't need to mess with these dialog boxes. I just didn't want you to be surprised or confused if they do appear.) When the Outlook Express window opens, it will look like the one shown in Figure 6.1.

The Outlook Express window consists of the usual menu bar and toolbar at the top. The work area starts out divided into two panes. Normally, the left pane contains the hierarchical list of message folders shown in Figure 6.1, but you might see a column of large icons for the folders instead. Initially, the right pane shows the Outlook Express start page, containing

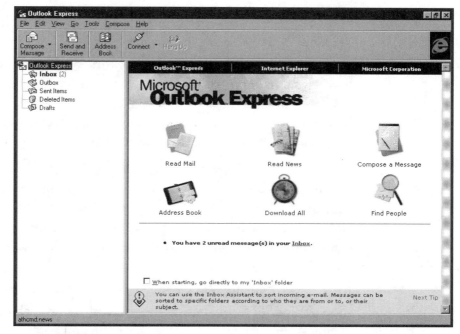

Figure 6.1

Behold the Outlook Express window.

icons for common tasks you'll perform in the program. The icons are attractive, but once you get familiar with Outlook Express, you'll probably want to skip this page and go directly to your Inbox folder, where you can read your mail. Since you can also start all the other tasks from the Inbox, there's really no point in displaying the opening page. You can bypass it in the future by checking the When Starting check box near the bottom of the page.

Setting Up Your E-mail Accounts

Before you can begin using Outlook Express to read and send mail, you'll need to set up the program with information about your e-mail accounts. Of course, that means you'll need to have the following information on hand:

✪   Your e-mail address, such as yourname@company.com

✿ The names of your ISP's mail servers for incoming and outgoing mail

✿ Your e-mail account name and password

Your Internet service provider or network system administrator should have given you this information when you set up your Internet access (and e-mail) accounts. Check the Welcome Kit you received when you signed up. If you signed up online, look for the scrap of paper where you jotted down all the IDs and passwords you knew you'd need later.

Another possible source of information is the ISP's Web site. Many ISPs post instructions on their Web site for configuring your software to work with their system. Look there if you need the names of their mail servers and instructions on how to derive your e-mail address and account name from your system logon ID (if the user ID and e-mail account name are linked).

If you can't find the information anywhere else, call the ISP's technical support line. (This will be a good test of the availability of your ISP's technical support. If it's Sunday afternoon and you need to get information from a corporate network system administrator, all I can say is "good luck.")

NOTE Did you notice that I've been using the plural when referring to e-mail accounts? That's because many people do have more than one e-mail account—one for work and another for personal use, and other family members might have their own accounts too—and because Outlook Express can be set up to handle multiple accounts easily.

When you have the information together and you're ready to proceed with setting up your e-mail accounts, follow these steps:

1. From the Tools menu in Outlook Express, choose Accounts. This will open the Internet Accounts dialog box, as shown in Figure 6.2.

2. Click on Add and then choose Mail from the submenu. This will launch the Internet Connection Wizard (see Figure 6.3) where you can define your e-mail account.

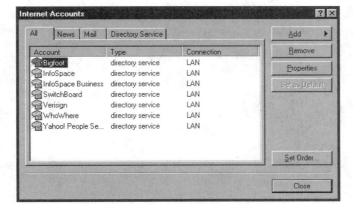

Figure 6.2

Outlook Express starts out with a number of directory services predefined, but you'll have to add your own e-mail accounts.

Figure 6.3

This Wizard takes you through the steps required to set up an e-mail address.

3. In the Display Name box, enter your own name as you want it to appear in the headers of the e-mail messages you send. Click on Next to proceed to the next page of the wizard, as shown in Figure 6.4.

4. Enter your e-mail address in the space provided. Be sure to enter your full address (such as yourname@company.com), not just the short form address (such as yourname) that others on the same network can use to send you mail. Remember, this is the address that users anywhere on the Internet should use to address mail to you. After entering the address, click on Next to advance to the next page of the wizard (see Figure 6.5).

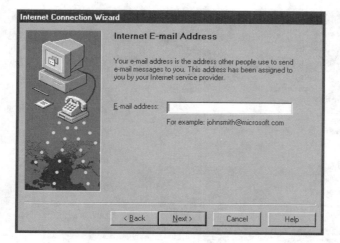

Figure 6.4

Enter your e-mail address here.

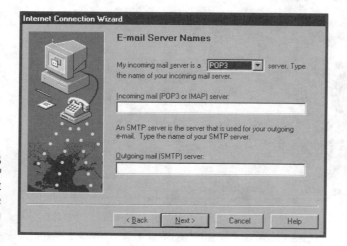

Figure 6.5

You'll need to get the names of the mail servers from your ISP.

5. Your ISP should furnish you with the information you'll need to enter on this page. Select either POP3 or IMAP from the drop-down list box near the top of the page, depending on the type of mail server your ISP provides for your incoming mail. (If you're not sure, stick with the default setting of POP3.) Then fill in the names of the incoming and outgoing mail servers in the corresponding text boxes. Typically, the server names will be something like

pop.company.com and smtp.company.com. Often, an ISP will use the same server name (such as mail.company.com) for both incoming and outgoing mail, so if your ISP gave you only one mail server name, enter it in both places. Sometimes the server address will be numeric (something like 121.212.121.2), but it will have the same effect as the words. Be sure you enter the server names exactly as supplied by your ISP, then click on Next. The wizard page, as shown in Figure 6.6, will appear.

6. Unless your ISP requires you to use Secure Password Authentication, click on the Log On Using option and then enter the account name and password you use to access your e-mail account. This is a separate name and password from the one you use to log on to the ISP's network. Occasionally, in an effort to reduce the number of names and passwords you must memorize, an ISP will assign you an e-mail account name and password that matches your system access ID and password. But that's the exception rather than the rule; usually the two name-and-password sets are separate and different. After entering the name and password, click on Next to proceed to the page, as shown in Figure 6.7.

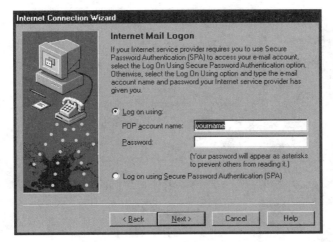

Figure 6.6

This is where you give Outlook Express the key to your online mailbox.

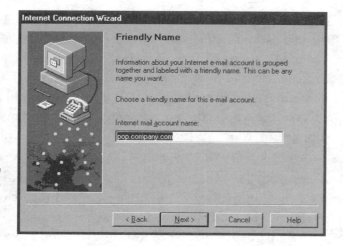

Figure 6.7

You get to make up
the friendly name
for the e-mail
account.

7. On this page, you enter the name you want to give this e-mail
account. This isn't something you got from your ISP—it's something you make up to identify where the account appears in
Outlook Express menus and dialog boxes. You can make it something descriptive, such as Office Mail, Personal E-mail, or Mike's
Messages. After entering the name, click on Next to advance to the
Choose Connection Type page, as shown in Figure 6.8.

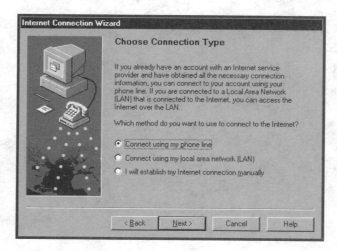

Figure 6.8

How do you want
Outlook Express to
connect to this
e-mail account?

8. This is where you tell Outlook Express how to connect to the Internet to check your mail. If you connect to the Internet using a modem and a Dial-Up Networking connection, click on the top option—Connect Using My Phone Line. Select the middle option—Connect Using My Local Area Network—if you have a full-time Internet connection through your local network. If you choose the bottom option—I Will Establish My Internet Connection Manually—Outlook Express will not be able to check your mail automatically unless you first establish an Internet connection. After making your selection, click on Next. What happens next depends on what kind of connection you chose. If you chose to connect using your phone line, the Dial-Up Connection page (shown in Figure 6.9) will appear. Otherwise, you'll skip that page and go directly to the Congratulations page.

9. On the Dial-Up Connection page, you can elect to create a new Dial-Up Networking connection or select an existing Dial-Up Networking connection to use when checking e-mail for this account. If you choose the Create a New option and click on Next, the wizard will lead you through the steps for creating a new dial-up networking connection. It's essentially the same process you went through in the Sunday Morning session. More often, though, you'll

Figure 6.9

Select a Dial-Up Networking connection to use for this e-mail account.

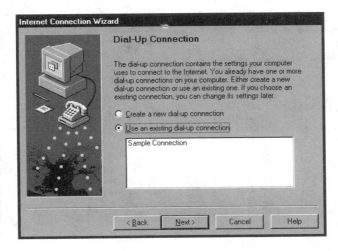

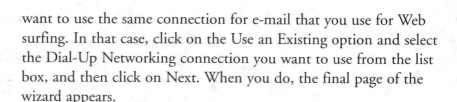

want to use the same connection for e-mail that you use for Web surfing. In that case, click on the Use an Existing option and select the Dial-Up Networking connection you want to use from the list box, and then click on Next. When you do, the final page of the wizard appears.

 NOTE Normally, you must access the Internet using the same ISP that provides your e-mail service to gain full access to your e-mail account. It's common for ISPs to configure their mail servers to refuse outbound mail that does not originate from within the same system. Sometimes all access to the mail server is restricted if you log on from outside that ISP's system. These restrictions came about in response to abuses by mass mailers sending thousands of messages from any mail server they could reach. Of course, this is a concern only if you have Internet access accounts with more than one ISP.

10. When the Congratulations page of the wizard appears, all you need to do is click on Finish. The Wizard dialog box disappears and the Internet Accounts dialog box reappears with your new e-mail account added to the list (see Figure 6.10).

11. Repeat Steps 1 through 10 for each e-mail account you want to access with Outlook Express.

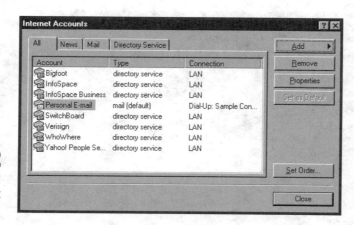

Figure 6.10

Your new e-mail account is now part of the list.

At this point, Outlook Express knows about your e-mail accounts and how to access them. But you're not quite ready to start sending and receiving messages yet.

Setting Other E-mail Account Properties

The wizard does a pretty good job of setting up your e-mail accounts in Outlook Express. However, there are a couple of settings that the wizard overlooks. To adjust these settings, or to edit any of the e-mail account settings, you can use the Properties dialog box for the e-mail account. Simply select the account you want to edit from the Internet Accounts dialog box and click on Properties. A dialog box similar to the one shown in Figure 6.11 will appear.

The Properties dialog box for an e-mail account gives you access to all the settings you specified in the account setup wizard and a few more besides. For example, the General tab (shown in Figure 6.11) includes spaces for the friendly name for the e-mail account, your name, and your e-mail address. In addition, there are boxes where you can specify your Organization and Reply Address. (The Reply Address is the e-mail address to

Figure 6.11

This dialog box will enable you to edit any of the settings for the e-mail account.

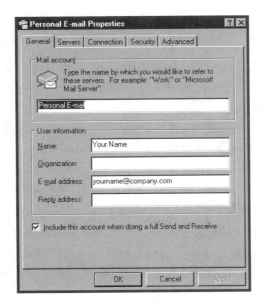

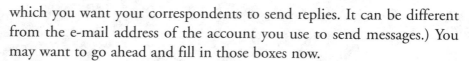

which you want your correspondents to send replies. It can be different from the e-mail address of the account you use to send messages.) You may want to go ahead and fill in those boxes now.

At the bottom of the General page, there is a check box that allows you to determine whether Outlook Express will include this e-mail account in the list of accounts it checks automatically when you click on the Send and Receive button in the main Outlook Express window. (I'll show you how to use Send and Receive shortly.) Naturally, if you have only one e-mail account, you'll want to make sure this option is checked. On the other hand, if you have several e-mail accounts, you may not want to access every account each time you check for new mail. If you disable this option for an e-mail account, you can still check for messages in that account by accessing it from the Outlook Express menus.

The Servers and Connection tabs let you edit the settings that specify the mail servers, account name and password, and how you access the Internet. That's the same stuff you did when you set up the account in the wizard. The Security tab is something special—it enables you to set up a digital ID for secure e-mail. However, that's an advanced feature that is rarely used.

Actually, the Advanced tab of the Properties dialog box for an e-mail account (shown in Figure 6.12) is, in some ways, less "advanced" than the Security tab. At least, you're more likely to need to adjust some of the settings found there. Certainly, the settings in the Server Port Numbers area are advanced settings; you'll want to leave them alone unless your ISP instructs you to change them. However, you can feel free to adjust the slider in the Server Timeouts area to tell Outlook Express to wait a little longer for a response from the mail server. You'll want to do this if you sometimes get an error message that mentions a timeout when you attempt to check the mail on this account.

The settings in the Delivery area are the ones you may want to change. By default, Outlook Express copies your e-mail messages from the mail server to your local hard disk and then erases the copies of those messages

Figure 6.12

You can adjust the Delivery settings to leave a copy of your e-mail messages on the mail server.

from the mail server. Normally, that's exactly what you want to do—you don't often need more than one copy of each message. However, there are some exceptions to this general rule. For example, you might want to use Outlook Express to check your office e-mail from home so you can get a sneak peek at some urgent messages you are expecting, but you'll probably want to leave those messages on the server so you can access them again tomorrow with your regular office e-mail program. If you don't want Outlook Express to erase the messages it downloads from the mail server, put a check mark in the Leave a Copy of Messages on Server check box. When you enable that option, you'll have a couple of additional options to choose from. You can instruct Outlook Express to automatically delete from the server any messages that are more than a certain number of days old. Or you can have Outlook Express remove messages from the server when the copy you downloaded is removed from the Deleted Items folder in Outlook Express.

After you adjust the settings in the Properties dialog box for an e-mail account, click on OK to close the dialog box and record the settings. This will take you back to the Internet Accounts dialog box.

Defining the Default E-mail Account

If you have more than one e-mail account, one of those accounts will be designated as the default. The default e-mail account is the one Outlook Express will use to send the outgoing messages that you compose in the program. The default designation has no effect on how you receive and read e-mail messages in Outlook Express—it affects only the outgoing messages.

Outlook Express will assume that the first e-mail account you defined should be the default account unless and until you choose another e-mail account as the default. (Obviously, if you have only one e-mail account, it will always be the default account and you won't need to change that designation.) The default account is clearly indicated as such in the account list in the Internet Accounts dialog box, as shown in Figure 6.13.

Only one e-mail account can be designated as the default at any given time and any messages you compose will be sent out to the Internet using the default account. However, you can send messages from any of your e-mail accounts by simply changing which account is defined as the default before you compose a message. To change the default account, just follow these steps:

1. Open the Internet Accounts dialog box (choose Accounts from the Tools menu) and click on the Mail tab to display just the e-mail accounts. (You can also change the default e-mail account from the All tab of the Internet Accounts dialog box, but working on the Mail tab is a little less confusing.)

2. Select the e-mail account you want to designate as the new default account by clicking on it in the account list. Remember, this is the account you want to use to send messages from.

3. Click on Set As Default. Outlook Express immediately marks the selected account with the (Default) designation.

4. Click on Close to close the Internet Accounts dialog box and record the new setting. The program will use the newly defined default account to send any new messages or replies that you compose in Outlook Express.

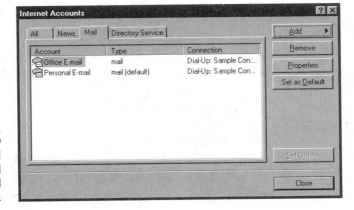

Figure 6.13

Click on the Mail tab to display and adjust the e-mail accounts.

Setting Up Access to a News Server

As I mentioned earlier, Outlook Express can handle more than just e-mail messages. The program also enables you to read and post messages on the public discussion forums known as Internet newsgroups. However, before you can use Outlook Express to access those newsgroups, there is some setup involved.

CAUTION

The term *newsgroups* is a little misleading. Most Internet newsgroups don't have anything to do with the kind of hard news that you probably associate with the morning newspaper or TV evening news program. Internet newsgroups are mostly unmoderated discussion forums that are open to all. The news they contain is more likely to be gossip, rumor, hearsay, or anecdotes than it is to be news in the journalistic sense. Still, there's a lot to be gained from the kind of informal information sharing that goes on in many newsgroups. Just be sure to approach newsgroups with an appropriate degree of skepticism. Remember that the message you read might be a carefully written exposition by a knowledgeable expert in the field under discussion, or it might be an off-the-cuff comment by an ill-informed crackpot. Newsgroups are populated by people from both extremes, and everything in between.

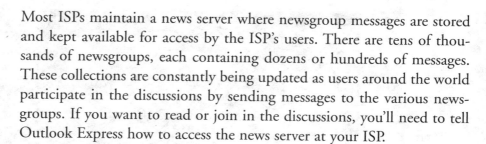

Most ISPs maintain a news server where newsgroup messages are stored and kept available for access by the ISP's users. There are tens of thousands of newsgroups, each containing dozens or hundreds of messages. These collections are constantly being updated as users around the world participate in the discussions by sending messages to the various newsgroups. If you want to read or join in the discussions, you'll need to tell Outlook Express how to access the news server at your ISP.

Setting up Outlook Express to access a news server is very similar to setting up the program to access an e-mail server. You'll use some of the same information you used to set up your e-mail account. In addition, you'll need one more key piece of information: the official name of your ISP's news server. The name of the news server should be included in the new account packet you received from your ISP. The information is probably also available on the ISP's Web site. If you don't find it there, call the ISP's technical support line.

When you have the name of the ISP's news server in hand, you can set up Outlook Express to access Internet newsgroups by following these steps:

1. Open the Internet Accounts dialog box by choosing Accounts from the Tools menu.

2. Click on Add and choose News from the submenu. This will launch the wizard that will lead you through the process of setting up an Internet news account. The first page of the wizard (shown in Figure 6.14) will look familiar from your experience setting up an e-mail account. It might look as though the program is starting to set up the wrong kind of account, but don't worry—the difference between a mail account and a news account will become apparent in later steps.

3. Type in your name as you want it to appear on the From line in the header of the messages you send to Internet newsgroups. Then click on Next to display the next page of the wizard (shown in Figure 6.15).

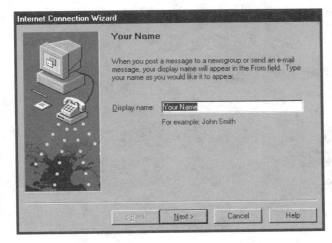

Figure 6.14

The News account
setup starts off
looking the
same as a Mail
account setup.

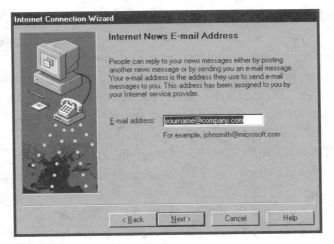

Figure 6.15

You'll need to
supply an e-mail
address, even for
newsgroups.

4. Enter your e-mail address in the space provided. When other newsgroup participants reply to a message you post, they can do so by
   posting a message on the newsgroup (if the reply might be of interest
   to the entire group) or by sending you a private e-mail message. Those
   e-mail messages will be delivered to the e-mail address you enter here.
   If you have more than one e-mail account, be sure to use the e-mail
   address of the account where you want to receive personal replies from
   any newsgroup messages you post. After entering your e-mail address,
   click on Next to proceed to the next page (shown in Figure 6.16).

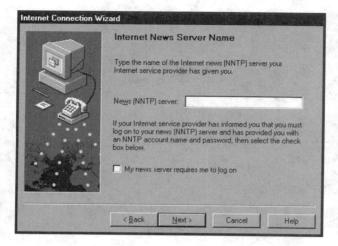

Figure 6.16

This is where you specify the name of your ISP's news server.

5. In the News (NNTP) Server text box, type the name of your ISP's news server. Typically, the server name will be something like **news.company.com**, but it could be a numeric address such as **255.128.255.10** or an unrelated name. Just be sure to enter the server name exactly as it was given to you by your ISP. Rarely, an ISP will require you to log on to the news server with a separate user ID and password. If that's the case, you can check the My News Server Requires Me to Log On option near the bottom of the page and the wizard will add a step to the setup that prompts you to enter that user ID and password. When you're ready to move on, click on Next to display the page, as shown in Figure 6.17.

6. The next step is to give the news account a friendly name. This is the name you'll see in the lists and menus in Outlook Express. The system suggests the news server name you just entered on the previous page, but you can type any name you want in the space provided. After naming the news account, click on Next to bring up the next page of the wizard, as shown in Figure 6.18.

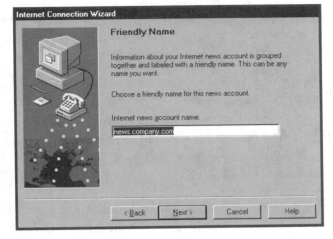

Figure 6.17

Now you get to name your news account.

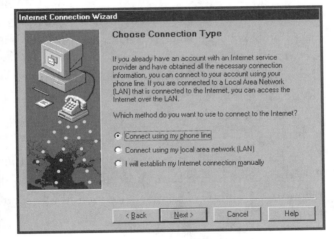

Figure 6.18

How will you connect to this news account?

7. Select the kind of connection you want to use to access your news account. Typically, you will choose the first option—Connect Using My Phone Line—to use a Dial-Up Networking connection to the Internet. Choose the second option—Connect Using My Local Area Network (LAN)—if you have a direct network connection to the Internet. If you choose the last option—I Will Establish My Internet Connection Manually—Outlook Express will not be

able to automatically initiate an Internet connection when you try to access the news server. Click on Next to proceed to the next page of the wizard (see Figure 6.19).

NOTE Normally, ISPs do not require you to log on to the news server, but they often limit access to the news server to their own customers by refusing access to anyone who is connecting to the Internet from outside of the ISP's system. This means you'll need to make sure you specify a dial-up connection to the same ISP where the news server is located.

8. If you chose to connect to the Internet using your phone line in the previous step, this page will appear to enable you to select (or create) the Dial-Up Networking connection you want to use. If you chose one of the other connection types in the previous step, the wizard will skip this page. You have two options. You can choose Create a New Dial-up Connection and click on Next to go through all the wizard steps to define a new connection. Normally, you will choose the second option, to use an existing dial-up connection, and select the desired connection from the list, then click on Next to display the final Congratulations page of the wizard.

9. When the Congratulations page appears, click on Finish to complete the news account setup process and return to the Internet Accounts dialog box. The newly defined news account will appear in the accounts list.

Now your news account is set up and ready to use. If you have access to other news servers at other ISPs, you can repeat the process to set up accounts for those news servers as well. Because there are so many different newsgroups, most ISPs don't try to carry them all on the news server. As a result, you may need to access more than one news server to find all of your favorite newsgroups.

After setting up a news account, you can select the account name in the list in the Internet Accounts dialog box and click on Properties to open a dialog box where you can edit the settings you created with the setup wizard.

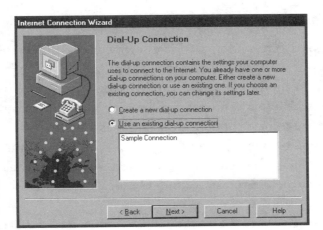

Figure 6.19

Choose your Dial-Up Connection.

If you have multiple news accounts, you'll need to define one of them as the default account Outlook Express will use for sending outgoing news messages. The procedure for setting the default news account is just like the one you used for setting the default mail account. You just click on the News tab in the Internet Accounts outbox, select the account name you want to designate as the default, and then click on Set As Default. That's all there is to it.

When you close the Internet Account dialog box after adding a news account, Outlook Express will ask if you want to download a list of the newsgroups available on the news server you just added. Just click on No for now. I'll show you how to update the list of newsgroups later. In the mean time, there are a couple of other configuration issues to get out of the way while you're dealing with setting up Outlook Express.

 NOTE In addition to e-mail and news, there is a third kind of account, or server, that Outlook Express can access. That is a directory service. Directory services are large databases that you can use to look up someone's e-mail address. Outlook Express comes with the addresses of several of the leading directory services, and it's unlikely that you will need to add directory services to the accounts list unless your network or ISP maintains a directory service listing local network users. In that case, your network or ISP will give you instructions on how to add the directory service to Outlook Express.

Configuring Outlook Express Options

Outlook Express offers a wide assortment of configuration options that allow you to tweak and fine-tune the program. Most of those options are found on the various tabs of the Options dialog box (shown in Figure 6.20), which you can open by choosing Options from the Tools menu. There are a lot of options available, but you won't have to go through them one by one, adjusting each setting. In general, the default settings will work just fine. However, there are a few settings you'll probably want to change before you start using Outlook Express.

TIP

If you want a brief explanation of an option in a dialog box, click on Help (the button marked with ? at the right end of the dialog box's Title Bar) and then click on the option you want information about. A tip box appears to display the explanation. Click anywhere to close the tip box.

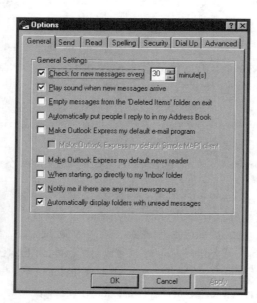

Figure 6.20

This dialog box gives you access to the many configuration options for Outlook Express.

Unless you plan to use another program as your primary e-mail or newsgroup access program, you'll want to make sure Outlook Express opens when you click on a Mail or News button in another program, such as Internet Explorer. You'll find the following options, along with several others, on the General tab of the Options dialog box:

- Make Outlook Express My Default E-mail Program
- Make Outlook Express My Default News Reader

Enable one or both options according to your preferences. If you have another program you'd rather use as the default e-mail or news program, make sure these options are cleared so your other program can be the default.

An important setting you'll probably want to change is located on the Send tab of the Options dialog box. Click on the Send tab to display the options, as shown in Figure 6.21. Notice the Mail Sending Format and the News Sending Format both offer the option of HTML or Plain Text. By default, the Mail Sending Format is set to HTML and the News Sending Format is set to Plain Text. I suggest that you select Plain Text in both areas.

- Mail Sending Format—Plain Text
- News Sending Format—Plain Text

A little explanation is in order here. Outlook Express is capable of composing and displaying messages that include much of the text formatting and effects that you commonly see on Web pages. To achieve those formatting effects, the program embeds formatting codes in the text of the message—the same HTML (Hypertext Markup Language) formatting codes that are used to define Web pages. As a result, your e-mail messages can include different fonts, text sizes, bold and italic effects, pictures, hyperlinks, and more. It's quite an improvement over the drab, plain-text e-mail messages that have been the standard in the past. So why disable a nice feature?

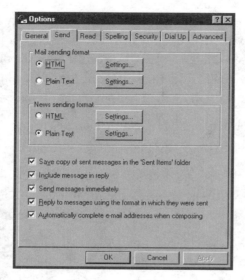

Figure 6.21

HTML formatting is a nice feature, but you'll probably want to disable it.

Outlook Express isn't the only e-mail and news reader program capable of handling messages that include HTML formatting. However, the capability is far from being universally available—and that's the problem. If you send e-mail messages that include HTML formatting to people who use Outlook Express (or another similarly advanced e-mail program), they will see an attractive and nicely formatted message, just as you intended. If, on the other hand, the recipient of the message is using an older e-mail program that doesn't support HTML formatting, the formatting codes embedded in the text can make your message nearly impossible to read. So unless you can be absolutely certain that the recipient of a message will be able to view the HTML formatting properly, you need to stick with plain text for the messages you send.

TIP

If you have a special message you want to send using HTML formatting, you can open the Options dialog box, click on the Send tab, choose HTML in the Mail Sending Format area, and then click on OK to enable the HTML formatting option. Compose your message, including the special formatting effects, and send it on its way. Just don't forget to reset the Mail Sending Format back to Plain Text when you're done.

Next, click on the Spelling tab to display the assortment of options, as shown in Figure 6.22. This is where you can tell Outlook Express how you want to handle spelling checks on the messages you compose and send. Certainly, you'll want to use the spell checking feature, so make sure there is a check mark beside the following options:

- Always Suggest Replacements for Misspelled Words
- Always Check Spelling Before Sending

Adjust the other settings according to your preferences. I usually check all the options in the When Checking Always Ignore box to reduce the number of obvious nonstandard words the spell checker flags as misspellings.

You'll probably be satisfied with the default settings on the Read, Security, and Advanced tabs of the Options dialog box—at least to start with. You can explore the options found on those pages later, at your leisure. The next option that I suggest you change is on the Dial Up tab (shown in Figure 6.23). In the When Outlook Express Starts area at the top of the page, choose Do Not Dial a Connection.

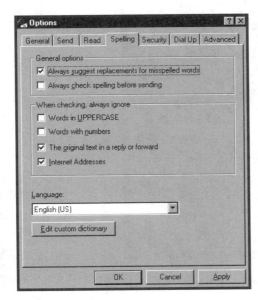

Figure 6.22

Catch those embareassing spellin mistaks and typng errars before you send your e-mail messages.

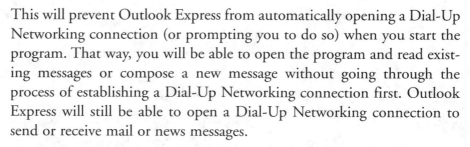

This will prevent Outlook Express from automatically opening a Dial-Up Networking connection (or prompting you to do so) when you start the program. That way, you will be able to open the program and read existing messages or compose a new message without going through the process of establishing a Dial-Up Networking connection first. Outlook Express will still be able to open a Dial-Up Networking connection to send or receive mail or news messages.

Also, you'll probably want to disable the Hang Up When Finished option. It sounds like a convenient feature to have the program automatically hang up the phone line when it finishes getting your messages, but it's likely that you'll be checking mail and checking out Web sites at the same time. It can be really annoying if Outlook Express kills the Internet connection when you're in the midst of downloading a Web page.

After adjusting the settings in the Options dialog box, click on OK to record the settings and close the dialog box. Now you're ready to start using Outlook Express to send and receive e-mail and news messages.

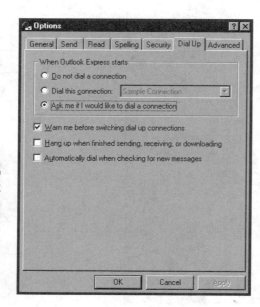

Figure 6.23

Stop Outlook Express from automatically initiating a Dial-Up Networking connection when you start the program.

NOTE   Another group of configuration options is located in the Window Layout Properties dialog box. (To open the dialog box, choose Layout from the View menu.) The settings in the dialog box control the arrangement of the major sections of the Outlook Express window, such as the folder list, the toolbar, and the Preview Pane (where you can view messages). The default settings work quite well and there's no need to change them, but you can explore the layout options on your own if you like.

Take a Break

Hey, how about taking a break now. Get up and stretch, take a short walk, see what the rest of the family is doing, or check the score of the game. (Now don't let yourself get distracted by the game. Just check the score and come on back. You can watch the highlights of the big plays on the news later.) When you return, you'll learn how to do something useful with this program you've been laboring to get set up.

Sending and Receiving E-mail with Outlook Express

After going through all the setup and configuration steps required to get Outlook Express ready to use, you might think that this is a complicated program that will be difficult to work with. But that's not the case at all. After the tedium of setting up accounts is out of the way, using Outlook Express is easy.

Reading Your E-mail Messages

Your home base for working with e-mail is the Inbox, one of the five default folders that Outlook Express provides for organizing your e-mail messages. (The other four default folders are Outbox, Sent Items, Deleted Items, and Drafts. You'll learn more about those other folders in a few

minutes.) The purpose of the Inbox is just what you would expect from its name—it's the place where incoming messages land when you download them into Outlook Express.

Read Mail

You can display the Inbox by clicking on the Read Mail icon in the Outlook Express start page (refer to Figure 6.1) or you can click on Inbox in the folder list at the left side of the Outlook Express window. If you choose to forego the Outlook Express start page, the program will go directly to the Inbox each time you start Outlook Express.

When you display the Inbox (as shown in Figure 6.24) you'll notice that the folder list remains the same, but the right side of the Outlook Express window splits into two panes. The top pane contains a list of the messages in your Inbox and the bottom pane shows a preview of the message that is selected in that list. Along the top of the Preview Pane there is a header bar that shows an abbreviated version of the message header—just the From, To, and Subject fields. The Preview Pane includes scroll bars to allow you to view other portions of the message.

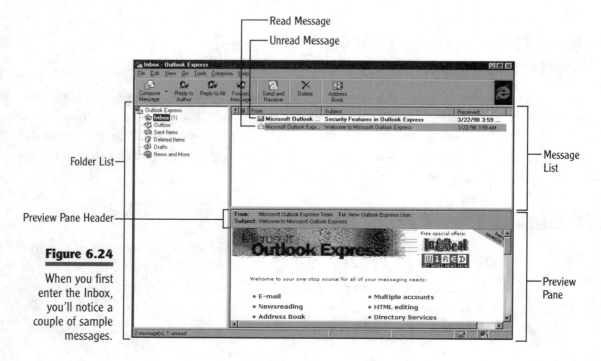

Figure 6.24

When you first enter the Inbox, you'll notice a couple of sample messages.

TIP

You can drag the dividing line between the Message List and Preview Pane up or down to change the relative size of the two panes. Try dragging the dividing line up so you can see more of the message displayed in the Preview Pane.

Using the Inbox couldn't be simpler. Each line in the Message List represents a different message and includes enough information about the message (who it's from, the subject, and the date and time it was received) to help you identify it. To view a message, you just click on an item in the message list to display the contents of that message in the Preview Pane. As the sample messages clearly show, Outlook Express can display messages that include text formatting and graphics in addition to plain text.

Unread messages appear in the Message List in bold type accompanied by an icon that looks like an unopened envelope. After a message has been displayed in the Preview Pane for a few seconds, Outlook Express marks it as "read" in the Message List by changing the text from bold to regular and by changing the icon to an open envelope.

The Preview Pane provides a quick and easy way to view your e-mail messages. However, sometimes you may want to view a message in a separate window. You can do that by simply double-clicking on an item in the message list to open a separate window and displaying the message in it (see Figure 6.25).

When you view a message in its own window, you have a few advantages over viewing the same message in the Preview Pane. For one thing, you see a slightly more complete header and you can do things like copy addresses from that header to your Address Book (more on that later, in "Using the Address Book"). For another thing, you have a full set of menus and toolbar buttons dedicated to managing and manipulating the e-mail message displayed in the message window. Actually, most of the same menu commands and buttons are available in the main Outlook Express window and you can use them to work with messages in the

Save This Message Reply to Author
  Print Reply to All
    Copy Forward
      Delete Previous Message
        Next Message

Address Book

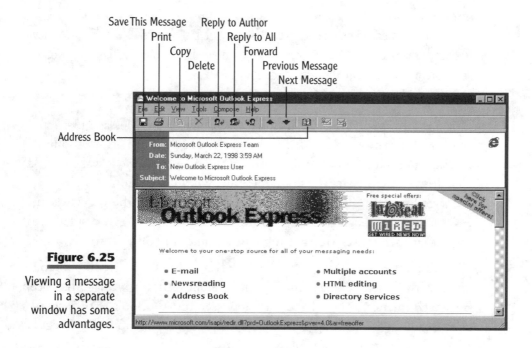

Figure 6.25

Viewing a message in a separate window has some advantages.

Message List. However, many people find them a little easier to use in a separate message window, if only because there is no room for ambiguity about what the command will apply to in the message window.

Finally, perhaps the best reason for viewing a message in a separate window is that you can easily move and resize the window, which makes it easier to compare the contents of a message to another document or message in another window on your desktop.

Checking Your Mail

All right, so you've read the sample messages that the programmers left in Outlook Express. (That's about as exciting as staring at the picture that came with your wallet.) Now it's time to check your electronic mailbox to see if there are any messages waiting for *you*.

Any e-mail messages addressed to you will be delivered to the mail server at your ISP and stored in your folder on the server until you pick them

up with an e-mail program such as Outlook Express. It's analogous to having a box at the local post office. Retrieving your messages with Outlook Express is like sending a messenger to the post office to pick up the mail from your box and deliver it to the In tray on your desk. Just as the messenger would have to have the combination or key to your post office box in order to pick up the mail, Outlook Express uses your account name and password to access your e-mail account on the mail server. You've already given Outlook Express all the information it needs to collect your messages for you. All that remains is to dispatch the messenger to fetch your e-mail.

Outlook Express gives you a choice of ways to start the process of collecting your e-mail messages from the server. You do any of the following:

- ✿ Click on the Send and Receive button in the Outlook Express toolbar. The program will automatically send outgoing messages and download incoming messages for all your e-mail accounts except those accounts you chose not to include in a full send and receive. (The option is found at the bottom of the General tab of the Properties dialog box for the e-mail account.)

- ✿ Open the Tools menu, point to Send and Receive, and choose All Accounts from the submenu. Outlook Express will automatically send outgoing messages and download incoming messages for all your e-mail accounts, one after the other.

- ✿ Open the Tools menu, point to Send and Receive, and choose a specific e-mail account name from the submenu. Outlook Express will send and receive messages for the selected e-mail account only.

When you tell Outlook Express to send and receive messages, you are launching the program on an automated process. Here's a summary of the steps the program will take:

1. Use the option defined for the first e-mail account to initiate a Dial-Up Networking connection (or confirm a LAN connection to the Internet) and wait for the Internet connection to be established.

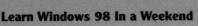

2. Log on to the e-mail server using the account name and password you defined in the mail account setup.

3. Check the Outbox folder for any outgoing mail messages waiting to be sent out using the current e-mail account and copy them to the mail server.

4. Download any incoming messages waiting on the server and save them on your hard drive. The messages appear in the Inbox folder in the Outlook Express window.

5. After successfully downloading the messages, erase the copies of those messages from the mail server.

6. Repeat Steps 1 through 5 for each e-mail account.

Once you start the send and receive process, Outlook Express does everything automatically. You won't have to do anything—except perhaps enter your user ID and password if it's required to complete a Dial-Up Networking connection. While it's actively working to establish a connection to the mail server and transfer messages, Outlook Express displays a message box to inform you of its status.

If you're checking multiple e-mail accounts that each require a separate Dial-Up Networking connection, the whole send and receive process could take several minutes. On the other hand, if you're already connected to the Internet and you check your mail on a single e-mail account that uses the same connection, it might take no more than the blink of an eye. (In other words, don't blink or you might miss it.) The number and size of the messages being downloaded can also significantly affect the length of time required for Outlook Express to transfer messages from the mail server and save them on your local hard disk. One or two short text messages will be transferred in just a few seconds. But if there are lots of messages to transfer, or if some of the messages are very long or include large attached files, Outlook Express might be busy for many minutes. If that happens, just be patient.

After your incoming messages are successfully downloaded from the mail server, Outlook Express adds them to the message list in the Inbox. You

can read the new messages (you did get some new messages, didn't you?) just as you did the sample messages that you saw when you first launched Outlook Express.

NOTE Typically, the first time you access a new Internet e-mail account, you will find a welcome message from your ISP waiting for you. But if you didn't get any incoming messages, don't worry. In the next section, you'll learn how to send messages. Then you'll be able to send messages to yourself so you can make sure the system and software are all working properly.

Composing and Sending E-mail

When you're ready to send your epistles out into the ether, Outlook Express provides the tools you'll need. Sending a message happens in two stages. First, you create the message. Outlook Express includes basic word processing, so you can compose your message without leaving the program. Then, after you finish the message, you send it to its intended recipients. Actually, Outlook Express doesn't send the message out over the Internet immediately. Instead, the program temporarily stores outgoing messages in the Outbox folder (one of the five standard folders, like the Inbox) until you initiate a connection to the mail server by doing a Send and Receive. Then Outlook Express completes the send operation by automatically handling the details of copying messages from the Outbox folder to the mail server at your ISP and sending them on their way to the proper addresses.

The hard part of composing e-mail messages is thinking about what you want to write and getting the words right. The mechanics of typing and sending those words in an e-mail message are simple. You just follow these steps:

1. Click on the Compose Message button in the toolbar or choose New Message from the Compose menu. Outlook Express will open

a New Message window like the one shown in Figure 6.26. You'll notice that it looks a lot like the message window you use to view individual messages, but all the header (address) information is missing and the message area is empty.

2. Begin by typing the recipient's e-mail address in the To field. (The cursor starts out in the To field by default, so you don't need to click there first.) Be sure to enter the address completely and accurately. You can enter more than one address in the To field by using a semicolon (;) to separate individual addresses.

TIP

Just to check out the system, make the first e-mail message you create and send from Outlook Express a message to yourself.

NOTE

Notice the small icons that look like Rolodex cards at the left end of the To, Cc, and Bcc fields. You can click on the icon to open a dialog box where you can select e-mail addresses from your Address Book and add them to the message header with a couple of mouse clicks. Right now, your Address Book is probably empty, so it won't do you much good. I'll show you how to use the Address Book later.

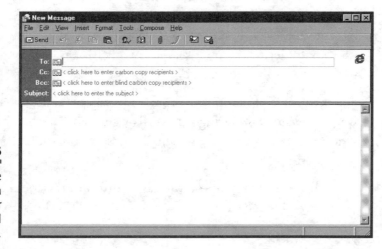

Figure 6.26

The New Message window provides a template for creating e-mail messages.

3. Click on the Cc field (the space where it says <Click Here to Enter Carbon Copy Recipients>) and enter the e-mail addresses of additional recipients of the message (if any). Do the same in the Bcc field if you want to add some blind copy recipients.

NOTE The difference between the To (To), Cc (carbon copy), and Bcc (blind carbon copy) fields is that all the recipients of the message will be able to see the e-mail addresses of other recipients listed in the To and Cc fields but not the Bcc field. There's no functional difference between the To and Cc fields, they simply continue the traditional address format for office correspondence.

4. Click on the Subject field (click where it says <Click Here to Enter the Subject>) and type a short phrase or title that describes your message. When you enter the message subject, Outlook Express mirrors the same subject information in the Title Bar of the message window, replacing the generic New Message title.

NOTE The subject line is a very important part of an e-mail message. It appears in the Message List in Outlook Express (and almost all other e-mail programs) and helps the recipient identify the message and decide how to handle it. Your message may be erased, ignored, or read immediately, depending on what you put in the subject field.

5. Click anywhere in the message area (the large blank workspace that occupies the bottom half of the message window) and begin typing your message. It's just like using a simple word processor. As you type, long lines of text automatically break to the next line to fit within the window; you only need to press Enter at the end of paragraphs. All the common text editing features are available. You can move the insertion point with the arrow keys or by clicking the mouse, you can use the Delete or Backspace keys to erase text, and you can insert text by simply typing. You can highlight text by

dragging the mouse pointer across it and then use buttons on the toolbar to Cut, Copy, and Paste the selected text or just use the mouse to drag the selected text to a new location.

6. To check for spelling errors in your message, open the Tools menu and choose Spelling. Outlook Express will scan your message looking for possible errors. If it finds words it doesn't recognize, Outlook Express highlights the first one and displays the Spelling dialog box, as shown in Figure 6.27. Like most spelling checkers, the program works by comparing each word in your message to its dictionary file and treats any word that doesn't appear in the dictionary as a potential misspelled word. Of course, the unrecognized word might be a misspelled word or a typing error, or it might be a proper name, technical term, or some other properly spelled word that just doesn't happen to be in the limited spelling dictionary.

The Spelling dialog box shows you the unrecognized word and suggests a properly spelled alternative in the Change To box. Other suggestions appear in the Suggestions list. If the word is properly spelled, you can click on Ignore to disregard the unrecognized word and make no change to the message, or you can click on Ignore All to skip all other occurrences of the same word in the message. If you're sure the word is spelled

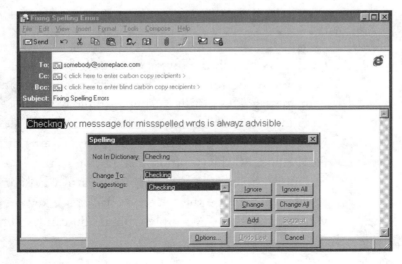

Figure 6.27

Fix your mistakes before anyone else sees how badly you spell.

correctly (and it's a name or term you'll be using frequently), you can click on Add to add it to the spelling dictionary.

If the highlighted word is misspelled, you need to get a correctly spelled replacement in the Change To box. Often, Outlook Express' first suggestion will be right. If one of the other words in the Suggestions list is the correct alternative, click on it to place that word in the Change To box. If none of the suggestions are appropriate, you must type the correct word in the Change To box. (Clicking on Suggest will display suggested alternatives to what you type in the Change To box. Basically, this performs a spell check on what you just typed.)

Once the properly spelled word is in the Change To box, you can click on Change to change the highlighted word in the message, or click on Change All to change all occurrences of the word in the current message. After changing or ignoring one unrecognized word, the spelling checker automatically moves on to the next word it can't find in its dictionary.

After you've dealt with all the unrecognized words in the message, the spelling checker displays a small message box that says the spelling check is complete. Click on OK to get rid of the message and return to your message.

TIP

■ ■

Actually, you don't have to manually initiate a spelling check on your message if you've set your Outlook Express options as I suggested. The program will automatically run a spelling check before sending the message.

■ ■

7. When you finish your message, click on the Send button located at the left end of the toolbar. Outlook Express will store the message in its Outbox folder. The next time you issue the Send and Receive command, the program will send the message to the mail server at your ISP and from there, it'll go on to the recipient.

Replying to an E-mail Message

Often, you'll be reading an e-mail message when you discover that you need to respond to it with a message of your own. Of course, you could compose a new message from scratch, but that isn't necessary because Outlook Express provides some features designed to facilitate quick replies.

When you are reading a message, you can click on the Reply to Author or Reply to All buttons in the toolbar. The buttons are available on the main Outlook Express toolbar when a message is highlighted in the message list. You'll find similar buttons on the toolbar of the message window when you view the message in a separate window. Clicking on one of the Reply To buttons causes Outlook Express to open a New Message window like the one you use to create new messages, but the program doesn't stop there; it fills in most of the header information for you and inserts a copy of the message you're replying to in the message area (see Figure 6.28).

If you click on the Reply to Author button, Outlook Express addresses the reply to the person who sent the message to you. If you click on the Reply to All button, Outlook Express addresses the reply to the author and also to all the people who were listed as recipients of the original message.

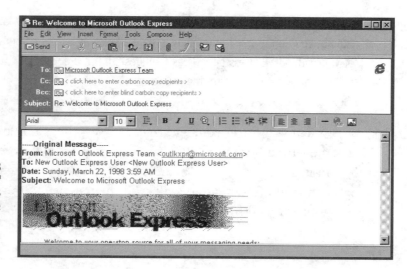

Figure 6.28

Outlook Express does most of the work for you when you reply to a message.

When you create a reply, Outlook Express automatically copies the subject of the original message to the Subject field of the reply and adds the RE: prefix. The program also copies the text of the original message and inserts it in the message area of the reply. That way, you and the recipients of the reply have the text of the original message available for easy reference. All you need to do is type your comments in the message area and then click on Send to send your reply on its way.

 NOTE Quoting the text of the original message in your reply is a helpful and widely accepted practice on the Internet. But don't overdo it! You should edit the text that Outlook Express copies from the original message so that only the specific passages to which you are replying remain in your message. Delete any extraneous information from the quoted text so it doesn't unnecessarily clutter your reply and make it longer than it needs to be.

Forwarding an E-mail Message

Forward Message

The Forward Message button is for those times when you are reading a message and you think of someone else who really should see it. Just click on Forward Message to send them a copy of the message you are reading. It works a lot like the Reply To buttons; Outlook Express copies the text of the original message and pastes it into the message area of a new message window. The subject gets copied also, and prefaced with FW. But unlike replies, when you Forward a message, Outlook Express doesn't copy any addresses from the original message. You'll need to enter the e-mail address of the person you want to send the message to. Then you can add a comment to the body of the message and click on Send to send the forwarded message.

Attaching a File to an E-mail Message

One very useful feature of modern Internet e-mail is the ability to attach a file to an e-mail message. Sending a file as an attachment to an e-mail message is a little like copying a file to a floppy disk and enclosing it in

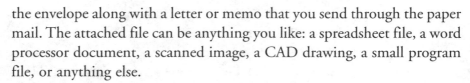

the envelope along with a letter or memo that you send through the paper mail. The attached file can be anything you like: a spreadsheet file, a word processor document, a scanned image, a CAD drawing, a small program file, or anything else.

Because the e-mail system is designed to handle text information only, transmitting a file that contains anything other than plain text characters through that system requires special handling. However, Outlook Express takes care of all the details for you—sending and receiving file attachments become simple drag-and-drop operations.

To send a file attached to an e-mail message, start by composing a normal e-mail message. Then, to attach a file to the message, simply drag the file's icon from your desktop or from an Explorer window and drop it on the message area of the new message window. Outlook Express adds a copy of the file to the message and displays the file's icon in a separate panel at the bottom of the new message window, as shown in Figure 6.29. After attaching the file, you can continue to compose and send the message normally.

When you receive a message that contains a file attachment, the attachment will be indicated by a small paper clip in the message list in the

Figure 6.29

A message window showing an attached file

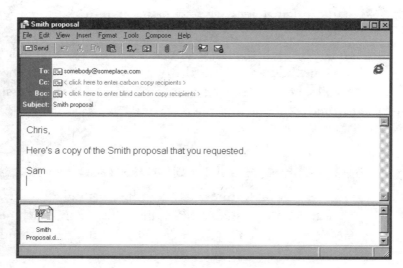

Inbox. The easiest way to work with the attached file is to double-click on the message item in the message list to open the message in its own window. The attached file will appear as an icon at the bottom of the window just as it does in an outgoing message. You can double-click on the file icon to open the file or drag the file icon from the message window and drop it on your desktop or an Explorer window.

Managing E-mail with Folders

Outlook Express manages your e-mail messages by storing them in different folders. You've already seen two of the default folders at work. The following list describes the purpose of the five default folders:

- ✿ **Inbox**. This is the folder where Outlook Express places the incoming messages it downloads from the e-mail server.

- ✿ **Outbox**. The Outbox is the temporary holding bin for outgoing messages that you have created but not yet sent to the mail server.

- ✿ **Sent Items**. After sending an outgoing message to the server, Outlook Express moves the local copy of the message from the Outbox folder to the Sent Items folder.

- ✿ **Deleted Items**. This folder is Outlook Express' version of the Recycle Bin. When you delete a message from another folder, it isn't erased immediately—it's just moved to the Deleted Items folder. The message isn't really gone until you delete it from the Deleted Items folder. You can delete messages from the Deleted Items folder manually or you can set an option to automatically clean out the Deleted Items folder when you exit Outlook Express.

- ✿ **Drafts**. Outlook Express automatically saves new messages in this folder while you are working on them. If you close a new message window before sending the message, you'll have the option of keeping the copy of the message saved in this folder. Later, you can reopen the message and finish it.

Those five default folders are just the beginning of your message organization system. Outlook Express enables you to create your own folders

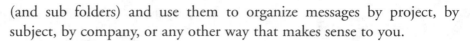

(and sub folders) and use them to organize messages by project, by subject, by company, or any other way that makes sense to you.

To create a folder, follow these steps:

1. Open the File menu, point to Folder, and choose New Folder from the submenu. This will open the Create Folder dialog box, as shown in Figure 6.30.

2. Type a name for the new folder in the Folder Name box.

3. Select a parent folder from the folder list. To create a top-level folder like Inbox and Outbox, click on Outlook Express in the folder list. Otherwise, click on an existing folder to make the new folder a subfolder within it.

4. Click on OK to close the Create Folder dialog box and add the new folder to the folder list on the left side of the Outlook Express window.

Using the folders to organize your messages is easy. Every folder basically works the same whether it is one of the five default folders or a new folder that you have created.

✪ Click on a folder name in the folder list to display the list of messages in that folder.

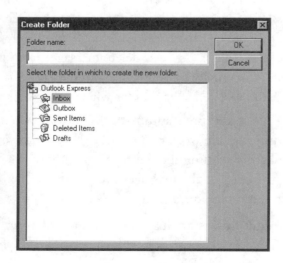

Figure 6.30

Use the Create Folder dialog box to define your own folders.

- ✿ To move a message to a different folder, simply drag it from the message list and drop it on the destination folder in the folder list.
- ✿ To delete a message from a folder, select the message in the message list and click on the Delete button in the toolbar.

If you ever want to delete an entire folder, click on the folder in the folder list and then click on the Delete button in the toolbar. Then you'll need to confirm the action because deleting a folder permanently deletes the folder and all the messages it contains.

Using the Address Book

Outlook Express includes an Address Book where you can keep e-mail addresses and other contact information for the people with whom you exchange e-mail messages. The Address Book is an important feature of Outlook Express because e-mail addresses are often long and complicated and one tiny mistake in typing an address can render your message undeliverable. Once you enter an e-mail address in the Address Book, you'll be able to add that address to a message by simply selecting it from a list instead of having to type it in each time.

You can open the Address Book by clicking on the Address Book button in the Outlook Express toolbar. The Address Book window (shown in Figure 6.31) displays a simple list of the addresses you've collected. It starts out empty, but it will become more useful as you accumulate addresses.

One way to add an address to the Address Book is to click on the New Contact button in the Address Book toolbar. This will open a blank Properties dialog box for an Address Book entry, like the one shown in Figure 6.32. Type the contact's name in the First, Middle, and Last boxes. (Why not enter your own name and contact information as your first entry in the Address Book?) Carefully type the contact's e-mail address in the Add New box and then click on Add to add the e-mail address to the E-mail Addresses list box. Note that each contact can have multiple e-mail addresses in the address book and you can set which one will be used as the default address for this contact.

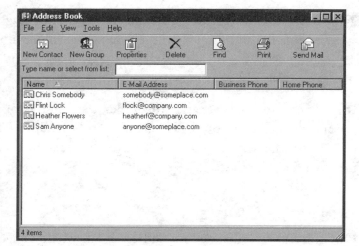

Figure 6.31

Keep those e-mail addresses handy in the Address Book.

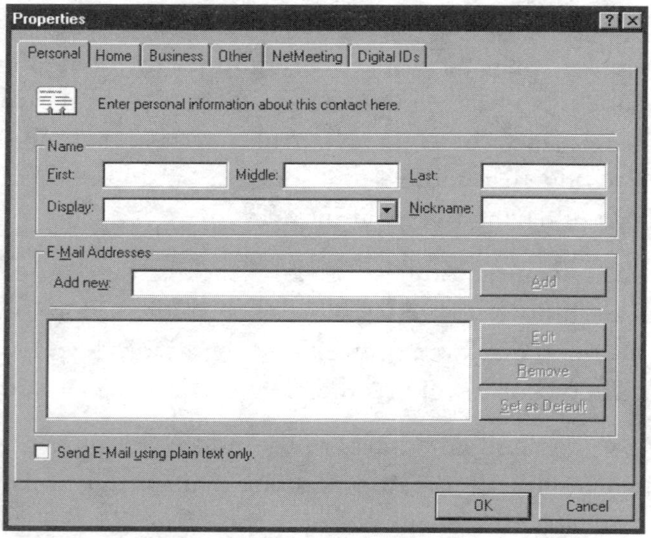

Figure 6.32

The various tabs of this dialog box store more than just an e-mail address for each contact.

The various other tabs in the dialog box provide space to keep track of lots of other information about each contact—you can enter as much or as little as you like. After entering information about the new contact, click on OK to close the Properties dialog box and enter the contact information in the Address Book.

Another, even better, way to add an entry to the Address Book is to copy the information from the header of an e-mail message. That eliminates the possibility of mistyping something critical—meaning anything in the e-mail address itself. To copy address information from an e-mail message, first display the message in a message window so you have access to the full header information. Right-click on a name or address in the header area of the message window and choose Add To Address Book from the short-cut menu. Outlook Express will open a Properties dialog box for the Address Book entry with the name and e-mail address already filled in. Edit or add to the contact information as needed and then click on OK to add the contact to your Address Book. The Address Book window doesn't need to be open to add contacts in this way.

 The whole point of creating a list of contacts in the Address Book is to be able to use those e-mail addresses to address the messages you create in Outlook Express. When you are creating a new message, you can access addresses from the Address Book by clicking on one of the little Rolodex card symbols in the To, Cc, and Bcc fields (refer to Figure 6.26). This will open the Select Recipients dialog box, as shown in Figure 6.33.

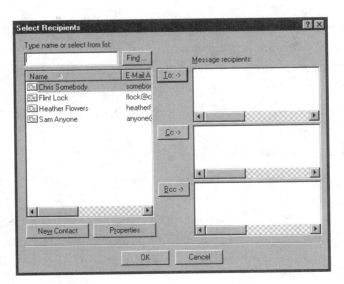

Figure 6.33

Adding an Address Book contact to the list of recipients for an e-mail message takes only a couple of mouse clicks.

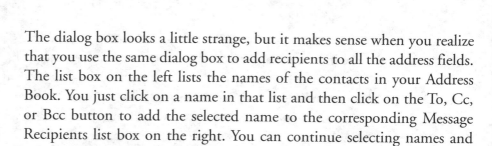

The dialog box looks a little strange, but it makes sense when you realize that you use the same dialog box to add recipients to all the address fields. The list box on the left lists the names of the contacts in your Address Book. You just click on a name in that list and then click on the To, Cc, or Bcc button to add the selected name to the corresponding Message Recipients list box on the right. You can continue selecting names and adding them to any of the Message Recipients categories.

When the Message Recipients lists are complete, click on OK to close the Select Recipients dialog box and update the address fields for the message you are creating. Notice that the address fields contain easy-to-read display names for each Address Book contact rather than their more arcane e-mail addresses. But you can rest assured that the complete e-mail address for each contact is recorded in the e-mail message.

Reading the News

At this point, you've covered the basics of using Outlook Express to handle your regular e-mail communications. Now it's time to learn about using Outlook Express to access the newsgroups that allow people from around the globe to participate in ongoing public discussions. Because newsgroups are really a variation on e-mail, many of the same tools and techniques you use for handling regular e-mail messages will apply to newsgroup messages as well. But despite the similarities, there are also some distinct differences between regular e-mail and newsgroups.

Connecting to a News Server

Before you can view newsgroup messages, you must connect to a news server and get a list of the newsgroups available on that server. You should already have an account set up for the news server at your ISP (remember, that was part of the Outlook Express setup that you did in the first half of this session) and it should appear as an item and the Outlook Express folder list.

To get things started, click on the news account in the folders list, then click on Yes when Outlook Express offers to download a list of newsgroups and click on Yes again if the program asks if you want to establish a connection to the server. Outlook Express will establish a connection to the news server and begin downloading the list of available newsgroups. Because there are typically many thousands of newsgroups available on a news server, the process may take quite a while. After the program finishes downloading the list of available newsgroups, it will display them in the Newsgroups dialog box. Fortunately, you'll only have to go through this process once for each news server. Outlook Express will maintain a list of available newsgroups for each server and update it automatically each time you connect to the server.

After the initial connection to the news server is complete, Outlook Express will handle most subsequent connections to the news server automatically, connecting and disconnecting as needed to get the message lists and messages you select—as long as the Dial-Up Networking connection is open. If you are not connected to the Internet, you'll need to click on the Connect button in the Outlook Express toolbar to initiate a Dial-Up Networking connection before you can do much of anything with newsgroups. Once the Internet connection is established, Outlook Express can handle the connections to the news server.

Finding News Topics

Once you get connected to the news server, the next step is to find a newsgroup on a topic that interests you. With tens of thousands of active newsgroups, you don't just scroll through the list to see if something catches your eye—you look for a particular topic or subject area. And it may take some searching to find what you're looking for. It's not usually a question of whether a newsgroup on a given topic exists, it's what the newsgroup is named and where it's located in the vast hierarchy of newsgroups.

News groups

To begin your search for an interesting newsgroup, click on the Newsgroup button in the Outlook Express toolbar. The Newsgroup dialog box appears (see Figure 6.34). By default, the All tab is selected so the list box shows all the newsgroups available on the news server.

At first, the newsgroup names probably don't make much sense and the list looks impossibly long. But there really is a strange logic to the newsgroup names. (The long strings of words separated by periods are really a series of categories starting with a general category on the left and progressing to more specific subcategories on the right.) And Outlook Express provides a search tool to help you find interesting newsgroup categories among the throng.

Suppose you wanted to locate a newsgroup where you could share what you're learning about Outlook Express and pick up tips from other users. To search for such a newsgroup, type **outlook** in the Display Newsgroups Which Contain box at the top of the Newsgroups dialog box. Outlook Express will display only those newsgroups with Outlook in the newsgroup name (see Figure 6.35).

Sure enough, there is a newsgroup that looks like it might fit the bill: microsoft.public.inetexplorer.ie4.outlookexpress. However, as you can see

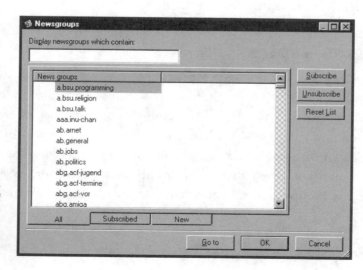

Figure 6.34

The Newsgroup dialog box is a search tool in disguise.

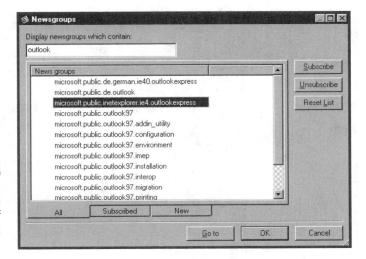

Figure 6.35

Use the built-in search capability to shorten the list of newsgroups to a manageable size.

from this newsgroup, the newsgroup names are descriptive but they often include abbreviations, run-together words, and elements that you might not expect. Furthermore, newsgroup names are often missing category descriptors that you would expect to be part of the name. For instance, if you had searched for the term e-mail, the Outlook Express newsgroup would not have shown up on the list even though it is definitely an e-mail program. As a result, you might need to use some imagination and try several alternative search terms in order to find a newsgroup.

Browsing a Newsgroup

When you find the name of a newsgroup that might be interesting, the next step is to check it out to see what kind of discussions are going on there. Select a newsgroup from the list in the Newsgroups dialog box and then click on Go To. Outlook Express will close the Newsgroups dialog box, download a list of message headers from the selected newsgroup, and display them in a message list arrangement (see Figure 6.36) much like the message list for e-mail.

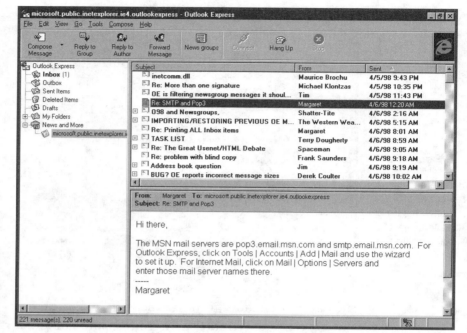

Figure 6.36

Viewing a
newsgroup is
similar to viewing
an e-mail folder.

Reading Messages

Reading news messages (sometimes called *news articles*) in Outlook
Express is essentially the same process as reading e-mail messages. You
select a message from the message list in the top portion of the window
and Outlook Express displays that message in the Preview Pane at the
bottom. One significant difference between reading e-mail messages and
reading news messages is that Outlook Express downloads the content of
your e-mail messages at the same time it downloads the message headers,
but when you read newsgroup messages, Outlook Express just downloads
the message headers and waits until you select a message from the
message list before downloading the body of that message. As a result,
you'll probably notice a slight delay between the time you select a message
header from the message list and the time the message appears in the
Preview Pane.

Following Threads

Another difference between e-mail messages and news messages is the concept of *threads*. A thread is a series of linked messages on the same subject. It starts when someone posts a message on the newsgroup and then someone else posts a reply to that message. A message and a reply starts a thread. Then someone else might post another message in response to that reply, and the thread grows. A thread is like an online conversation with exchanges going back and forth between two or more participants.

Outlook Express groups all the messages belonging to the same thread together in the message list. Initially, the thread occupies only a single line in the message list even though it may consist of several messages. A thread is indicated by a plus sign (+) in a box next to the small message icon in the message list. Click on the + and Outlook Express will expand the thread just like an Explorer window displaying the subfolders within a folder. Figure 6.37 shows a number of threads in the message list—some are expanded and some are not.

Subscribing to Newsgroups

When you locate a newsgroup using the Newsgroups dialog box, you can view that newsgroup, download the list of message headers, read messages, and post messages and replies. You can go to another newsgroup and then return. Outlook Express lists the newsgroups you've visited in the folder list and maintains the list of message headers in each newsgroup—until you exit Outlook Express. When you close Outlook Express, the list of newsgroups you visited gets erased.

If you want to be able to return to a newsgroup without having to search for it in the Newsgroups dialog box, you can subscribe to the newsgroup. Outlook Express won't erase its records of newsgroups that you have subscribed to. When you return to the program, the subscribed newsgroups

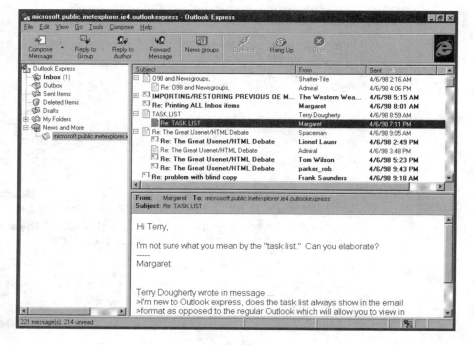

Figure 6.37

Related news messages are grouped together in threads.

will be listed in the folder list and you can click on a newsgroup to display the list of messages that were available the last time you are connected to the news server. Then, all you need to do is click on Connect to go back to the news server and update the newsgroup.

The best way to subscribe to a newsgroup is to visit the newsgroup first and check it out. Then you can right-click on the newsgroup name in the Outlook Express folder list and choose Subscribe To This Newsgroup from the shortcut menu. Outlook Express will darken the newsgroup's icon in the folder list to indicate that it is a subscribed newsgroup. It won't be erased when you close the program. If you ever want to reverse the effect of subscribing to a newsgroup, you can right-click on a subscribed newsgroup in the folder list and choose Unsubscribe From This Newsgroup from the shortcut menu. The next time you close Outlook Express, the unsubscribed newsgroup will be erased from the folder list.

Posting Articles You've Written

You don't have to confine your participation in Internet newsgroups to the role of spectator, just reading messages posted by others. Outlook Express gives you all the tools you need to become an active participant, creating and posting original messages and replies. In fact, you already know how to use those tools because they are essentially the same as the ones you use to create e-mail messages and replies. The only difference you'll see between regular e-mail messages and news messages is the address the messages go to. Here's a quick summary of the news message creation options:

- ❂ **Compose Message.** Clicking on Compose Message while viewing a newsgroup opens a New Message window that is almost identical to its e-mail counterpart. The difference is that instead of the To field in the address header, you'll find a Newsgroups field, and Outlook Express automatically inserts the name of the current newsgroup. The only other significant difference is that the Send button in the toolbar is replaced by the Post button. That's a useful reminder as well as a simple name change: when you send something, you know exactly where it's going; when you post it, you post it for the whole world to read.

- ❂ **Reply to Group.** Clicking on this button while reading a news message is equivalent to clicking on the Reply to Author button while reading an e-mail message, but instead of addressing the reply to the author of the message you're replying to, Outlook Express addresses it to the newsgroup.

- ❂ **Reply to Author.** Sometimes you may want to send a private e-mail reply instead of posting a response on the newsgroup. That's what this button does. It's exactly the same as using the Reply to Author button to create a reply to an e-mail message.

- ❂ **Forward Message.** You can forward a news message to someone else just like you can forward an e-mail message.

In addition to the address differences, there are some behind-the-scenes differences in how outgoing messages are routed to servers, but Outlook Express handles that automatically.

What's Next?

The next order of business is a break from the computer and a nice Sunday evening meal. Is that fresh bread that I smell baking?

After dinner, there is one more session in this weekend of Windows 98. In it, you'll learn how to add Web pages directly to your Windows desktop and how to update your copies of those Web pages automatically by using channels and subscriptions.

Bringing the Web to Your Desktop

- What Is Active Desktop?
- Making Windows Act Like a Web Page
- Adding Web Content to Your Desktop
- Subscribing to Web Content
- Offline Viewing

Hello there, I'm glad to see that you're back. I hope you're not feeling sluggish after consuming a big Sunday evening dinner, because there's some exciting stuff to cover in this final session of your Windows 98 weekend. You could say that I've saved the best for last.

In this evening's session, you'll learn about integrating content from the Internet and the World Wide Web into your Windows working environment. You'll learn how to set up your desktop so that you can access Web content from the Internet as easily as you access documents stored on your local hard drive. Specifically, you'll get a chance to explore the following topics:

- ✿ Understanding the new Active Desktop
- ✿ Setting up the Web style and the other Active Desktop features
- ✿ Subscribing to Web content from Channels and from regular Web pages
- ✿ Viewing subscription content whether you're connected to the Internet or not

Well, so much for the teaser headlines. It's time to see how this stuff really works.

What Is Active Desktop?

Active Desktop is one of the hallmark features of Windows 98. It's often mentioned as one of the new features that sets Windows 98 apart from its predecessors—which is a bit of an overstatement; you could have Active Desktop on a Windows 95 system if you installed the Internet Explorer 4 enhancements. I guess Active Desktop gets a lot of attention because it's a dramatic, visible change from the familiar classic Windows 95 desktop and it can make a significant difference in the way you use your computer. Active Desktop is a standard feature of Windows 98, whereas it's only available on Windows 95 systems that have been upgraded with all the latest add-ons.

Also, many of the other new features of Windows 98 are in areas such as support for new kinds of hardware devices that aren't yet in widespread use. They don't make nearly such good selling points now, though they'll come in handy later.

Okay, so Active Desktop is a high-visibility feature of Windows 98, but that doesn't explain what it does. Actually, Active Desktop is hard to sum up in a short, succinct definition because it gives Windows a whole collection of new capabilities.

One feature that falls under the general Active Desktop umbrella is the new Web style interface that lets you open objects with a single mouse click, like clicking on hyperlinks in a Web page. You learned about the basics of Web style in the Friday Evening session.

The main features of Active Desktop are outgrowths of Windows 98's built-in ability to display Web pages. (Yeah, that's part of the "integrated Web browser" feature that has been the subject of lawsuits and lots of press coverage.) Add to that the ability to define a Web page background for the Windows desktop (and for any other folder, for that matter) and a number of interesting things become possible. Your desktop and folders can include graphics and interactive elements that were previously impossible to implement and display. Most of all, you can customize your

Windows environment in unprecedented ways. For example, it's easy to add background graphics to folders as well as to add whole Web pages and interactive elements to your desktop. Background graphics behind the icons in your folders aren't a significant development, but Web pages floating on your desktop (as shown in Figure 7.1) can be really cool.

Another feature, called Web page *subscriptions*, is totally separate from Active Desktop. Subscriptions enable you to automatically update Web pages stored on your system and view them offline. Combining subscriptions with the Web pages on your desktop means that those Web pages can be automatically updated with the latest information. The result is a different kind of desktop environment, one that sets new standards in making information convenient and accessible.

The rest of this session is devoted to learning how to set up Active Desktop and Web page subscriptions, so you can begin exploring this world of accessible Web-based information.

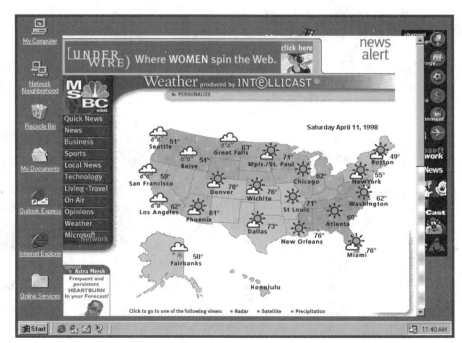

Figure 7.1

Active Desktop enables Windows 98 to display Web-related content directly on the desktop.

Making Windows Act Like a Web Page

What does it take to get Web content to show up on your Windows desktop and in your folders? It would be really great if there was one simple option that you could enable to turn on all the Web content capabilities of Windows 98. But that's not the case. Instead, you'll need to adjust several different settings if you want to take full advantage of Active Desktop. Fortunately, the inconvenience of having to adjust several settings is at least partially offset by the ability to mix and match and fine-tune each of the settings to get just the effect that you want and need in your copy of Windows.

Choosing the Web Style (or Not)

In the Friday Evening session, you learned the difference between the Web style Windows desktop, with its underlined icon labels and its point-to-select and click-to-open mouse actions, and the Classic style Windows desktop, with its traditional appearance and its click-to-select and double-click-to-open mouse style. I even gave you instructions for switching between the two styles.

Now, you're going to have to make a decision that might necessitate giving up a familiar old friend—the Classic style Windows desktop. You simply can't take full advantage of the Active Desktop if you stick with the pure Classic style. The obvious alternative is to use the Web style Windows desktop, and the Web style does, indeed, work very well with Web content on the Active Desktop.

But that doesn't mean you will be forced to convert totally to the Web style to be able to display a Web page on your desktop or in a folder. There is a third option, the Custom style, that allows you to pick specific elements of the Web style for use on your Windows desktop. So, if you want, you can keep the mouse-clicking characteristics of the Classic style and still enable Windows to display Web-related content.

If you're already using the Web style Windows desktop, then your system is already configured to accept Web-related content on the desktop. If, however, you've been using the Classic style Windows desktop, you'll need to either switch to the Web style or follow these steps to create a Custom style that supports Web-related content:

1. Click on the Start button on the taskbar and then choose Settings, Folder Options from the Start menu. This will open the Folder Options dialog box, as shown in Figure 7.2.

2. Select the Custom, Based On Settings You Choose option. Then click on Settings to open the Custom Settings dialog box, as shown in Figure 7.3.

3. Select the Enable All Web-Related Content on My Desktop option. This is the essential setting that allows Active Desktop to do its thing by displaying Web pages on your desktop.

4. Select other options in the Custom Settings dialog box according to your preferences. If you like the Classic style mouse actions, be sure

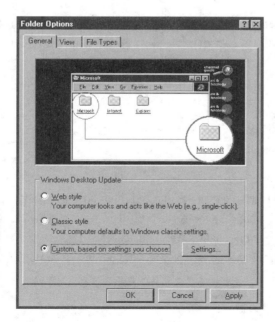

Figure 7.2

If you plan to use Active Desktop, you'll have to give up on the Classic style.

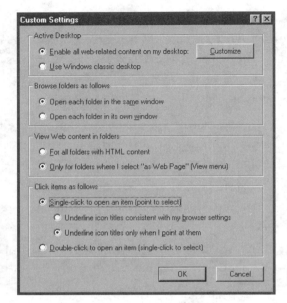

Figure 7.3

Mix and match
settings to define
your own Custom
style desktop.

to select Double-Click To Open in the Click Items As Follows area
at the bottom of the dialog box. Also, you may want to select Only
For Folders in the View Web Content In Folders area so you can
choose whether to display Web content in individual folders on a
case-by-case basis.

5. Click on OK to close the Custom Settings dialog box and return to
the Folder Options dialog box. Then click on Close to close the
Folder Options dialog box.

TIP

If you are using the Classic style Windows desktop, you can quickly activate Web-related
content by right-clicking on the desktop and choosing Active Desktop, View As Web Page.
Windows will automatically switch to a Custom desktop style that retains the Classic
style mouse actions but enables Web-related Active Desktop content. It's quicker than
creating your own Custom desktop style, but not quite as flexible.

Customizing Folders

Active Desktop affects more than just your Windows desktop; it affects the way folders appear in Explorer windows as well. For example, the graphics on the left side of the Explorer window shown in Figure 7.4 appear courtesy of Active Desktop and show up only when the folder is viewed as a Web page.

If you are using the Web style Windows desktop or you are using a Custom style desktop and you chose to display Web content in all folders, you'll see this kind of graphics in almost every folder. The only exceptions are likely to be folders on floppy disks, CDs, and network drives that were created before you installed Windows 98.

If you create a Custom style desktop and choose the Only For Folders option, you'll be able to choose which folders display Web content and which do not. To view the Web content in the folder you're viewing in an Explorer window, pull down the View menu and choose As Web Page. To hide the Web content again, simply repeat the same command.

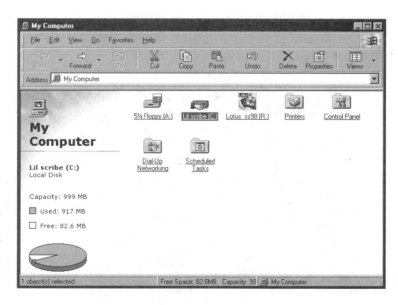

Figure 7.4

Often, the Web content in a folder provides information about the selected item.

Theoretically, you could customize your folders by editing the HTML file that forms the folder's Web page background. However, it's not very practical for average users to mess with the kind of HTML file Windows automatically generates and places in each folder—leave that to the programmers. What you can do is make some cosmetic changes to the folder by selecting an image to go behind the icons in the folder. Here's how you do it:

1. Right-click on the background of a folder window and choose Customize This Folder from the shortcut menu. Windows will open the Customize This Folder dialog box, as shown in Figure 7.5.

2. Select the middle option—Choose a Background Picture—and then click on Next to open the next page of the Wizard, as shown in Figure 7.6. You can ignore the top option—Create or Edit an HTML Document—it's for advanced HTML programmers only. The bottom option—Remove Customization—will come in handy later if you decide you don't like the effect of a background picture in the folder.

3. The list box shows the picture files available in your Windows folder. When you select a file in the list, a preview of the picture appears in the box on the left.

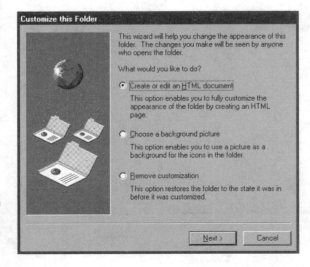

Figure 7.5

Pick how you want to customize the folder.

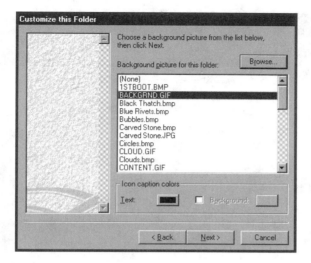

Figure 7.6

Pick a picture to display as the background of your folder.

4. Click on the Text button near the bottom of the dialog box to open a Color palette where you can select a color for the text labels in the folder. Click on a color and then click on OK to record the color selection. If you would like each label to have a background box behind the text, click on the Background check box and then click on Background and select a background color. After selecting the picture and the colors you like, click on Next to proceed to the last page of the Wizard.

5. Click on Finish to record your settings and apply them to the folder. Figure 7.7 shows an example of a folder customized with a background picture.

If you decide to customize your folders with background pictures, be sure to choose the pictures very carefully. If the background picture is too busy or distracting, the text and icons in the folder will be very difficult to read.

Adding Web Content to Your Desktop

The Web content that appears in folders is a nice touch, but it's kid stuff compared to what you can do with Active Desktop on the Windows

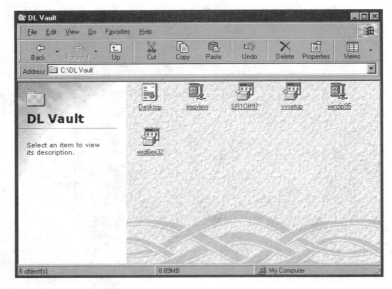

Figure 7.7

You can customize
your folders with
background
pictures.

desktop itself. You can make your favorite Web pages part of your desktop
so that they are always instantly available.

One of the nicest things about the way you add Web content to your
desktop is that it's so easy to do. Just follow these steps:

1. Start by viewing the Web content you want to add to your desktop.
   Typically, you'll do that by viewing the Web page in the Internet
   Explorer Web browser.

 NOTE If you want to use a Web page that is stored on your local hard drive, you can simply
open the folder containing that file in Internet Explorer or in Windows Explorer. You can
drag the file's icon from the Explorer window just as you can drag a hyperlink from the
Internet Explorer window.

2. Locate a hyperlink to the page you want to add to your desktop.
   Alternatively, if you want to add the page currently displayed in the
   Internet Explorer window, locate the icon beside the page's URL in

the Address box near the top of the Internet Explorer window. Right-drag the hyperlink or icon from the browser window and drop it on your Windows desktop.

3. Choose Create Active Desktop Item Here from the shortcut menu. Windows will display a small Security Alert message box asking you to confirm that you want to add an item to your Active Desktop. Click on Yes. Windows may also display another small dialog box notifying you that you are not only adding the Web page to your active desktop, you're also subscribing to the page. For now, just click on OK. (Later you'll learn more about how to customize and edit subscriptions.) Windows adds a small window to the desktop containing your Web content, as shown in Figure 7.8.

4. Now all you need to do is size and position the Web page window on your desktop. Initially, the window appears to have no border or title bar, just scroll bars on the bottom and right side. However, when you point to the window, a thin border appears around it.

Figure 7.8

Your new Active Desktop item starts out as a small square box.

You can drag that border to adjust the size of the Web page window, just as you would resize any other window. When you point to the top of the window, a thicker border (a sort of blank Title Bar) appears along the top edge of the window. You can drag this thicker border to move the Web page window, just as you would move a normal window by dragging its Title Bar. After you move and resize the window, you'll be able to see the contents of the Web page (see Figure 7.9).

That's all it takes to add Web-related content to your desktop. The Web page, in its window on your desktop, behaves basically like a Web page in an Internet Explorer Web browser window. However, one significant difference becomes apparent when you click on a hyperlink. Instead of loading the target page into the window on your desktop, Windows opens a new Internet Explorer window to display the target of the hyperlink.

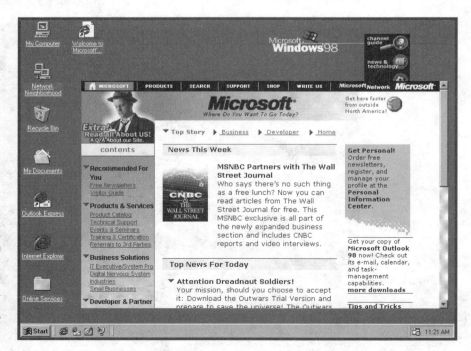

Figure 7.9

Moving and resizing the window completes the task of adding a Web page to your desktop.

Now it's your turn. Try visiting one of your favorite Web sites and adding that page to your Active Desktop.

Turning Desktop Web Content On and Off

Having Web pages displayed on your desktop is pretty cool, but it's also easy for your desktop to become crowded with too many Web pages. You may not want *all* your desktop Web pages displayed *all* the time.

Hiding a Web page that is currently visible on your desktop is easy. Just point to the top edge of the Web page window until the top border appears and then click on the Close button located at the right end of the top border. Windows will close the desktop Web page just as it would close any application window.

Turning on a Web page window that isn't currently displayed on the desktop is only slightly more involved. Just follow these steps:

1. Right-click on the desktop and choose Properties from the shortcut menu to open the Display Properties dialog box.

2. Click on the Web tab to display the settings, as shown in Figure 7.10. The list box shows all the available Active Desktop elements with a check box beside each one. A check mark indicates an item that will appear on the desktop and an empty check box indicates an item that is available but hidden.

3. Click on the check boxes to select the Active Desktop items you want to display. To permanently delete an item, click on it and then click on Delete.

4. When you are satisfied with the list of Active Desktop items to be displayed, click on OK to close the Display Properties dialog box and update your Windows desktop with the new selection of Active Desktop items.

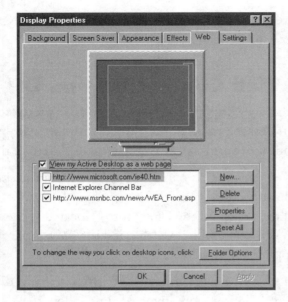

Figure 7.10

Select which Active Desktop items you want to display.

Take a Break

This is a short session, so you might not need to take a break in the middle, but if you'd like to pause for an intermission, this is a good place to do it. So far, you've learned how to use the Active Desktop. When you return from your break, you'll learn about subscribing to Web sites.

Subscribing to Web Content

How many times do you return to the same Web site over and over again to check for the latest information? For some of your favorite sites, the answer is probably "frequently."

Fortunately, the Favorites list makes it easy to find a site again once you add a site to the list. But the process doesn't happen instantly. First, you must initiate the procedure by selecting the site you want to visit from the Favorites list. Then you wait. The Internet Explorer window opens and then the system must establish a Dial-Up Networking connection before you can access the Internet.

After the Internet connection is established, Internet Explorer connects to the Web server and begins downloading the page you requested. If the page includes many graphics, that can take a while. Finally, Internet Explorer displays the Web page and you can check out the new information you are looking for. But wait, what you see onscreen is the same thing you saw the last time you visited this site. The new information that you were expecting to see hasn't been posted yet. You've just wasted a few minutes looking for information that wasn't there. What's worse, you'll have to try again later.

Subscriptions are a solution to exactly this kind of problem. Instead of manually revisiting Web sites to check for updated information, you can instruct your computer to automatically check Web sites to see if they have been updated since your last visit. Windows can notify you (via e-mail) that a Web site has been updated, or download the Web page to your hard drive so you can view it whenever you like, or both.

NOTE   The term *subscriptions* can be a little confusing for some people. It suggests an analogy to magazine or newspaper subscriptions, where the publisher is responsible for sending you each new issue. But a Web page subscription in Windows 98 is more like having an assistant who checks the newsstand on a regular basis and picks up the new issue for you when it's available.

Subscribing to a Regular Web Site

Basically, subscriptions are a powerful new dimension that has been added to the Favorites list. So, naturally, you'll use some of the same tools to define subscriptions that you use to define regular Favorites. The process of defining a subscription starts out by defining a Favorite, then expanding on that by giving the computer instructions for downloading the page to your hard drive, checking for future updates, and notifying you when updates occur.

To create a subscription to a Web page, follow these steps:

1. First, locate the page you want to subscribe to and display it in the Internet Explorer Web browser.

2. Pull down the Favorites menu and choose Add to Favorites. This will open the Add Favorite dialog box, as shown in Figure 7.11. This is the same dialog box you used to add a Web page to your Favorites list in the Sunday Morning session, so you already know how to use some of its features.

3. Give your new Favorite a name by editing the entry in the Name box. Then click on Create In to expand the dialog box to show the list of subfolders, and select the subfolder (submenu) that will be home to this new favorite item.

4. To create a subscription to this Web page instead of just a Favorites list item, choose one of the two options that begin with the word Yes. (Remember, to create a simple Favorites list item, you chose No Just Add The Page To My Favorites.) Which of the Yes options you choose depends on what kind of subscription you want to create. Normally, you'll want a full-service subscription, so choose the one that begins Yes Notify Me Of Updates. If you don't want to download the Web page for offline viewing, choose Yes But Only Tell Me When This Page Is Updated. (If you choose Yes But Only..., the program will display only Steps 7 and 9 when you start to customize the subscription settings.)

Figure 7.11

Subscribing to a Web page starts out like adding a page to your Favorites list.

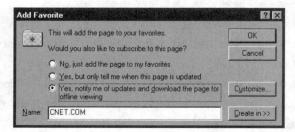

NOTE

If you choose a notification-only subscription, Windows won't check the Web page for updates on any fixed schedule. Instead, the program will do its checking in the background when you are connected to the Internet and browsing other Web pages.

5. Click on Customize to open the Subscription Wizard (see Figure 7.12), which will lead you through the process of customizing your subscription settings for this Web page.

6. Choose whether you want to download only the current Web page, or the current page and also all the pages that are hyperlinked to the current page. After making your selection, click on Next. If you chose to download link pages in addition to the current page, the Wizard will present an extra page where you can specify how far to follow links. The default is to follow links one page deep, but you can increase that number if you want. Just use caution, because the number of linked pages can quickly multiply to the point that they will require excessive download times and may overrun the available storage space on your hard drive. Click on Next to advance to the next page, as shown in Figure 7.13.

Figure 7.12

The Subscription Wizard will help you define the subscription settings.

Figure 7.13

Do you want to be notified of updates?

7. When Windows discovers that a subscribed page has been updated, it adds a red star to the page's icon in the Favorites list. If you would also like to receive an e-mail message notifying you of the update, select the Yes Send an E-mail option. The e-mail message will be sent to the address listed under the option. If you need to change the address, click on Change Address. After specifying the notification options, click on Next to go to the Wizard page, as shown in Figure 7.14.

8. This is where you choose whether you want to initiate subscription updates manually or have the computer update the subscription automatically according to a predefined schedule. If you opt for scheduled updates, you'll also need to specify a schedule. The program comes with predefined schedules for daily, weekly, and monthly updates. If you want to use one of those schedules, you can simply select it from the drop-down list box. If none of those schedules fit your needs, you can click on New to open the Custom Schedule dialog box where you can define your own update schedule. After you define and name a custom schedule, it will appear in the drop-down list and you'll be able to select it for this, and other, subscriptions. If you use a dial-up networking connection to connect to the Internet with a modem, be sure to enable the Dial

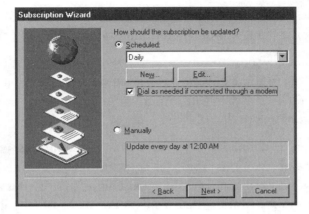

Figure 7.14

You can opt for manual or scheduled updates.

As Needed option in the middle of the dialog box. Otherwise, Windows will only be able to update your subscription if you happen to be connected to the Internet at the scheduled time. When the schedule is complete, click on Next to advance the next (and last) page of the Wizard, as shown in Figure 7.15.

9. Most Web pages don't require you to log on with a user name and password, but if the Web page you're subscribing to is an exception to that rule, select the Yes option and enter your user name and password in the spaces provided. When you finish, click on Finish to close the Subscription Wizard and return to the Add Favorite dialog box.

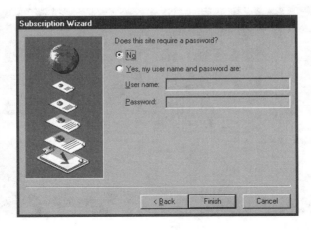

Figure 7.15

If you must use a password to access the Web page, enter it here.

10. Click on OK to close the Add Favorite dialog box and add the new favorite item, with its subscription information, to your Favorites list.

Now you know how to subscribe to a Web page. Now it's your turn to try subscribing to some of your favorite sites. After you've done it a couple of times, you'll find that you can create a subscription in much less time than it took me to describe the process.

After you've defined a few Web page subscriptions, you can choose Manage Subscriptions from the Favorites menu in Internet Explorer to open a window like the one shown in Figure 7.16. This is a special version of the Explorer window that displays the status of all your subscriptions (including the pages you placed on your Active Desktop) and provides a place for you to handle all those maintenance chores such as deleting unneeded subscriptions. Also, you can right-click on a subscription item and choose Properties from the shortcut menu to open a dialog box where you can edit all the subscription settings.

Subscribing to a Channel

Channels are Web sites specifically designed for viewing as part of your Windows desktop. They include some special features to allow the Web site developer to specify some of the subscription settings such as the update schedule and whether to download linked pages. After all, who

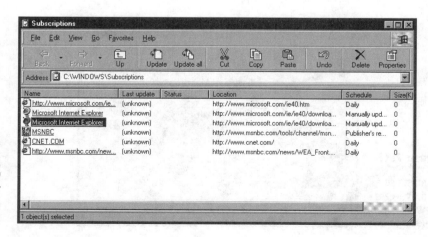

Figure 7.16

Manage your subscriptions from this window.

besides the Web site developer will know more about how often the site will be updated and how many pages will be changed each time. Channels also often include lots of graphics, special effects, and custom programming, which is stuff that isn't commonly found on normal Web pages. As a result, a channel might appear on your Active Desktop looking very much like any other subscription Web page, or it might take on a totally different appearance and function as an animated screen saver or a ticker tape.

I can't tell you very much about the specifics of how to work with channels, because channels vary so much. But I can give you an overview of the steps required to add a channel to your Active Desktop.

1. First of all, you need to locate the Web page that contains a link to the channel you want to add to your active desktop. To get you started, Microsoft includes two versions of its Channel Bar in Windows 98. One Channel Bar appears on the default desktop when you enable Active Desktop. The other Channel Bar appears in the Internet Explorer window when you click on the Channel Bar button in the Internet Explorer toolbar. Clicking on buttons in the Channel Bar will eventually take you to the Web pages of some of Microsoft's business partners that offer channels. Other Web developers offer channels as well. You'll find those channels by surfing the Web and by various word-of-mouth promotions. On the channel developer's Web page (see Figure 7.17), you'll find a button labeled Add Active Channel, or something to that effect.

2. Now this is the hard part: Click on the button and wait while Internet Explorer downloads some files to your hard drive. Shortly, a Modify Channel Usage dialog box similar to the one shown in Figure 7.18 will appear.

3. You can customize the subscription settings for the channel if you want, but normally you'll simply click on OK to accept the channel developer's settings. Other dialog boxes may appear and more file downloads might occur, depending on the specific features the channel installs. For example, the c|net channel installs a screen

saver that displays headlines from the current technology news. When all the downloads are complete, the channel should be installed and ready to use.

Some active channels will appear as separate windows on your desktop, while others will be accessible from the Channel Bar. After the channel is installed, clicking on its button in the Channel Bar will display the channel content saved on your hard drive instead of taking you to the Web page from which you installed the channel.

Figure 7.17

Where is that button that installs the Active Channel?

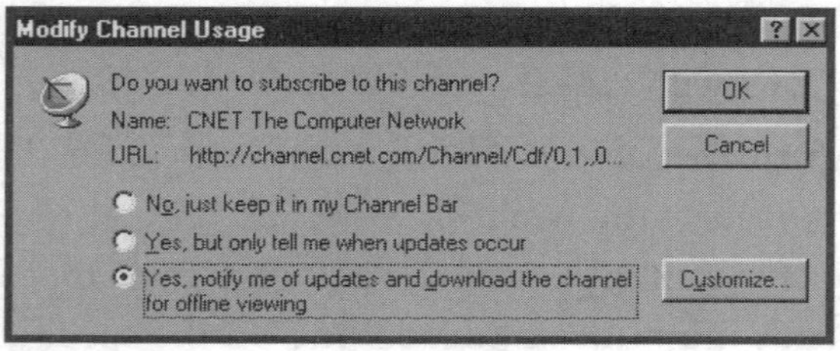

Figure 7.18

This is your opportunity to customize the subscription settings for the channel you are adding to your Active Desktop.

Getting Subscription Updates Manually

As you saw when you were defining a Web page subscription, you have two options for updating a subscription. You can initiate and update manually, or you can let Windows update your subscriptions automatically according to a predefined schedule.

Manual updates might seem like a bother, but they are often the best way to go. You have complete control over when the updates occur and you're sure to get the absolute latest information. Manual updates are easy to do. You can use any of the following techniques:

✿ Right-click on the desktop and choose Active Desktop, Update Now from the shortcut menu. Windows will update all your active subscriptions.

✿ Display the Favorites list, then right-click on a subscription item in the list and choose Update Now from the shortcut menu. Windows will update the selected subscription.

✿ Open Internet Explorer, pull down the Favorites menu, and choose Manage Subscriptions to open the subscriptions window. Then you can select an individual item and click on the Update button in the toolbar to update that one subscription, or click on the Update All button in the toolbar to update all the subscriptions at once. Now wasn't that easy?

TIP ■
If you're leaving on a trip with a laptop computer and want to read your subscribed Web pages offline while you're on the road, performing a manual Update All just before leaving is a good idea even if you have automatic updates scheduled. That way, you'll be sure to have the latest information downloaded.

■ ■

Getting Subscription Updates Automatically

You just saw how to initiate subscription updates manually. The other option is to let Windows do the subscription updates automatically. Manual updates are easy to do, but automatic updates are even easier—you don't have to do anything; Windows does it all for you. The subscription updates occur automatically at a predetermined time, so as to view updated Web pages at your leisure.

Of course, for automatic subscription updates to work, everything must be set up properly. Obviously, your computer must be turned on at the time when the updates are supposed to occur and it must be connected to the Internet—or else Internet Explorer must be configured to connect automatically using the correct Dial-Up Networking connection.

If you connect to the Internet using a modem, that last point is particularly important. You'll want to double-check the appropriate Internet Explorer settings. To do so, open the View menu and choose Internet Options to open the Internet Options dialog box. Click on the Connection tab, select the Connect To Internet Using Modem option, and then click on Settings to open the Dial-Up Settings dialog box, as shown in Figure 7.19.

Make sure the correct connection is selected and confirm your user ID and password. Then, make sure the Connect Automatically To Update Subscriptions option is enabled. When that's done, click on OK twice to close both dialog boxes and record the settings. That should allow Internet Explorer to make the necessary connections when it comes time to automatically update your subscriptions.

NOTE The exact times of your automatic subscription updates will vary from the scheduled times because Internet Explorer adjusts the scheduled times to avoid conflicts that might occur from too many subscriptions being updated at the same time.

Figure 7.19

If you plan to update Web subscriptions automatically, you must make sure that the connection is properly configured.

Offline Viewing

One of the great advantages of Web page subscriptions is that you can download Web pages and save them on your hard drive. Then you can view those pages offline, when you're not connected to the Internet. The pages are stored on your hard drive, so they load almost instantly—no waiting. And you can take as long as you like to read a page because you're not using up Internet connection time as you read.

If you're accustomed to thinking of Web browsing as something that requires an Internet connection to do, then you might think that you would have to do something special to be able to view a Web site offline. Well, you're in for a pleasant surprise. There are no special techniques required for offline viewing of subscribed Web pages.

TIP

Windows adds a small red star to the icon for any subscription page in the Favorites list that has been updated since you viewed the page last.

To view a Web page on your active desktop, all you'll need to do is close or minimize any open windows that are obscuring your view. To view any other subscription page, just select it from your Favorites list. Internet Explorer opens automatically and downloads the selected Web page from your hard drive. That's all there is to it. Depending on the way you have Internet Explorer configured, the program might automatically initiate a Dial-Up Networking connection when it opens. If that happens, just cancel the connection and choose to work offline; you won't need an Internet connection to view your subscription.

What's Next?

This is only the beginning. In this weekend, you've learned the basics of how to work with Windows 98. Now you've got the tools you need to get some work done, but there's a lot more to Windows and to the programs you can run on a Windows-based computer. You're off to a good start, but don't let that be the end of it. Pick an area that interests you and learn more about it. Read another book; do some exploring on your own. Learning is such a great adventure, enjoy it!

Installing Windows 98

Many computer users never have to deal with installing Windows 98, or any other operating system for that matter. A personal computer is nearly useless without an operating system, so computer manufacturers rarely sell a computer without an operating system preinstalled at the factory. As a result, when you purchase a new computer, plug all the components together, and start it for the first time, you can expect to see the operating system start up automatically. On the overwhelming majority of personal computers sold today, the operating system will be Windows 98.

NOTE Sometimes, the installation of Windows 98 on a new computer is not quite complete. When you start the computer for the first time, the Windows 98 installation program appears and asks a few questions (such as your time zone and whether you want to install a printer) before proceeding through the final stages of the installation process. Then the computer will automatically reboot itself and Windows 98 will appear, ready to use.

The only time you, as the computer user, are likely to need to install Windows 98 is if you have an existing computer running an older version of Microsoft Windows and you want to upgrade the operating system to the current standard—Windows 98. That's the scenario I'll address in this appendix.

Upgrading to Windows 98 from Windows 95

Windows 95 has been on the market for roughly three years. Although the basic product has remained the same, it has gone through several minor revisions and upgrades in that time. Some of the revisions have been to fix bugs, while others have added or improved features. The most dramatic change comes with the addition of Internet Explorer 4, which not only adds the latest version of Microsoft's Web browser, but also makes some (optional) changes in the look and feel of the Windows 95 desktop and other operating system elements. If you recently purchased a new computer with Windows 95 installed, you probably got the latest version that includes all the available updates. If you have an older version of Windows 95, you can download files from the Microsoft Web site that will upgrade your copy of Windows 95 with most (but not all) of the updated features.

Windows 95 with Internet Explorer 4 and all the available system upgrades installed comes very close to matching Windows 98 in look and feel and in major features. However, the trick is getting all those system upgrades installed on Windows 95. Downloading and installing dozens of upgrade files one by one can be tedious and time-consuming. If your copy of Windows 95 is more than about a year old, it's probably easier to upgrade to Windows 98 than it is to bring your system up to date by adding all the necessary upgrades to Windows 95. On the other hand, if your copy of Windows 95 is fairly new and it came with (or you have added) Internet Explorer 4, then you probably won't need Windows 98 unless you decide to add some new hardware that Windows 95 doesn't support. The system requirements for Windows 95 and Windows 98 are about the same. Just about any computer with a 486 or Pentium processor and at least 8MB of RAM should be adequate to run Windows 95, but a faster Pentium with 16MB of RAM and a fast video card makes a more comfortable platform for Windows 95 or Windows 98. If you plan to run multiple programs, 32MB (or more) of RAM is preferred, and adding more RAM generally improves performance. Modern Windows programs tend to be quite large, so a 1GB (or larger) hard drive is recommended. You really need a CD-ROM drive—both for playing multimedia titles and games and for the more mundane task of installing programs. A sound card and speakers are optional. A modem (or a connection to the Internet via a local area network) is highly desirable.

Because the system requirements and the major features of the Windows 95 and Windows 98 operating systems are so similar, the upgrade from Windows 95 to Windows 98 is a relatively simple transition. If that's what you're looking at doing, skip on to the "Installing the Windows 98 Upgrade" section now.

Upgrading to Windows 98 from Windows 3.1

Upgrading from Windows 3.x to Windows 98 is a profound change. There are many advantages to using the newer operating system (the power and efficiency of 32-bit programs and the convenience of long file names are just a couple of the more obvious examples) including the new and easier to use user interface that relies on the Start menu and taskbar instead of the antiquated Program Manager. Probably the most compelling reason to upgrade your operating system is because you need features of some new version of an application program that is only available for 32-bit operating systems such as Windows 95 or Windows 98. You could achieve most of the same advantages by upgrading to Windows 95 as to Windows 98, but there is no point in upgrading to Windows 95 now that Windows 98 is the current standard.

One major factor that you must consider before upgrading your operating system is the system requirements of Windows 98. Windows 98 simply requires a more powerful computer. So you'll need to ask yourself whether your old Windows 3.x computer has what it takes to run Windows 98. If not, some serious hardware upgrades may be in order before you attempt to install Windows 98. In some cases, the cost of upgrading your computer may be so high that it's more practical to replace it with a new system. (And if you buy a replacement computer, it'll probably come with Windows 98 already installed.)

Windows 3.x needs a 386-based computer with 4MB to 8MB of RAM. A 486-based computer with 8MB to 16MB of RAM is plenty for Windows 3.x. According to Microsoft's promotional material for Windows 95, it's supposed to run on a 386 computer with 8MB of RAM—but don't expect to be happy with it if you want to do anything but watch screen savers!

A fast 486 or a Pentium computer with at least 16MB of RAM is the minimum practical configuration for Windows 95 or Windows 98. A faster Pentium processor and 32MB of RAM is a better choice—and more RAM is better. You'll also need a CD-ROM drive and a fast video adapter. A sound card and speakers are optional and a modem (or an Internet connection via a local area network) is highly desirable.

You should consider replacing any old components for which drivers designed for Windows 95 and Windows 98 are not available. Continuing to use the old real-mode drivers you used with Windows 3.x after upgrading to Windows 98 will significantly impair the performance of your system.

NOTE

If you got your computer and its various components prior to the time Windows 95 was released on the market, the installation disks that came with your hardware will not include modern 32-bit drivers. However, you can usually find the 32-bit drivers you need to use your existing hardware with Windows 95 or Windows 98 by requesting them from the hardware manufacturer's technical support department. Often, you can find the drivers available for download on the manufacturer's Web site.

If you plan to install Windows 98 and an assortment of application programs, you'll want to have at least a 1GB hard disk—anything smaller will quickly fill up and get cramped. You'll need about 250MB or more of free space on your hard drive just to install Windows 98. The actual amount of space required depends on what components you install and whether you elect to save backup copies of your existing Windows (and DOS) files so you can remove Windows 98 later. Windows 98 won't consume all that space permanently, but the setup program needs lots of room for temporary files during the installation.

Once you determine that your hardware is up to the task of running Windows 98, you can proceed with the installation. The process is mostly automatic. The Windows 98 installation program may not do as good a job of transferring programs and preferences from Windows 3.x to Windows 98 as it can do when upgrading from Windows 95 to Windows 98. However, reinstalling programs and customizing your system settings in Windows 98 is not difficult—you'll learn how by reading this book.

NOTE   Before upgrading to Windows 98, it's a good idea to clean up your Windows 3.x system by removing unneeded programs and files and editing the Windows system files (WIN.INI and SYSTEM.INI) to remove obsolete entries. If you don't have the expertise you need to do this yourself, try to find a friend, co-worker, or consultant who does. You can upgrade to Windows 98 without doing this cleanup first, but the cleanup can help reduce the chances of having minor problems with the upgrade.

Installing the Windows 98 Upgrade

The actual procedure for installing the Windows 98 operating system upgrade is fairly simple and basically the same whether you are upgrading from Windows 3.x or Windows 95. The Windows 98 setup program takes care of the difficult parts automatically. All you really have to do is follow these instructions:

1. Boot your computer and start your existing version of Windows.
2. Exit any programs that were started automatically when you started Windows.
3. Insert the Windows 98 upgrade CD in your CD-ROM drive.
4. Start the Windows 98 setup program using one of the following techniques:

   ✿ If you're using Windows 95 with the AutoRun feature enabled, you will see a message advising you that the CD contains a more recent version of Windows than you are currently running and asking if you want to upgrade your computer to the new version of Windows 98 now. Click on Yes to start the upgrade.

   ✿ Click on the Start button in the Windows 95 taskbar and choose Run from the Start menu. When the Run dialog box appears, type in **x:\startup.exe** (substitute the correct letter for your CD-ROM drive in place of x) and click on OK.

   ✿ In the Windows 3.x Program Manager, open the File menu and choose Run. When the Run dialog box appears, type in **x:\startup.exe** (substitute the correct letter for your CD-ROM drive in place of x) and click on OK.

5. Follow the on-screen instructions as the Windows 98 Setup program installs the new version of Windows on your computer.

Basically, that's all there is to it. The Windows 98 Setup program does its thing automatically with minimal input from you. The process takes about an hour or so, and in that whole time you'll only need to click on a few on-screen buttons to do things like accept the Microsoft license agreement and accept or reject a few installation options.

The installation program begins by scanning your hard disk for errors and performing some other essential system tests. After your system passes these tests, the Windows 98 Setup Wizard is installed. The Windows 98 license agreement appears. Click on the I Accept The Agreement radio button and then click on Next.

After some more system checks, the setup wizard gives you the option of saving your existing MS-DOS and Windows system files so you can uninstall Windows 98 if necessary. Click on the Yes (Recommended) radio button and then click on Next to proceed.

After saving your system files, the setup Wizard will prompt you to enter the product identification number from the Certificate of Authority you got with your Windows 98 update CD. Type the number in the spaces provided and then click on Next.

Next, you'll be asked to select your country or region from a list so the setup Wizard can install the appropriate Internet channels. Select United States (or your native country) from the list and then click on Next.

The Windows 98 Setup Wizard will display a series of messages that describe new features of Windows 98 while it copies files from the CD to your hard drive. You might as well relax and read the messages—the file-copying process will take a while.

After copying the files, the setup Wizard automatically restarts your computer. The reboot may take a long time, so be patient. Then the setup program searches for installed hardware and Plug-and-Play devices. This, too, takes a while. Next, the setup program goes about its business setting up Control Panel, programs on the Start menu, Windows help, and MS-DOS program settings. The setup program moves applications on your hard drive so they will start faster and then updates your system configuration. All of this takes time—go get a cup of coffee (or lunch).

After all this setup and configuration is complete, the Windows 98 Setup Wizard performs another automatic reboot of your computer. At least, it's supposed to be automatic. You may need to manually toggle the power switch off and back on if the automatic reboot stalls. Booting the computer takes a while as the system goes through more Plug-and-Play scanning and lots of setting up personalized settings for various programs. But when it's all complete, Windows 98 appears on your screen, ready to use.

Now that you have Windows 98 installed and running on your computer, you can return to the Friday Evening session in this book and begin learning how to use your new operating system.

GLOSSARY

Active Desktop. A feature to customize your desktop to display information you can update from the Internet. A term that is synonymous with viewing your desktop as a Web page.

Active Window. The window that is currently open for use. The active window is designated by a different color toolbar than other open windows.

America Online (AOL). A widely used online service offering access service to the Internet as well as proprietary information created by AOL. This proprietary information includes news, financial planning, homework help for students, chat lines, and much more.

Application. Computer program designed to enable users to perform specific job functions. Word processing, accounting, and engineering programs are examples of application programs.

AT&T WorldNet. A widely used Internet access service.

Bitmap. A graphic file format made up of small dots. A specific kind of bitmap file with the .BMP extension is the format Windows uses for desktop wallpaper.

Border (of a window). A line that delineates the edge of a program window; it's also a tool for resizing the window.

Briefcase. A special folder on the Windows desktop used to keep documents up to date when shared between computers.

Browser. A software program especially designed for viewing Web pages on the Internet.

Button. A graphical representation of an option or a command that activates the option. Clicking on an onscreen button precipitates an action like pressing a physical button on a household appliance.

Byte. The amount of space needed to store a single character, such as a number or a letter. 1,024 bytes equals one kilobyte (1 KB).

Card. A removable circuit board that is plugged into an expansion slot inside the computer (such as a graphics card, sound card, or fax card).

CD-ROM. Compact Disc-Read Only Memory. Means of data storage using optical storage technology. A single CD-ROM can hold more than 650 MB of information, or half a billion characters of text.

Channels. A specialized Web site designed to work with the Windows 98 subscription feature to automatically download information from the Internet and store it on your computer for later viewing.

Channel Bar. A window containing a set of buttons that enables you to link to specially designed Web sites. The Channel Bar is an optional feature of the Active Desktop and it's also available in the Internet Explorer window.

Check Box. Check boxes are used to present options requiring individual on/off decisions in dialog boxes. A check box appears as a small square ballot box beside an option description. A check mark in the box indicates the option is enabled. If the box is empty, the option is disabled. Clicking on a check box toggles the check mark on or off.

Choose. To use the mouse or the keyboard to pick a menu item or dialog box option that initiates an immediate action. Compare with select.

Classic Style. A Folder Options setting that tells Windows how to interpret mouse actions and display certain on-screen items. In Classic Style, you click on an item to select it and double-click on an item to open it. Compare with Web Style.

Click. To quickly push and release the main (usually the left) mouse button when the onscreen mouse pointer is positioned over the desired item.

Clipboard. An area of computer memory where text or graphics can be temporarily stored. It is a holding place for items that have been cut or copied. The item remains on the Clipboard until you cut or copy an additional item or until you turn off the computer.

Close. To shut down or exit a dialog box, window, or application.

Close Button. The small button with an X on it located at the right end of the title bar of most windows. Clicking on the Close button will close (exit) the dialog box, document, or program displayed in that window.

Command Button. A button in a dialog box, such as Open, Close, Exit, OK, or Cancel, that carries out a command.

CompuServe. A widely used online service that offers access to the Internet, as well as proprietary content and information.

Connect Charge. The fee a user must pay for the privilege of having access to an online service or the Internet. Generally, a connect charge is based on a monthly rate.

Copy. To take a selection from the document and duplicate it on the Clipboard or to make a duplicate of a file.

Cursor. A symbol (usually a blinking horizontal or vertical bar) that designates the position on the screen where text or codes will be inserted or deleted. Compare with mouse pointer.

Cut. To take a selection from the document and move it to the Clipboard.

Default. A setting or action predetermined by the program unless changed by the user.

Desktop. The screen background and main area of Windows where you can open and manage files and programs.

Dialog box. A sort of on-screen form where you can fill in the blanks, make selections from lists, and choose various combinations of options and settings.

Dimmed. Describes the appearance of an icon, a command, or a button that cannot be chosen or selected.

Directory. An organizational tool used to store groups of files on a hard disk or similar computer storage medium. Synonymous with folder, directory is an older term used in MS-DOS, older versions of Windows, and the Unix systems frequently found on the Internet.

Document. A letter, memo, proposal, or other file that is created in a software application.

Double-Click. Pushing and releasing the main (usually the left) mouse button twice in rapid succession when the on-screen mouse pointer is positioned over the desired item.

Drag and Drop. To move text or an object by positioning the mouse pointer on the item you want to move, pressing and holding the mouse button, moving the mouse, then releasing the mouse button to drop the object into its new location.

Drag. Pressing and holding the main (usually the left) mouse button while moving the mouse, then releasing the mouse button when the pointer reaches the desired destination. Normally used for moving on-screen items and selecting text.

Driver. A computer software program that tells Windows about the special features of a particular device and how to access them. For example, a printer needs a driver to communicate with the computer.

Drop-Down List Box. A compact way to present a list of options in a dialog box. The box displays a single selected item, but clicking on the little arrow button at the right end of the box causes a list to appear. You can scroll through the list and select an item by clicking on it.

Ellipsis. A punctuation mark consisting of three successive periods (...). Choosing a menu item or command button with an ellipsis opens a dialog box.

E-mail. The exchange of text messages or computer files over a local area network or the Internet.

Exit. To leave a program.

Explorer Window. A multi-purpose window used by Windows 98 to display just about everything. For example, in addition to My Computer, the Network Neighborhood, the Recycle Bin, and the My Documents folder all appear in Explorer windows.

FAT. File Allocation Table. A table, or list, within the operating system that keeps track of a user's files and their locations. The system uses this table as users create and modify files.

FAT32. A new variation on the traditional File Allocation Table that stores data more efficiently—especially on large hard drives.

File Format. The arrangement and organization of information in a file. File format is determined by the application that created the file.

File. Information stored on a disk under a single name.

File Name. The name given to a file, which a user uses to identify the contents of the file, or which a program uses to open and save a file.

Folder. An organizational tool used to store files. Synonymous with directory, but folder is the newer, preferred term.

Font. A group of letters, numbers, and symbols with a common typeface.

Function Keys. A set of keys, usually labeled Fl, F2, F3, and so on, used by themselves or with the Shift, Ctrl, and Alt keys to provide quick access to certain features in an application.

Gigabyte. Approximately one billion bytes. Abbreviated as GB.

Graphical User Interface (GUI). The concept of allowing users to interact with a computer by manipulating symbols on the screen as opposed to typing text commands. Windows is an example of a GUI, whereas MS-DOS is a text-based operating system.

Handle. An on-screen marker that indicates where on or around an object that you can drag to resize or move the object. The handles for toolbars in the taskbar and Explorer windows appear as vertical ridged lines at the left end of each toolbar. The handles for a selected graphic object appear as small black boxes at the corners and on the sides of the selection box that surrounds the object.

Header. In an e-mail message, the header is the address and routing information at the beginning of the message. Outlook Express displays an abbreviated version of this information at the top of the message window when you view the message.

Help. A feature that gives you instructions and additional information on using a program.

Highlight. To change to a reverse-video appearance when a menu item is selected or an area of text is blocked.

Hypertext link. A connection from the current document to another document or to a document on the World Wide Web.

HyperText Markup Language (HTML). The standard for embedding formatting instructions and hyperlinks in a text document to be viewed by a Web browser. Originally developed for World Wide Web, HTML is now widely used for all sorts of formatted documents.

Icon. A small graphic image that represents an application, command, or a tool. An action is performed when an icon is clicked or double-clicked.

Inactive Window. A window that is not currently being used. Its title bar changes appearance, and keystrokes and mouse actions do not affect its contents. An inactive window can be activated by clicking on it.

Input. The process of entering data into a computer from a keyboard or other device.

Internet. An international network connecting businesses, government agencies, universities, and other organizations for the purposes of sharing information.

Internet Explorer. A program made by Microsoft and included in Windows 98 that is used to view Web documents—typically, you access those documents on the Internet.

Intranet. An intra-company network designed to distribute information, documents, files, and databases. Similar to the Internet except it is contained within an organization.

Extranet. An inter-company network designed to distribute information, documents, files, and databases. Similar to the Internet except it is limited to a certain number of companies that share information.

Kilobyte. (KB) 1,024 bytes of information or storage space.

Link. A connection between two objects that allows data to be passed between them. Used with OLE as well as with the Internet.

List Box. A box that displays a list of choices. When a list is too long to display all choices, it will have a scroll bar, so that you can view additional items.

Log In or Log On. The process that a user goes through to begin using a computer system. Usually involves entering some type of identification, followed by a password.

Log Out or Log Off. The process a user goes through to end a session on the computer.

Mailbox. An area of memory or disk that is assigned to store any e-mail messages sent by other users.

Maximize. To enlarge a window to its maximum size so that it fills the entire on-screen desktop.

Megabyte. Approximately one million bytes (MB) 1024 kilobytes (1,048,576 bytes) of information or storage space.

Memory. A generic term for storage areas in the computer. The area in a computer where information is being stored while being worked on. Information is only temporarily stored in memory.

Menu. A list of options displayed onscreen from which you can select a particular function or command.

Menu Bar. The area at the top of a window containing headings for pull-down menu items.

Message Box. A box, similar to a dialog box, that appears with information, a warning, an error message, or a request for confirmation to carry out a command.

Microsoft Network. A widely used online service offering access service to the Internet and propriety content and information.

MIDI. Musical Instrument Digital Interface. A format that allows communication of musical data between devices, such as computers and synthesizers.

Minimize. To reduce a window to its minimum size so that it is represented onscreen only by a button on the taskbar. Minimizing a window hides a program from view but doesn't close the program or the document you were working on.

Modem. A device used to connect a personal computer with a telephone line, so that the computer can be used for accessing online information or communicating with other computers.

Mouse Pointer. A symbol that indicates a position on-screen as you move the mouse (or other pointing device) around on your desk.

Multimedia. A generic term for computer applications and files that combine standard computer capabilities with other media, such as video and sound.

Multitasking. The capability of a computer to perform multiple operations at the same time.

My Computer. The default name for a desktop icon that opens an Explorer window displaying information about your system's disk drives and also special system folders such as the Printers folder and the Control Panel.

Netiquette. Network etiquette. Internet rules of courtesy for sending e-mail and participating in newsgroups.

Netscape Navigator. A popular browser made by Netscape to view documents on the World Wide Web.

Network. A connection between two or more computers that allows them to communicate and to share files, printers, and other resources.

Network Neighborhood. A desktop icon that opens an Explorer window giving you access to network resources (if your computer is connected to a Windows network).

Newsgroups. An Internet forum of discussions on a range of topics. It consists of articles and follow-up messages related to a specific subject.

Object. A picture, map, or other graphic element that you can place in a document.

Open. To start an application, to insert a document into a new document window, or to access a dialog box.

Operating System. Software that controls how a computer performs basic operations between the hardware and software. An operating system creates a platform on which to run other, more specialized software programs.

Option. A choice inside a dialog box.

Password. A secret code that restricts access to a file, system, or network. Without the password, the resource cannot be opened.

Paste. To retrieve information stored on the Clipboard and insert a copy of it into a document.

Path. A convention for designating the location of a file by listing the drive, folder, and nested subfolders in which the file is stored.

Pixel. Short for *picture element*. A pixel is the smallest dot that can be represented on a screen or in a paint (bitmap) graphic.

Plug & Play. A set of hardware standards followed by computer manufacturers to allow for better compatibility between computers and software. Also known as *PnP*.

Port. A connection device between a computer and another component, such as a printer or modem. For example, a printer cable is plugged into the printer port on the computer so information can be sent to the computer.

Print Queue. The list of print jobs waiting to be sent to a particular printer.

Print Spooling. The process of sending documents to a storage area on a disk, called a buffer, where they remain until the printer is ready for each one in turn.

Printer Driver. The enabling software that tells Windows about the features of a printer and how to access them to print documents.

Prodigy. A widely used online service offering access service to the Internet, as well as proprietary content and information.

Program. A set of instructions for a computer to execute. Software designed for a certain use, such as word processing, e-mail, or spreadsheet entries. Sometimes called an *application*.

Program Buttons. Buttons on the taskbar representing the currently running programs.

Quick Launch Toolbar. A toolbar on the taskbar that provides shortcuts to frequently used features, such as the desktop, the Web browser, Outlook Express, and channels.

Radio Button. One of a set of buttons found before options in a dialog box. Only one radio button in a set can be selected at a time.

RAM. Random Access Memory. The main memory that holds the application program and data that is currently being used.

Recycle Bin. An icon on the desktop that represents a temporary holding place for files that are deleted.

Redo. To reverse the last Undo action.

Registry. A central file that Windows 98 uses to store information about the hardware, software, and preferences on a specific computer.

Restore. To return a window from its minimized state to its normal size. Also, to copy files from a backup storage device to their normal location.

Right-click. To quickly push and release the secondary (usually the right) mouse button when the on-screen mouse pointer is positioned over the desired item.

Right-drag. Pressing and holding the secondary (usually the right) mouse button while moving the mouse, then releasing the mouse button when the pointer reaches the desired destination.

ROM. Read Only Memory. The part of a computer's main memory that contains the basic programs that run the computer when it is turned on. ROM cannot be erased.

Save As. To save a document with a new name or properties.

Save. The process of taking a document residing in the memory of the computer and creating a file to be stored on a disk.

Scroll Bar. The bar on the right side or bottom of a window that lets you move vertically or horizontally through a document.

Select. To identify a command option (from menus or dialog boxes) to be applied to an object or block of text. Compare with *choose*. Also to highlight or mark an object such as an icon or a text passage to be acted upon by the next command.

Serial Port. A port on a computer through which data is sent and received one bit at a time.

Shortcut. An icon that represents a quick way to start a program or open a file or folder.

Shortcut Key. A keystroke or keystroke combination that gives you quick access to a feature.

Shortcut Menu. The pop-up menu that appears when you right-click on something. Shortcut menus list commands that pertain to the object you clicked on.

Shut Down. The process of saving all settings before a computer is physically turned off. Accessed from the Start menu.

Sliders. A dialog box control that allows you to set a value by visually positioning a marker to indicate where the desired value should fall in a range.

Software. The instructions created from computer programs that direct the computer in performing various operations. Software can also include data.

Start Button. The button in the lower-left corner of the taskbar that is used to access programs.

Status Bar. The line at the bottom of a window that shows such information as the path, page information, or location of the insertion point.

Submenu. An additional list of menu items opening from a single menu item.

Subscribe. The capability to receive updated information from a Web site on a regular basis.

System Tray. The area of the status bar in the lower right than contains icons for programs running in the background.

Tabs. Dialog box controls that provide a way to access multiple pages of options in one dialog box.

Taskbar. The bar (usually at the bottom of the screen) that lists all open folders and active applications. The taskbar also contains the Start button, System Tray, and other toolbars.

Temporary File. A file that a program creates when it is running. Temporary files are deleted when the program is exited properly.

Text Boxes. A data entry area in a dialog box where you simply type in text information.

Text File. A file saved in ASCII file format. It contains text, spaces, and returns, but no formatting codes.

Thread. In an Internet newsgroup, a thread is a message and its replies that constitute conversation on a topic.

Tile. A display format for open windows. Tiled windows are displayed side by side, with no window overlapping any other window. Compare with *cascade*.

Title Bar. The colored bar across the top of the window that lists the name of the application and the name of the current document. The Title Bar changes color to indicate which program window is currently active.

Toggle. A term used to refer to something (such as a feature) that turns on and off with the same switch (such as a keystroke).

Toolbar. A row of one or more buttons that provide quick access to programs, options, or commands. Toolbars in program windows generally appear just below the Menu bar.

Trackball. A pointing device consisting of a small platform with a ball resting on it, similar in size to a mouse. Unlike a mouse, the platform remains stationary, while the user manipulates the ball to move the pointer on the screen.

Undo. To reverse the last action.

Views. Ways of displaying documents to see different perspectives of the information in that document.

Wallpaper. A photograph, drawing, or pattern displayed on the background of the Windows 98 desktop.

Web. Short for World Wide Web, the term has come to be used to refer to anything associated with the World Wide Web or using the same HyperText Markup Language that was developed for World Wide Web documents.

Web Style. A Folder Options setting that tells Windows how to interpret mouse actions and display certain on-screen items. In Web Style, you point to an item to select it and click on an item to open it, just as you do when viewing Web pages in a Web browser. Compare with Classic Style.

Window. A movable, resizable on-screen box, in which to display a program's operations. You can have several program or application windows open and displayed onscreen at the same time and the windows can overlap without interfering with each other, in much the same way that you can have several sheets of paper from different projects in an overlapping stack on your office desk.

Windows Explorer. A variation of the ubiquitous Explorer window that is optimized for file management chores by the addition of a hierarchical display of the drives and folders available on your system.

Wizards. The interactive programs supplied with Windows 98 to assist users through a project or problem by asking a series of questions.

World Wide Web. A series of specially designed documents, all linked together, to be viewed on the Internet.

Work Area. The large open space occupying most of a program window. It is used by the program to display the document or data that you're working on.

WYSIWYG. What You See Is What You Get. Refers to a computer screen display that approximates the printed page, showing fonts and graphics in correct proportions.

INDEX

... (ellipsis), 66
? (Help button), 284
16- and 24-bit color, 116, 118
16- and 32-bit computer code, 8, 347
16-bit sound card, 153
386/486 systems, 8, 116, 348
32-bit drivers, 348
3-D graphics, 153
56K modems, 154

A

accessories, Windows 98, 58–59, 62, 86–92
account properties, e-mail, 273–275
Active Desktop
    adding Web content to desktop, 327–331
    as complement to Web Style, 17
    customizing folders, 325
    enabling Web-related content, 323–324
    interacting with, 16–17
    main features of, 320–321
    turning Web content on and off, 331
ActiveMovie Control, 91
Add New Hardware Wizard, 156, 159, 167,
    193–194
Add New Printer Wizard, 157, 167, 197
address, device, 149, 179
address book
    Outlook Express, 297, 305–308
    Phone Dialer, 89

Address box, Internet Explorer, 234–235
Address toolbar, 113
addresses
    e-mail, 267, 297, 305–308
    Web page, 233–235, 236
AGP video card, 153
alarms, laptop, 138–139
All Folders bar, 45
America Online (AOL), 188, 189, 210, 262
applets, 86
application programs
    closing, 24
    defined, 5
    DOS-based, 92–96
    installing/removing, 55–61, 92–96
    migration from DOS to Windows, 8
application windows. *See* windows.
ASCII, 80
AT command, 189
ATA-2 interface, 153
AT&T WorldNet, 210
attaching files to e-mail, 302
audio
    CDs, 91, 133–134
    files, 91
    playback and recording settings, 132–133
Auto Arrange, 28, 50
Autoexec.bat, 95, 99
AutoHide, 108, 109–110

automatic updates, Web page subscriptions, 342
AutoRun, 58

B

Back button, Internet Explorer, 230
background, desktop, 20
Backspace key, deleting text with, 70–71
backups, system, 200
base address, 149
Baseball theme, 130
.BAT files, 95
batteries, conserving, 137–139
Bcc (blind carbon copy) field, e-mail, 297
beeps, system, 175
BIOS, 165, 176, 200
bitmap images, 119
blank screen, troubleshooting, 174–176
.bmp images, 119
bookmarks, 238
boot disk, 154–155
border, window, 34
browser. *See* Web browser.
burn-in, monitor, 122
Buttons setting, Mouse Properties, 126

C

card game, 88
Cc (carbon copy) field, e-mail, 297
CD Player, 91, 133–134
CD-ROM drive, 153, 348
Channel Bar, 21, 31, 231, 248, 339
channels, subscribing to, 338–340
Channels button, Internet Explorer, 231
Character Map, 90
chat rooms, 208
check boxes, 39
Classic Style desktop
   contrasted with Web Style, 17
   features, 14–15
   limitations of, 322–323

Clear command, 71
Clipboard, 48, 71, 73–74
clock, 22, 107, 110, 112, 136–137
Close button, 34, 35, 64
closing
   documents, 81–82
   files, 81–82
   programs, 24, 35
   Windows 98, 51–52
color resolution, 115–118
color schemes, 124–126
.COM files, 95
COM ports, 149, 159, 171–172
command line mode, 11
commands, ways of issuing, 64–66
communications ports, 149, 159, 171–172
communications programs, 88–89, 184, 188
Compression Agent, 90
compression program, 90
CompuServe, 188, 210, 262
computer code, 16- and 32-bit, 8
computer operating system. *See* operating system.
computer system. *See also* hardware; My
   Computer.
   components, 26, 29, 40–44
   improving performance, 90–91
   maintenance, 91, 349
   personalizing user settings, 139–141
   shutting down, 51–52
Concentric Network, 211
conferencing, online, 225
Config.sys, 95, 99
configuring new hardware, 165–171
Conflicting Device List, 151, 185–186
Content Advisor, Internet Explorer, 252–254
Control button, 35
Copy command, 73–74
copying
   files and folders, 47–49
   text, 72–76
CP/M, 7

crashes, system, 199–201
Create New Folder button, 79
cursor (.cur) file, 127
Custom Style Windows desktop, 322, 324, 325
customizing
 desktop, 12–14, 107, 115–131
 folders in Explorer windows, 325–327
 Internet Explorer, 246–256
 Start menu, 102–103
 taskbar, 107–115
cut and paste, 73–75
Cut command, 71, 73–75

D

Dangerous Creatures theme, 130
databases, Web page, 242
date and time, setting, 112, 136–137
Daylight Savings Time, automatic adjustment for,
 137
defragmenting hard disk, 90
DejaNews, 243
Deleted Items folder, e-mail, 289, 303
deleting
 color and font schemes, 126
 e-mail messages, 275
 Favorites list entries, 241
 files and folders, 29, 50–51
 graphics, 70–71
 sounds, 129
 text, 70–71
desktop, Windows 98
 arranging icons on, 28
 color schemes, 124–126
 configuration options, 12–14
 customizing, 12–14, 107, 115–131
 defined, 12
 determining and changing active view, 17–18
 fonts, 124–126, 134–136
 major components, 20–22
 personalizing for multiple users, 139–141, 144

styles
 Classic Style, 14–15, 17–19, 322–323
 Custom Style, 322, 324, 325
 Web Style, 15–19, 322–323
 wallpaper, 119–121
Desktop Themes, 58, 130–131
Desktop toolbar, 113
desktop wallpaper, 58, 119–121
Details button, 79
device address, 149
device conflicts, 151, 185
device drivers. *See* drivers.
Device Manager, 148–151, 172, 185
diagnostics, system, 11
dial tone, problem getting, 187–188
Dialing Properties, 160
dialog boxes, 37–39, 284
Dial-Up Adapter, 213
Dial-Up Networking, 88, 161, 189–190, 216–224,
 271–272
digital ID, 274
DIMM, 153, 175
Direct Cable Connection, 89
directories, Web, 242
directory services, 283
discussion forums. *See* newsgroups.
Disk Cleanup, 90
Disk Defragmenter, 90
disk drive
 backing up, 200
 changing to different, 78–79
 defragmenting, 90
 displaying contents of, 42
 improving performance of, 90–91
 installing additional, 153
 troubleshooting, 177–178
display resolution, 115–118, 162–163
documents
 closing, 81–82
 converting to other formats, 80–81
 creating new, 85

displaying large, 36
opening saved, 82–83
saving, 30, 76–81
selecting, 69–70
Documents menu, 25
DOS
    commands, 26
    file names, 8, 78
    role in Windows start-up, 10
    text-based interface, 7
DOS-based programs
    creating shortcuts for, 100–102
    installing, 92–96
    in MS-DOS mode, 99
    problems with games, 94, 192
    running, 26, 99
    troubleshooting, 96–100
double-clicking, 15, 16, 127
Drafts folder, e-mail, 289, 304
drag-and-drop, 28, 47, 48, 75–76
drive. *See* **disk drive.**
Drive Converter (FAT32), 90
drivers
    32-bit, 348
    defined, 165
    getting from Microsoft Web site, 187
    installing/reinstalling, 166, 186, 200
    modem, 160, 186, 190
    printer, 199
    sound card, 193–194, 196
    video card, 181–182
DriveSpace, 90
drop-down list boxes, 37–38
DVD disks, 9

E

EarthLink, 211
Edit button, Internet Explorer, 232
editing
    images, 87
    Web pages, 232

EIDE interface, 153
electronic mail. *See* **e-mail.**
ellipsis (...), 66
e-mail
    accounts
        choosing default, 276
        establishing multiple, 266
        friendly name, 270, 273
        setting up, 265–275
    address, 267
    Address Book, 297, 305–308
    defined, 262
    digital ID, 274
    directories, 283
    messages
        attaching files to, 302
        checking for spelling mistakes, 287, 298
        collecting, 293–294
        composing and sending, 295–300
        deleting, 275
        delivery options, 274–275
        forwarding, 301
        leaving on server, 274–275
        managing, 303–305
        organizing, 289–290
        plain text *vs.* HTML formatting, 285–286
        quoting from original message, 301
        reading, 289–292
        replying to, 300–301
    passwords, 269
    program, setting default, 264, 285
    Reply Address, 273–274
    security, 274
    server timeouts, 274
    software, 225, 232
emergency boot disk, 154–155
Empty Recycle Bin, 51
energy, saving, 123, 137–139
"Energy Star Compliant" monitors, 139
entertainment utilities, 91–92

error messages
　floppy drive failure, 176–177
　hard drive failure, 177–178
　memory error, 178–179
　operating system failure, 178
EtherExpress, 214
.EXE files, 95
exiting Windows, 51–52
Explorer windows, 40–44
extensions, file, 8, 59, 78, 95

F

fan, power supply, 174
Favorites bar, 231, 248
Favorites button, 231
Favorites list
　adding Web pages to, 239–242
　contrasted with Web page subscriptions, 332–333
　deleting entries, 241
　organizing, 241–242
　purpose of, 25, 238–239
　renaming entries, 241
Favorites menu, 25, 238
file extensions, 8, 59, 78, 95
file formats, 80
file management, 8, 44–51
File Manager, Windows 3.*x*, 8
file names, 8, 78
file properties, changing, 98–100
File Transfer Protocol, 236
files
　attaching to e-mail, 302
　closing, 81–82
　deleting, 29, 50–51
　moving and copying, 47–49
　opening saved, 82–83
　renaming, 46–47, 49
　restoring deleted, 50
　saving, 30, 80–81
Find menu, 25–26
firmware updates, 200

FlashNet, 211
floating toolbars, 113
floppy drive failure, 176–177
folders
　creating, 46, 304
　customizing with Active Desktop, 325–327
　deleting, 29, 50–51
　displaying contents of, 42–43
　managing e-mail with, 303–305
　moving and copying, 47–49
　renaming, 46–47, 49
　restoring deleted, 50
　saving files in, 78–79
fonts
　changing type and size, 124–126
　cutting and pasting from Character Map, 90
　deleting font schemes, 126
　displaying installed, 134
　installing, 134–136
　Large Fonts setting, 118
　Small Fonts setting, 118
forums, 208
Forward button, Internet Explorer, 230
forwarding e-mail messages, 301
Freecell, 87
friendly name
　e-mail account, 270, 273
　news account, 280–281
FrontPage Express, 58, 225, 232
ftp://, 236
Fullscreen button, Internet Explorer, 231
Fullscreen mode, Internet Explorer, 248–249

G

games
　display resolution considerations, 115–116
　DOS-based, 94
　troubleshooting sound problems, 192–193
　video card considerations, 153
　Windows 98, 58, 63, 87–88
Graphical User Interface, 7, 9

graphics
  3-D, 153
  deleting, 70–71
  screen saver, 122–124
  selecting, 66–70
  wallpaper, 119–121
graphics programs, 86–87, 162
graphics tablets, 16
GUI, 7, 9

H

handles
  selection, 67–68
  toolbar, 247
Hang Up When Finished option, Outlook Express, 288
hard disk
  backing up, 200
  defragmenting, 90
  displaying contents of, 42
  improving performance of, 90–91
  installing additional, 153
  troubleshooting, 177–178
hardware. *See also* **My Computer.**
  configuring new, 165–171
  device addresses and IRQs, 149, 179, 185
  identifying current system components, 148–152
  installation process, 147–148, 156
    modems, 159–161
    monitors, 162–163
    networks, 164
    PC cards, 163–164
    printers, 157–159
    scanners, 161–162
  testing, 11, 165–171, 173
  troubleshooting
    general, 173–179
    modem problems, 184–190
    printer problems, 196–199
    sound problems, 190–196
    system crashes, 199–201
    video problems, 180–184
  upgrading, 148, 153–154, 173

hardware requirements, Windows 98, 347
Hayes commands, 189
Hearts card game, 88
Help system, 26, 96–97, 284
hiding
  taskbar, 108, 109–110
  toolbars, 113
  Web page on Windows desktop, 331
High Color, 116, 118
history, personal computer operating systems, 7–10
History bar, Internet Explorer, 231, 248
History button, Internet Explorer, 231
History list, Internet Explorer, 235–238
Home button, Internet Explorer, 231
home page, 228, 256
HotBot, 243
HTML formatting of mail and news messages, 285–286
http://, 236
https://, 236
Hyper Terminal, 89
hyperlinks, 226, 232
Hypertext Markup Language, 285–286
Hypertext Transfer Protocol Secure, 236
Hypertext Transfer Protocol, 236

I

IBM Internet Connection, 211
icons
  adding to toolbars, 115
  arranging, 28
  default location, 26–27
  functions of standard, 29–30
  moving, 28
  reducing size on Start menu, 110
  selecting
    on Classic Style desktop, 15
    on Web Style desktop, 15–16
  shortcut, 27
IDE interface, 153, 154

images
  bitmap, 119
  editing, 87
  screen saver, 122–124
  wallpaper, 119–121
Imaging program, 87
IMAP mail server, 268
Inbox, e-mail, 265, 289–291, 303
indexes, Web, 242
Infoseek, 242
Input/Output Range, 186
Inside Your Computer theme, 130
Install button, 59, 60
Install New Modem Wizard, 159
installing
  hardware, 147–148, 156
    modems, 159–161
    monitors, 162–163
    networks, 164
    PC cards, 163–164
    printers, 157–159
    scanners, 161–162
  network software, 213–216
  Outlook Express, 263
  programs, 55–61, 92–96
  Windows 98 upgrade, 349–352
Interactive CD Sampler and Trial Programs, 92
Internet
  choosing a service provider, 207–213
  connecting, 206–207
    via local area network, 224–225
    via modem, 216–224
  content filter, 252–254
  as distinguished from World Wide Web, 227
  hardware and software requirements, 213–216
  logging on, 222–224
  security, 249–254
  software, 225
Internet Connection Wizard, 29, 206, 228, 266–273
Internet e-mail. *See* **e-mail; Outlook Express.**

Internet Explorer, 29
  Address box, 234–235
  allocating hard disk space for, 256–257
  buttons and functions, 230–232
  content filter, 252–254
  customizing, 246–256
  Fullscreen mode, 248–249
  History list, 235–238, 256
  Home Page setting, 256
  opening multiple copies of, 233
  purpose of, 225
  Search bar, 243–246, 249
  security features, 249–254
  starting, 227–229
  toolbars, 229, 246–247
Internet newsgroups. *See* **newsgroups; Outlook Express.**
Internet Service Providers. *See* **ISPs.**
Internet zone, 251
Interrupt Requests. *See* **IRQs.**
intranets, 250, 262
IRQs, 149, 150, 151, 152, 179, 185
ISA sound card, 153
ISPs
  choosing, 207–213
  contrasted with online services, 208–209
  Dial-Up Networking settings, 220–222
  e-mail accounts, 262
  establishing connection via modem, 216–224
  mail servers, 266, 268–269, 272, 274
  news servers, 263, 278, 280, 282
  problems during peak periods, 190
  regional and local, 210
  setup programs, 211–213
  typical services of, 207
  user IDs and passwords, 266
  Welcome Kit, 266

K

Kflex modems, 154

L

Landscape printing, 172
laptops
  advantage of using Web Style on, 16
  PCMCIA slot, 163
  power management, 137–139
  Standby mode, 139
  using Start menu from keyboard, 24
  Windows key, 24
Large Fonts setting, 118
Links toolbar, 113
Linux, 7
list boxes, 37, 38
List button, 79
local area network, 206–207, 224–225
Local intranet zone, 250, 251
Log Off command, 26, 141
logo screen, Windows 98, 11
long file names, 8, 78
Lycos, 243

M

Mac OS, 7
mail. *See* e-mail; Outlook Express.
Mail button, Internet Explorer, 232, 264
Mail command, Explorer, 264
Mail Sending Format, 285
mail servers, 262, 266, 268–269, 272, 274
maintenance utilities. *See* system utilities.
Maintenance Wizard, 90, 91
Make New Connection Wizard, 218
manual updates, Web page subscriptions, 341
Maximize button, 34, 35, 64
maximizing
  program windows, 32, 34, 35
  Web pages, 248–249
media clip, 91
Media Player, 91
memory
  adding, 153, 175
  determining amount of installed, 148, 149

  flawed chip, 200
  installation problems, 175, 178–179
  minimum requirements for Windows, 348
  specifications, 153
  video card, 118
Menu bar, 35, 63
Microsoft Network, 209, 210
Microsoft Office, 262
Microsoft Update, 187
MIDI configuration settings, 133
MindSpring, 211
Minesweeper, 88
Minimize button, 34, 35, 64
minimizing
  program windows, 22, 32, 35
  Web pages, 249
misspelled words, 287, 298
modems
  driver software, 160, 186, 190
  establishing connection for Internet access, 216–224
  installing, 159–161
  internal *vs.* external, 159
  recommendations for buying, 154, 159
  selecting port, 171–172
  setup string, 188, 189
  software supplied with, 172
  troubleshooting, 184–190
monitors
  burn-in, 122
  contrast and brightness controls, 175
  "Energy Star Compliant," 139
  energy-saving features, 123, 139
  flickering display, 182–184
  image controls, 180
  installing, 162–163, 175
  refresh rate, 173, 180, 182, 184
  resolution considerations, 115–116, 162–163
  super-VGA, 163
  troubleshooting, 175–176
  VGA, 115, 163
motherboard, PCI, 153

Motion setting, Mouse Properties, 128
mouse actions
    on Classic Style desktop, 15
    drag-and-drop, 28, 47, 48, 75–76
    right-drag, 48
    selecting text and graphics, 68–69
    on Web Style desktop, 15–16
mouse buttons, reconfiguring, 126–127
mouse pointer
    changing appearance of, 58, 127
    correcting sluggish, 126–128
Mouse Properties, 126–128
movie files, 91
moving
    files and folders, 47–49
    icons, 28
    text, 72–76
    toolbars, 115
MS-DOS. *See* **DOS.**
MSN, 209, 210
multimedia
    devices, 131–134
    tools, 91–92
Multiple Users feature, 11, 139–141
Multi-User Settings Wizard, 140
music CDs, playing, 91, 133–134
My Computer, 26, 29, 40–44
My Documents, 30

N
NE2000, 214
nested folders, 43
NETCOM, 211
NetMeeting, 225
Netscape Navigator, 238
network adapter, 213–216
network and security features, Windows NT, 10
Network Neighborhood, 29
network protocol, 213
networks, installing, 164

news account
    default, 283
    friendly name, 280–281
    setting up, 278–283
news reader, 263, 285. *See also* **Outlook Express.**
News Sending Format, 285
news servers, 263, 278, 280
newsgroups
    connecting to news server, 309
    defined, 277
    messages
        following threads, 313
        plain text *vs.* HTML formatting, 285–286
        posting, 315–316
        reading, 311–313
    searching categories, 309–311
    setting up news account, 278–283
    subscribing to, 313–315
    using Outlook Express to access, 277–278
NNTP news server, 280
Notepad, 86
NTR.net, 211

O
offline viewing, Web page subscriptions, 343–344
online conferencing, 225
online services
    chat rooms and forums, 208
    contrasted with ISPs, 208–209
    free trials, 209
    list of leading, 210
    setup programs, 209–210
    startup kits, 188
operating system
    alternatives to Windows, 7
    choosing, 9–10
    defined, 5–6
    failure, 178
    history, 7–9
    network and security features, 10
    text-based, 7

Organize Favorites, 241–242

OS/2 Warp, 7

Outbox, e-mail, 289, 300, 303

Outlook 98, 261–262

Outlook Express

configuration options, 284–289

    disabling HTML formatting, 285–286

    Hang Up When Finished, 288

    reading and composing messages offline, 287–288

    setting default e-mail program and news reader, 285

    spelling checker, 287, 298

    window layout, 289

contrasted with Outlook 98, 261–262

directory services, 283

e-mail functions

    attaching files to messages, 302

    checking for mail, 293–295

    composing and sending messages, 295–300

    forwarding messages, 301

    managing message folders, 303–305

    reading messages, 289–292

    replying to messages, 300–301

    using Address Book, 297, 305–308

icon, 30

installing, 263

newsgroup functions

    connecting to news server, 309

    posting messages, 315–316

    reading newsgroup messages, 311–313

    searching newsgroup categories, 309–311

    subscribing to newsgroups, 313–315

purpose of, 261–262

setup

    e-mail accounts, 265–276

    news server, 277–283

starting, 263–264

P

Paint program, 86–87

Paint Shop Pro, 162

paragraph, selecting, 69–70

passwords

attaching to screen saver mode, 124

changing, 142–143

confirming on start-up, 11

e-mail, 269

Internet, 212, 222, 224

managing, 141–143

for multiple-user systems, 139, 140

Passwords Properties, 142–143

Paste command, 73–75

patterns, desktop, 119, 121

PC. *See* **hardware.**

PC cards, 163–164

PC troubleshooting. *See* **troubleshooting.**

PCI motherboard, 153

PCI sound card, 153

PCI video card, 153

PCMCIA, 163

Pentium, 8, 153, 348

performance, improving system, 90–91

personal computer. *See* **hardware.**

personal computer operating system. *See* **operating system.**

Phone Dialer, 89

PhotoShop, 162

.PIF files, 95, 96, 97

plain-text files, 80, 86

sending mail and news as, 285

Play Sound button, 128

playback and recording settings, audio, 132–133

Plug-and-Play, 165

printers, 196

sound cards, 193

video cards, 180

pointer. *See* **mouse pointer.**

Pointers setting, Mouse Properties, 127

pointing devices. *See also* **mouse pointer.**

executing double-click with, 16

using Start menu with, 24

POP3 mail server, 268

port, selecting, 171–172

Portrait printing, 172
Power Management controls, 137–139
Power Schemes, 138
power supply fan, 174
preferences, multiple-user system, 11, 139–141, 144
Preview Pane, Outlook Express, 289, 290–291
Print button, 83, 232
printers
    canceling print request, 84
    changing settings, 83–85, 172–173
    driver software, 199
    ink or toner problems, 198–199
    installing, 157–159, 199
    Plug-and-Play compatible, 196
    troubleshooting, 196–199
printing Web pages, 232
Problem Devices, 152
Procomm, 89
Prodigy Internet, 188, 210
Program buttons, 21–22, 64
Program Manager, Windows 3.*x*, 8, 15, 22
program windows. *See* windows.
programs
    closing, 24, 35
    installing, 55–61, 92–96
    minimizing, 22, 34, 35
    removing, 55–61
    switching between, 20, 36
    troubleshooting DOS, 96–100
Programs toolbar, 107
properties, changing file, 98–100
public discussion forums. *See* newsgroups.
publishing, Web, 226–227
push technology, 31. *See also* Active Desktop; Channel Bar.

Q

Quick Launch toolbar, 21, 107, 112

R

radio buttons, 38–39
RAM, 348
rating systems, Web site, 252
recording and playback settings, audio, 132–133
Recycle Bin, 29, 50–51, 51
Redo, 72
Refresh button, Internet Explorer, 231
refresh rate, video card, 173, 180, 182, 184
Registry, Windows, 60
relative URL, 236
removing programs, 55–61
Reply Address, e-mail, 273–274
replying to e-mail messages, 300–301
resizing
    toolbars, 115, 247
    windows, 34
resolution, display, 115–118, 162–163
Resource Meter, 90
Restore button, 64
restoring deleted files and folders, 50
Restricted sites zone, 251
reverse video, 67
RTF (Rich Text Format), 80
Run command, 26

S

Safe Mode, 11, 163
Save As, 80
Save command, 77
saving
    documents, 30, 76–80
    energy, 123, 137–139
    Web pages, 256
ScanDisk, 90
scanners, 161–162
scenarios, configuring new hardware, 165–171
schemes
    color and font, 124–126
    sound, 128–129, 130

screen resolution, 115–118, 162–163

screen savers, 100, 122–124

scroll bars, 36

SCSI, 153–154

Search bar, Internet Explorer, 243–246, 249

Search button, Internet Explorer, 231

search engines, 242–246

Secure Password Authentication, 269

security, Internet, 249–254

selecting text and graphics, 66–70

selection handles, 67–68

Sent Items folder, e-mail, 289, 303

sentence, selecting, 69

serial port, 159

Server Port Numbers, 274

Server Timeouts, 274

Settings menu, 25

setup files, 95

setup programs, 59, 166
    ISPs, 211–213
    online services, 209–210
    Windows 98, 349–352

setup strings, modem, 188, 189

shared files, 61, 78

shortcut keys, 65, 100

shortcut menus, 24

shortcuts
    conflicts between DOS and Windows, 100
    creating, 49–50, 100–102
    defined, 27
    for maximizing and minimizing windows, 34
    putting on Start menu, 101, 103
    for renaming files and folders, 47
    for selecting text and graphics, 69–70

Show Desktop button, 112

Shut Down command, 26, 51–52

SIMM, 153, 175

sliders, dialog box, 39–40

Small Computer System Interface, 153–154

Small Fonts setting, 118

Solitaire, 58, 87–88

sound card
    diagnostic program, 190–192
    drivers, 193–194, 196
    installing software supplied with, 172, 193–194, 196
    Plug-and-Play compatible, 193
    recommendations for buying, 153, 193
    SoundBlaster, 153, 192–193
    troubleshooting, 190–196
    volume control, 22, 92, 134, 194

sound files
    associating with events, 128–129
    audio playback and recording settings, 132–133
    playing, 91

Sound Recorder, 91

SoundBlaster, 153, 192–193

Sounds Properties, 128–129

speaker
    icon, 194
    problems, 190–196
    settings, 132–133

spelling checker, Outlook Express, 287, 298

spiders, 242

Sprint Internet Passport, 211

SpryNet, 211

Standby mode, laptop, 139

Start button, 20–21, 107

Start menu
    customizing, 102–103
    items found on, 24–26
    launching programs from, 24, 62
    opening, 22
    putting shortcuts on, 101, 103
    reducing size of icons on, 110
    submenus accessible from, 22–23

start-up, Windows 98, 10–12, 17, 154–155

Startup Disk, Windows 98, 154–155

static, modem line, 188–189

Status bar, 64

Stop button, Internet Explorer, 231

Stretch option, wallpaper, 119, 120

Subject field, e-mail, 297

subscribing
to channels, 338–340
to newsgroups, 313–315
to Web pages, 321, 332–338
Subscription Wizard, 335
super-VGA monitors, 163
Switchboard, 243
switching
program windows, 20, 33, 36
views, 18
system clock. *See* **clock.**
system components. *See* **My Computer.**
system crashes, 199–201
System Information utility, 90, 151–152
System Properties, 148
system requirements, Windows 98, 347
System Tools, 90
System Tray, 20–22, 107, 111–112
system utilities, 22, 90–91, 151–152, 156
SYSTEM.INI, 349

T

tabs, dialog box, 39
Task Scheduler, 22
taskbar
changing size of, 110–111
customizing, 107–115
features, 21–22, 107
hiding, 108, 109–110
location and purpose of, 20–21
TCP/IP, 213, 216, 220–222
telephone dialer program, 89
Temporary Internet Files, 256
Terminal program, Windows 3.1, 89
text
deleting, 70–71
moving and copying, 72–76
selecting, 66–70
text boxes, 37, 38
text labels, 246
text processing, 86
text-based operating systems, 7

Themes, Windows, 130–131
threads, newsgroup, 313
three-dimensional graphics, 153
tiled wallpaper, 119, 120
time and date, setting, 112, 136–137
timeouts, server, 274
tips
Active Desktop, enabling Web-related content on Classic Style Windows desktop, 324
files and folders
shortcuts for renaming, 47
using Cancel button to abort copy or move command, 49
using Ctrl key to move or copy multiple, 49
hardware
installing new devices, 165
scheduling system maintenance with Maintenance Wizard, 91
Help system
using Help (?) button to display information on dialog box options, 284
using mouse pointer to display brief description of buttons, 64
Internet Explorer
disabling request for user name and password, 224
making Search bar visible in Fullscreen mode, 249
opening multiple copies of, 233
setting up multiple dial-up networking connections, 219
shortcut for opening Web pages, 235
starting from QuickLaunch toolbar, 228
using Favorites bar to check several Web sites, 239
laptops
reading Web page subscriptions offline with, 341
using Start menu from keyboard, 24
modems, shortcut for installing new, 159
monitors, changing refresh rate, 180
mouse, installing additional pointer schemes, 128
Outlook Express
changing relative size of Message List and Preview Pane, 291
running spelling check automatically, 299
sending a test e-mail message, 296
sending messages in HTML formatting, 286

Paint program, turning pictures into desktop wallpaper, 87

printer, using Print button to identify default, 83

program windows, shortcut for maximizing and minimizing, 34

scanner, using TWAIN-compatible, 162

screen savers

   installing Windows 98, 122

   using as security system, 124

start-up mode, using F8 key to bring up menu, 12

system clock, shareware program that adjusts automatically, 137

taskbar

   displaying program or file name for program button, 111

   hiding to save space on desktop, 108

video cards, utility program for setting refresh rate, 184

Web page subscriptions

   reading offline with a laptop computer, 341

   red star to identify updated pages, 343

Title Bar, 34

To field, e-mail, 297

toggle commands, 65

toolbars

   adding icons to, 115

   floating, 113

   hiding, 113

   Internet Explorer, 246–247

   moving, 115

   program, 35–36, 64

   resizing, 115, 247

   Windows 98 desktop, 20–21, 112–115

touchpads, 16, 24

trackballs, 16

Transmission Control Protocol/Internet Protocol. *See* **TCP/IP.**

troubleshooting

   DOS programs, 96–100

   general, 173–179

   modem problems, 184–190

   printer problems, 196–199

   sound problems, 190–196

   system crashes, 199–201

   video problems, 174–176, 180–184

   Windows 98, 11

troubleshooting mode, 11, 163

True Color, 116

Trusted sites zone, 250, 251

TWAIN-compatible scanners, 162

tweaking computer system, 90–91

U

underlining, on Web pages, 232

Undo, 71–72

Uniform Resource Locator. *See* **URL.**

uninstalling programs, 55–61

Unix, 7

Up button, 43

Up One Level button, 79

Update Device Driver Wizard, 186, 196

updates, Web page subscriptions, 341–342

Upgrade Your PC In a Weekend, **148**

upgrading

   books about, 148

   firmware, 200

   hardware, 148, 153–154, 173

   Windows 98, 346–352

URL

   anatomy of, 236

   defined, 233–234

   shortcuts for entering, 234–235

USB ports, 9

Usenet news. *See* **newsgroups.**

username/user ID, 141–143

user settings, personalizing, 139–141

utilities

   entertainment, 91–92

   system, 22, 90–91, 151–152, 156

V

VGA monitors, 115, 163

video, setting window size, 133

video card
drivers, 181–182
installation problems, 174, 176, 180–184
memory, 118
Plug-and-Play compatible, 180
recommendations for buying, 153
refresh rate, 173, 180, 182, 184
video files, 91
view. *See* **desktop, Windows 98.**
View Channels button, 112
View Desktop button, 79
Views button, 44
viruses, 252
VLB video card, 153
volume control, 22, 92, 134, 194

W

wallpaper, 58, 119–121, 130
Web address. *See* **URL.**
Web browser. *See also* **Internet Explorer.**
defined, 226
launching, 29
Netscape Navigator, 238
Web page
adding to Windows desktop, 327–331
addresses, 233–235, 236
defined, 226
editing, 232
History list, 235–238
maximizing and minimizing, 248–249
printing, 232
setting default, 228
shortcut for opening, 235
software for creating, 225
viewing more than one, 233
Web page subscriptions
defined, 321
manual *vs.* automatic updates, 341–342
setting up, 332–338
viewing offline, 343–344

Web publishing, 226–227
Web Publishing Wizard, 58
Web search engines, 242–246
Web servers, 236
Web sites
adult content, 252
defined, 226
Favorites list, 25, 238–242, 332–333
returning to previously visited, 237–238
searching for information at, 242–246
security zones/levels, 250–252
Web Style
as complement to Active Desktop, 17, 322–323
contrasted with Classic Style, 17
features, 15–17
Web-related content, enabling, 323–324
WebTV for Windows, 9
Welcome to Windows, 90, 139
WIN command, 10
Window Layout Properties, Outlook Express, 289
windows
defined, 32
maximizing and minimizing, 32
resizing, 34
standard features, 34–36
switching between, 20, 33
Windows 3.*x*, 7–8
Control button, 35
file names, 8.78
hardware requirements, 348
Program Manager, 8, 15, 22
upgrading to Windows 98 from, 347–349
Windows 95
hardware requirements, 348
improvements over Windows 3.*x*, 8–9
upgrading to Windows 98 from, 346–347
Windows 98
Active Desktop, 320–321
advantages over other operating systems, 7–10
beginner's tour and instruction booklet, 90
closing, 51–52

desktop
    color schemes, 124–126
    customizing, 12–14, 107, 115–131
    fonts, 124–126, 134–136
    major components, 20–22
    personalizing for multiple users, 139–141, 144
    wallpaper, 119–121
Desktop Themes, 130–131
earlier versions, 7–9
hardware requirements, 347–349
installing/removing components, 55–57
Internet and Web access features, 9, 225
Outlook Express and Outlook 98, 261–262
setting operating mode, 11–12
Setup Wizard, 351–352
starting, 10–12
tools and accessories, 58–59, 62, 86–92
upgrading
    from Windows 95, 346–347
    from Windows 3.*x*, 347–349
Windows Clipboard. *See* **Clipboard.**
Windows Explorer, 44–51
Windows for Workgroups 3.11, 8
Windows key, on laptops, 24
Windows NT, 10
Windows Registry, 60
Windows Themes, 130–131
WIN.INI, 349
Wizards
    Add New Hardware, 156, 159, 167, 193–194
    Add New Printer, 157, 167, 197
    Install New Modem, 159
    Internet Connection, 29, 206, 228, 266–273
    Maintenance, 90, 91
    Make New Connection, 218
    Multi-User Settings, 140
    Subscription, 335
    Update Device Driver, 186, 196
    Web Publishing, 58
    Windows 98 Setup, 351–352

word processing
    with Notepad, 86
    with WordPad, 23, 63, 86
WordPad, 23, 63, 86
work area, 36, 64
World Wide Web
    distinctive characteristics of, 226
    relationship to Internet, 227
    searching for information on, 242–246
WorldNet, AT&T, 210

X

X2 modems, 154

Y

Yahoo, 242

Z

zones/levels, Web site security, 250–252